Child Poverty in Wales

Child Poverty in Wales

Exploring the Challenges for Schooling Future Generations

Edited by

Lori Beckett

UNIVERSITY OF WALES PRESS
2023

www.uwp.co.uk

British Library Cataloguing-in-Publication Data
A catalogue record for this book is available from the British Library.

ISBN 978-1-83772-060-6
eISBN 978-1-83772-061-3

The University of Wales Press gratefully acknowledges the funding support of the Higher Education Funding Council of Wales and Bangor University in publication of this book.

Typeset by Richard Huw Pritchard
Printed by CPI Antony Rowe, Melksham, United Kingdom

the *Well-being of Future Generations (Wales) Act* itself is becoming a tool of Wales's 'soft power' in the world, where its very existence tells you about the characteristics of a nation open to change and prepared to be responsible for future generations.

Jane Davidson (2020). #Futuregen.
Lessons from a Small Country

For the children of Wales and future generations

CONTENTS

ACKNOWLEDGEMENTS

This edited book has been five years in the making, with time out in 2020 with Covid-19 lockdown, which is a remarkable team effort under the circumstances! So, first and foremost, thanks must go to the organisers of the Policy Forum for Wales (Fforwm Polisïau Cymru), who accepted my request to attend their keynote seminar on school standards and the National Education Plan in Cardiff in early 2018. This followed my retirement after twelve years as Professor of Teacher Education at Leeds Metropolitan University.

It was a truly remarkable experience to listen to a variety of speakers on schooling and education in Wales, which was seemingly so distinctly different to the model promoted in England. Arwyn Thomas, the managing director of the North Wales Regional School Improvement Service (gwasanaeth gwella ysgolion rhanbarthol Gogledd Cymru), known as GwE, reported on some innovative strategies for developing the organisation in support of schools, which again contrasted so markedly to what I had heard in England.

This chance meeting resulted in an invitation from Arwyn Thomas to visit GwE in North Wales, meet and discuss my concerns about poverty and schooling but also my impressions of Wales's system of school improvement, all set against the background of my work in teacher education in Australia and England. This ultimately led me to Bangor University, where I met the head of the School of Education Sciences, Professor Carl Hughes, and Caryl Elin Lewis, who had won the competitive tender for the 2018–19 Welsh Government-sponsored *Children First* needs assessment on Trem y Mynydd, to use its pseudonym. This resulted in an invitation to join a lively group of frontline workers, including the school Head, multi-agency workers and managers, all gravely concerned about the lot of resident families, including children and young people.

The upshot was an edited book proposal, which brought me to the University of Wales Press, so my sincere thanks go to Llion Wigley for expert editorial advice and for considerate understanding as the contributing authors came to juggle sickness with Covid and then the fall-out in terms of work commitments. I am also grateful to the anonymous reviewers of the book proposal and of the book manuscript, and Dafydd Jones and the production team.

This extends to Emeritus Professor Bob Lingard (University of Queensland), who not only provided me with critical feedback on our ideas but who provided invaluable directions on what it takes to be working in a nation-state that espouses social democracy. A glimpse of the depth and breadth of these ways can be gleaned from a cursory glance at his prestigious published work, which has had a profound effect on the tenor of our work.

I am particularly grateful to Honorary Professor Ruth Lupton (University of Manchester), who stepped up to write the foreword in an act of great generosity given her retirement and my need for a very prompt response. She brought such insight and acumen to the task, which was not surprising given her prestigious published work, which likewise has had a profound effect on our moving forward on policy advocacy. I am also especially grateful to Professor Philip Alston (University of New York), who brought more clarity to the twin ideas of systemic and structural change, building on his 2018 probe into *Extreme Poverty and Human Rights in the UK*, and another public statement on the cost-of-living crisis in the UK reported by Harry Clarke-Ezzidio in the New Statesman, 30 August 2020.

The necessity to develop a keen sense of poverty and inequalities on site and the potential of contextualised school improvement sparked a curiosity in local histories, which meant academic partners also embarked on documentary research. So sincere thanks to staff in Llangefni library and curatorial staff in the Bangor University Archives, Gwynedd Archives, and Wales's National Museums including the Bangor Museum and National Slate Museum, as well as Wales's National Library and the so-called National Library in London.

Finally I would like to acknowledge and thank colleagues in the School of Education Sciences at Bangor University, in particular Head of School Professor Carl Hughes and Deputy Head of School Graham French for the support they lent to the Bangor PLUS project and to my nomination as Visiting Professor. I would also like to acknowledge and thank Professor Parlo Singh and Dr Sue Whatman (Griffith University) for the support they lent to the idea of a multi-cities ethnography and to my nomination as Adjunct Professor. The multi-cities project, which includes Bangor and Brisbane, was a direct result of colleagues working on the BERA Commission into Poverty and Policy Advocacy reaching out to colleagues in the AARE equity network, who all in their own ways provided support for continuing the Bangor PLUS project.

In closing I would also like to give heartfelt thanks to my family and friends who unfailingly provide love and support, but especially Lin Williams, Mary Roddick and Steve Roddick in Wales, Sibyl Fisher and Paul Hughes in England, along with John Beckett, Ann Stewart, Chris Evans, Barb Hollard, Mela Cooke and Beryl Cooke in Australia. Last but by no means least, grateful acknowledgement must go to the team of contributing authors and resident families on Trem y Mynydd, who showed me such fighting spirit in their quest to battle against rising poverty and inequalities because it demands so much more than simply an abstract moral argument.

LIST OF FIGURES

Image 1: reproduced with kind permission from *iStock.com/tracy-williams-photography*.

Penrhyn Castle was home to the Penrhyn family dynasty and designed to showcase its power and enormous wealth garnered in its slate quarries in North Wales but also in its sugar plantations in Jamaica. It was gifted to the National Trust in 1951 by Lady Janet Harper in lieu of death duties.

Image 2: reproduced with kind permission from Wales National Museums.

This posed photo of a quarryman, positioned at a slate rock face and harnessed by a rope secured cliff top in the Snowdonia mountains, shows the working conditions at the heart of the lengthy and bitter 1900–3 Penrhyn Quarry dispute that also included trade union rights and pay.

Image 3: reproduced with kind permission from Wales National Museums.

This slate workshop shows the mechanisation introduced in the nineteenth century to speed up the production of roofing slates during the Industrial Revolution, which came to dominate not only the landscape of Gwynedd but its way of life given the employment of 20,000 people in industries prior to the First World War.

Image 4: reproduced with kind permission from Wales National Library.

This train engine was named after Linda Blanche Douglas-Pennant (1889–1965), granddaughter of the second Lord Penrhyn, George Sholto Gordon Douglas-Pennant (1836–1907), who was a protagonist in the Penrhyn Quarry dispute in 1900–3.

Image 5: reproduced with kind permission from Wales National Library.

These train waggons were a feature of the pioneering rail/port arrangement carrying dressed slate tiles from the Penrhyn Quarry on a 6-mile journey to Port Penrhyn, where they were then loaded onto a fleet of sail/steamboats destined for domestic and overseas markets.

Image 6: reproduced with kind permission from Bangor University.

The Penrhyn Arms Hotel in Bangor, built in 1799 as a coaching inn, became the first site of the University College of North Wales, which opened on 18 October 1884. Funds were raised by quarrymen among the 8,000 workers who subscribed to the university. Note the 'knowledge is power' motto.

Image 7: reproduced with kind permission from Wales National Library.

This shows the 4th Lord Penrhyn (middle/seated), Hugh Napier Douglas-Pennant (1894–1949), who sold parcels of land to Bangor City Council, some for social housing following enticements from the UK Government in Westminster to local councils to mitigate housing shortages in the interwar years.

Image 8: reproduced with kind permission from Gwynedd Archives.

This extract of a letter to the editor of the North Wales Chronicle, dated 13 December 1935, provides some insight into the public debates about Bangor City Council's plans for social housing that amounted to hundreds of new houses being built. Note the reference to future generations.

Image 9: reproduced with kind permission from Gwynedd Archives.

This front cover of a booklet prepared by Bangor City engineer, B. Price Davies, provides a glimpse of Bangor City Council's concern about standards in regards the planning and economics of housing design as well as public administration, all peer-reviewed in an open competition, and prize-winning.

Image 10: reproduced with kind permission from Gwynedd Archives.

This shows Port Penrhyn with sail boats ready for loading dressed slates at the quay built in 1821. These were likely part of a fleet owned by the Penrhyn family and though others had shares in shipping, in 1897 the 2nd Lord Penrhyn purchased a fleet of steamers from the Anglesey Shipping Co.

Image 11: photo reproduced by kind permission from Gwynedd Council.

This front cover of a booklet prepared by Llechi Cymru provides details of the key areas of the slate landscape located in Gwynedd and the vision to protect, conserve and enhance its Outstanding Universal Value. Inside it notes the heritage industry contributes £180m to the local economy.

Image 12: reproduced by kind permission from Storiel Bangor.

This photo of a Welsh Not artefact held in Bangor Museum was hung around a child's neck for speaking Welsh in nineteenth-century schools, a consequence of anti-Welsh bias notably in the 1847 Reports of the Commissioners of Inquiry into the State of Education in Wales, later known as the Blue Books.

FOREWORD

Ruth Lupton

Out of the gloom

The context in which I write this foreword seems exceptionally gloomy. There is war in Europe and an accelerating climate emergency. Public services and communities are only just managing after more than a decade of austerity and a global pandemic. And we now face another potential humanitarian disaster as energy prices soar. Although one might expect all this to stimulate bold and innovative policy responses, the social policy of the Westminster government has been almost paralysed for nearly seven years first by Brexit and then by Coronavirus, and has become apparently very hard to influence through academic research and evidence. From my position in England, it sometimes feels that nothing is being done, and maybe nothing can be done.

But of course things *can* be done, even in an unfavourable national policy context, and we need to hear about them! This is why I am particularly pleased to have the opportunity to write a foreword to this inspiring edited book, *Child poverty in Wales: Exploring the challenges for schooling future generations*. Both in the way it has been put together and its messages, it points to some of the possibilities of change, not just the challenges (although these are also pertinently highlighted).

Shedding light on the present

One thing that the book demonstrates is that, working together, local residents, front-line workers in schools and in multi-agencies, academic partners and critical friends can articulate and narrate the issues facing low-income neighbourhoods in detailed, careful and compelling ways, so that they can be seen and heard by people with the power to make things change. The majority of academic work on poverty takes place inside universities, working with statistics and surveys. Important journal articles using large scale data can influence policy and build careers without anyone leaving the office. Illuminating the day-to-day reality of life on the end of failed policies is more difficult. Academics working in and with communities rarely gain plaudits or promotions. Residents and front-line workers don't necessarily want students and 'boffins' poking around in ways that don't make any difference to them. So books like this, with academic partners mentoring and supporting practitioners co-developing research perspectives, are hard to pull off, and they are unusual.

But they are important, because they have the potential to reconnect policy making with the 'lived experience' of those experiencing policy effects or omissions. Reading about the detail of the daily work in the school office (Ch.6), for example, must make politicians, advisers and policy makers ask questions about their education plans and proposals. What do they mean by a 'community school?' Why is it better to 'send in' Family Engagement Officers, rather than provide more funding to the school to support its existing family support work? Why should low-income households need to pay £60 for a 'support letter' in order to make the case for re-housing? What resources do schools need if they are going to be providing this kind of support? These are difficult questions that are nor posed by more distant or abstract work, and they demand answers.

Demonstrating the importance of history

Perhaps even more important than this, the book rams home the importance of history as it plays out in the present, which should spark some intense debate about the place and its people. This is in marked contrast to policy cycles that are short. Politicians only have a short time, and usually not much spare money, to make their mark. There's a real temptation to launch high profile initiatives targeting the pressing problems of the day. But these come and go. When I researched twelve of the poorest neighbourhoods in England and Wales, back in the late 1990s/early 2000s,[1] most of them had seen a variety of short-lived programmes and initiatives over the years. Some had helped. But the problems that these neighbourhoods faced had been decades in the making.

The detailed 'back story' of each place mattered, as it matters in Trem y Mynydd. But there were common histories of decline and underinvestment. Globalisation and technological change had favoured more competitive places. Privatisation and the shrinking state had stripped out the foundational services people need. Cuts to the welfare state had punished the poor and widened inequality. So short term, small-scale interventions could not, on their own, make a significant difference. Policy solutions needed to have the same long term time span as the underlying problems, and the same attention to structural causes, economic geography and the politics of class relations.

This edited book, which has grown out of the Bangor Poverty and Learning in Urban Schools (PLUS) project, has collected, though images and archival work, shared knowledge of labour, achievement and pride, but also of injustice, exploitation and resistance. It provides an invaluable resource through which current residents (especially young people) can connect with past identities, events and struggles, and reimagine their futures. More than that though, it provides a deep, critical and informed historical account which must make it hard for politicians to fall back on short term, superficial fixes.

In my experience, it is all the more powerful when accounts such as these from different places are joined up, making the structural causes visible over and over again. Projects which link across national boundaries, like this one, with Sue Whatman's work in Brisbane, are rare. More similar links would further add to the value of this book, and it highlights work already done in trying to pull together a multi-cities ethnography across the UK and Australia.

How things can change

In a time of policy paralysis at the UK level, it is good to be reminded of the power of local action, and the determination and capacity that exists in almost every school-community for what Richardson (2008) called 'DIY Community Action'.[2] This is striking here, as is the need for institutional trust and funding agility to get behind the social action that people with front-line knowledge of their own communities are already organising, responding quickly and appropriately to the pressing issues.

But Trem y Mynydd's problems demand wider action too. You will draw your own conclusions about what needs to happen as the account of Trem y Mynydd's struggles unfold in the chapters that follow. Three major things struck me.

One was the deep and sustained reinvestment that is needed in places made poor over decades. Short term funding streams, thinly spread, are not going to produce the economic and social regeneration that is needed. This point is increasingly being made in UK-wide debates around what is commonly referred to as 'levelling up'. For example, the UK 2070 Commission argued that the UK needs a sustained, 50-year, 'levelling up' plan, with major reinvestment in skills, devolution of power, transport and economic investment. It should 'go big or go home'.

Experts including the Centre for Cities[3] have pointed out that what the UK needs now to tackle in regional inequalities is economic investment on the scale of that seen in East Germany after the fall of the Berlin Wall. Sustaining huge inequalities between the South East of England and the rest of the country is socially unjust and economically foolish. Hard and shortened lives cost us all. But it needs political will and ambition, from Westminster as well as Cardiff.

The second was the need to reconnect education policy with wider social and economic policies. In our recent book,[4] Debra Hayes and I argued that trying to fix 'disadvantage gaps' in education in isolation from the accelerating problems of child poverty and unequal childhoods has been one of the 'great mistakes' of education policy in both England and Australia in recent years. Here, from Wales, we also hear loud and clear about the pressure educators feel to respond to thin and meaningless targets (disconnected from local realities) and to do so through standardised pedagogical and leadership approaches.

This edited book is a clarion call to the Welsh Government (and those in other nations and jurisdictions too) first of all to make sure that the problems of child poverty are adequately addressed by decent social security and multi-agency approaches, not left to schools, and secondly to entrust heads and teachers with developing curricula and pedogogy that engage, energise, empower and connect children and young people. It is salient that an Australian academic is a key player in this project. Many of the good examples of contextualised schooling in disadvantaged communities come from that country.[5]

Third, I was struck by the need for greater imagination and courage to embrace new ideas in economic and social policy. This book draws on foundational economy thinking. FE highlights that traditional growth models neglect the fact around 40 per cent of the workforce is engaged with providing basic goods and services, upon which wellbeing and 'civilised life' depends. The primary role of public policy should be to secure basic goods and services as forms of collective consumption. Education, training, economic development and climate action should be linked to an area's 'foundational economy', as in the case of the Not-NEET's project described here.

But the foundational economy is just one among a number of emerging developments in economic thought and action which offer new ways of meeting the current challenges of economic change, inequality (and associated costs of social welfare) and climate emergency in more holistic ways. They include Inclusive Growth, Doughnut Economics, Community Wealth Building and Wellbeing Economy. In social policy, there is international interest in moving from traditional welfare state models to the provision of Universal Basic Income (UBI) or alternatively to Universal Basic Services (UBS) or a form of 'Social Guarantee'.

Whilst in England, there is a distinct lack of interest, at national governmental level, in these developments in economic and social policy, this is not the case in Wales, which is a leader internationally, and widely looked as a leading exemplar of new social democratic thinking. Translating the ideas and top-level statements into changed investment priorities and practical, funded action on the ground is still a work in progress, as this book demonstrates. But the Welsh context certainly creates cause for hope that old policy mistakes will not just be rehearsed, and new more radical directions will be taken, with more equitable consequences. All the more important, then, that cases like Trem y Mynydd's are made visible.

Call to action

In many ways, it is a shameful reflection on contemporary UK society that this book has to be written. Surely no-one can come to these chapters without feeling shock and shame at the deep poverty still endured in Trem y Mynydd and the failures of the policies of the last quarter century to make things better.

But the book is also a call to action. It demonstrates how local communities, working with allies from universities, charities and government, can embrace, exemplify and drive change, and it articulates the support and imagination they need from local and national government. At a time of general gloom, I feel sure that those who read it will be moved and inspired by its honesty, courage and radicalism. I hope that it plays its part in stimulating action not just for Trem y Mynydd, but for the many communities across the UK and internationally that continue to be held back by similar injustices.

Notes

1   R. Lupton (2003) *Poverty Street: the dynamics of neighbourhood decline and renewal.* Bristol: Policy Press.
2   L. Richardson (2008) DIY Community Action: neighbourhood problems and community self-help. Bristol: Policy Press.
3   See *What can German reunification teach the UK about levelling up? | Centre for Cities* Lupton (accessed 28 April 2023).
4   Lupton, R and Hayes, D. (2021) *Great Mistakes in Education Policy: and how to avoid them in the future* Bristol: Policy Press.
5   Hayes, D., Hattam, R., Comber, B., Kerkham, L., Lupton, R. and Thomson, P. (2017) *Literacy, Leading and Learning: Beyond Pedagogies of Poverty.* Abingdon; New York: Routledge. Hayes, D., Mills, M., Christie, P. and Lingard, B. (2005) *Teachers and Schooling Making a Difference: Productive Pedagogies, Assessment and Performance.* Sydney: Allen and Unwin. Munns, G., Sawyer, W. and Cole, B. (eds) (2013) *Exemplary Teachers of Students in Poverty.* London and New York: Routledge. Thomson, P. (2007) 'Making Education More Equitable: What can Policy Makers Learn from the Australian Disadvantaged Schools Programme?', in R. Teese, S. Lamb, and M. Duru-Bellat (eds) *International Studies in Educational Inequality, Theory and Policy.* Dordrecht: Springer Netherlands, pp. 239–56

EDITORS' INTRODUCTION

'THE LITTLE CASE THAT CAN' CONJOIN THE LOCAL AND NATIONAL TO ADDRESS CHILD POVERTY

Lori Beckett (Bangor University)

Introduction

This book, edited by an academic partner to the Trem y Mynydd school-community, recounts the work of a determined group of school staff, multi-agency workers and academic partners who joined forces with resident families and critical friends to push back against child poverty, especially its ongoing influence on schooling success. Trem y Mynydd is a pseudonym, in line with ethical protocols to protect the identity of these people and anonymise this place, which has a fascinating history that is tied to the Penrhyn family dynasty of slate-mining infamy in North Wales and beyond. Its history of disadvantage is in the present, marked by successive UK government policy choices, which sees the locals battling the damage done by de-industrialisation, unemployment, exploitation of the working poor, universal credit, benefit cuts and Brexit.[1] These lived experiences were all exacerbated by the Covid-19 pandemic, which saw people here dealing with a social emergency that melded into the cost-of-living crisis rightly called a humanitarian disaster.[2] Yet they show not only remarkable fortitude but also ingenuity in devising local solutions to these problems of poverty and inequalities.[3] These are then linked to projects that guard against children, young people and adults joining the ranks of those not in employment, education and training, which is to take advice from the Child Poverty Action Group (2017: 208) that the best strategy is to ensure that they should not be poor.

I came to this school-community through a series of referrals via the North Wales regional school improvement consortia GwE and Bangor University,[4] where I met Caryl Elin Lewis, who had won the competitive tender for the 2018–19 Welsh Government-sponsored *Children First* needs assessment (health and well-being). She invited me to Trem y Mynydd, specifically the sessions she had designed to solicit professional advice and input from participants, including the school Head, multi-agency workers and managers, and local authority workers, on improving the lot of resident families but specifically children and young people. This dovetailed with the 2015 Well-being and Future Generations (Wales) Act, a cornerstone of Wales's suite of progressive policies from its devolved government. In a brainstorming session to plug into Lewis's final report and strategic plan that included practical policy recommendations to Gwynedd Council and Welsh Government, the ongoing need for further research was made known.[5] This was the subject of intense debate, especially given local residents had made it known that they wanted nothing to do with research that made no difference to their lives.

I stepped up to canvass support for building a place-based action study to become part of a multi-cities ethnography that was just coming into being given the recommendations from our BERA commission on poverty and policy advocacy (see Ivinson et al., 2018; Ivinson and Thompson, 2020). The Bangor Poverty and Learning in Urban Schools (PLUS) project[6] was then developed in Trem y Mynydd, with support from Bangor University's head of the School of Educational Sciences, Professor Carl Hughes, who sponsored two series of six-monthly seminars designed to mentor and support practitioners to become research- and policy-active. My role was then formalised as a Visiting Professor at Bangor University, which coincided with my working with colleagues as an Adjunct Professor at Griffith University in Brisbane. The first series of seminars overlapped with the release of UN Special Rapporteur Philip Alston's (2019) probe into *Extreme Poverty and Human Rights in the UK*, which featured Wales and which drew our attention on human rights and the Welsh Government's response to the report. This culminated in a planned presentation to invited guests: Wales's then Children's Commissioner Sally Holland, and Alasdair Macdonald, an adviser to Wales's then Education Minister, Liberal Democrat Kirsty Williams.

This intentional move laying the ground for engaging in research-informed policy advocacy at local/national levels instructed the substance of the second series of seminars, which intended to plug into the multi-cities ethnography taking shape across the UK and Australia. The core Bangor PLUS team of research-active practitioners assembled here then decided to work towards an edited book. I reached out to international policy scholar Bob Lingard (University of Queensland) to discuss ideas, given that he was well placed to provide feedback on a social democratic social imaginary, which is reflected in successive Welsh governments' progressive policy frameworks.[7] Thinking about how things might be otherwise infused the Bangor PLUS team's efforts to articulate how the situation on Trem y Mynydd might be different to the ways things are now. Our work was then majorly interrupted by Covid-19 when everyone had to re-orient their work practices as 2020 unfolded month-by-month, but we re-grouped in January 2021 and reaffirmed the decision to publish the team's case stories. It should be noted at the outset that these are shared and reiterated across this book, notably because of the complexities that require attention in myriad ways by contributing authors who have different professional responsibilities and who are variously situated in work settings on this housing estate. As we were submitting the manuscript, I reached out to Ruth Lupton (University of Manchester) to write the foreword: her work had been equally inspiring (see Lupton, 2003; Lupton and Hayes, 2021).

All the contributing authors in this edited book share the view that if, in this tumultuous era, Wales's national and regional governments in Cardiff and Caernarfon are to respond to local needs on the Trem y Mynydd housing estate, the emphases needs to be placed on reconstructing the welfare state in the first instance, but simultaneously on local research-informed policy advocacy with appropriate models for doing it (see Calder et al., 2012). *Children First* inspired the Bangor PLUS team, and together they provide a model way of working given it is a school-community-university partnership,[8] but none of this has been straightforward: Welsh Government did not provide funding to follow through on the findings of the *Children First* needs assessment, and the Bangor PLUS team have worked together through their own volition.[9] Residents' need for emergency welfare support on this housing estate, including that provided by the school, is relentless, made worse by Covid-19 and the cost-of-living crisis that followed. Covid-19 intermittently grounded various team members and their families, including the school Head who was struck with long Covid. Likewise resident families were hit, with parents so often distracted by distress, sickness and worries rooted in their lived experiences of poverty. None of this can be understated.[10]

In this chapter, I describe what it means to be an academic partner with a belief in the feasibility of practical thinking for working in a school-community in challenging circumstances, which requires a social imagination that comes with engagement in a constructive analysis of the present, including the history in the present, and of possible and probable futures.[11] I then introduce Lewis's *Children First* needs assessment on Trem y Mynydd and tease out the practical-political obligations to resident families in her ethnographic narrative about their lived experiences of poverty. This pre-empts an 'ethnography that makes a difference' that points to tackling inequalities in this school-community.[12] I elaborate on the composition of the Bangor PLUS team to emphasise the involvement of practitioners outside academic institutions and to recognise the perspectives and contributions of experts in the practice work setting, and highlight the worth of their responsive educative work that runs across a number of portfolios. I describe the efforts of forging a notion of school-community development, which coordinates with solutions that can all be reasonably done locally to institute regenerative and sustainable practices at the heart of the 2015 Well-being and Future Generations (Wales) Act, and which has the potential to permanently lift resident families out of poverty. I then present my conclusions, which requires Wales's governments in Cardiff and Caernarfon to enact education as a public good as a cornerstone of a foundational economy, buttressed by a business case for public investment in our local solutions allied to their projects to avert becoming NEETs, and promoted here to realise Wales's promises on well-being and 'prosperity for all'. This is all in marked contrast to the ways families including children and young people in poverty are stigmatised in neo-liberal discourses.[13]

History in the present

Working as an academic partner[14] with schools in challenging circumstances is akin to a supervisory role of student teachers, meeting school staff, engaging conversations and observations, mentoring and supporting these colleagues new to the profession confronting educational and social inequalities, but it is more expansive. This requires deep learning about the local context, reaching out to the school-community and networking, operating with sensitivity, respect and regard for resident families functioning under duress and for those on the frontline working in stressful time-pressured situations. The intention over time is to build trust going every which way, create opportunities for stimulating informal conversations and being open to knowledge – building as a collaborative and cooperative venture. This also requires thinking and theorising about child poverty in relation to the practical-political realities with a view to mentoring and supporting colleagues to be both research- and policy-active, then acting in a secretarial role to publicise their case stories.[15] It is no doubt a challenge to conventional ways of working both in and out of a university,[16] but it is one way to broach the apparent breakdown in the research-policy-practice nexus to improve the lot of resident families.

A study of local history triggers deep learning about the local context.[17] The images with captions spread across this book provides a backdrop to the Trem y Mynydd housing estate, which was once 70-odd acres of open-space farmland sold in 1937 to Bangor City Council by the fourth Lord Penrhyn, Hugh Napier Douglas-Pennant (1894–1949). He was the grandson of the second Lord Penrhyn, George Sholto Gordon Douglas-Pennant (1836–1907), who had earned his notoriety in the Penrhyn Quarry lockout over three years at the turn of the twentieth century. This was said to be the longest running industrial dispute in Britain and it condemned the slate quarrymen to penury (see Jones, 1981; Lindsay, 1974, 1987; Jones, 1903). The Penrhyn family home, a fantasy castle, boasts vast displays of intergenerational wealth and grandeur that showcases what it means to be rich and powerful as well as the extent of the yawning gap between rich and poor.[18] Of particular interest were the negotiations over the sale price of £4,000 for Trem y Mynydd, which signalled then central and local governments' substantial public investment in social housing. This was no doubt a source of great pride for new tenants, workers in Penrhyn's quarries and Port Penrhyn, who were being re-located from the city centre then undergoing re-generation.[19]

The history of disadvantage in the present was impressed upon me by my first drive onto the Trem y Mynydd housing estate, which brought to mind Lupton's (2003) work on neighbourhood decline given that this place is marked by urban degeneration, notably in dilapidated public buildings, the ruins of the social club and some unkempt houses and landscapes. It is important not to be blinded by the obvious signs of being poor and disadvantaged, where residents do not have the money for home improvements and decorative gardens, but to critically consider the plight of living in poverty in a rich country. As the Child Poverty Action Group (2017) has it, poverty is something that is done to people and it is affected by political decisions. Most influential have been consecutive UK Conservative government prime ministers' hallmark policies promoting neo-liberal logics for a global economy: Thatcher's de-industrialisation, Cameron's austerity and Johnson's Global Britain agenda apropos Brexit, not to forget his oversight of the Covid-19 pandemic.[20] These have had some devastating effects on Wales with the nation reeling from the economic fallout from the loss of industry in Gwynedd, which came after the decline of the slate and allied industries. This was followed by decades of Westminster governments' budget cuts with Johnson and most recently his replacement Prime Ministers Liz Truss and Rishi Sunak committing the UK to a continuation of conservative economic policy dogma.

These sorts of informed discussions in the school-community precipitate a critical understanding of child poverty broadened out to the neo-liberal drivers of the global economy and what they mean for children's schooling. Lingard's work with colleagues (see Rizvi and Lingard, 2010; also Thomson, Lingard and Wrigley, 2012) has been crucial here, especially where they spotlight national governments that are keen to realign their educational priorities to what they perceive to be the imperatives of globalisation. This is to be found in Wales's devolved system of education given Labour education minister Jeremy Miles's concerns with 'raising attainment' and 'closing the gap', which is surprising only to the extent that such neo-liberal policy emphases do not sit well with a purported commitment to social democracy. As the Child Poverty Action Group (2017) argued, recent government policy emphasis (across the UK) tends to hone in on low educational achievement, worklessness, family instability, addictions and mental health, as well as poor parenting. These sort of foci, the group indicated, directs attention towards people's behaviour and away from the real structural and political causes of poverty, which point to the importance of current income and immediate everyday well-being. As they put it:

the effects of poverty & hardship upon children are so large and so immediate ... that it is impossible to discount the basic importance of [parents'] present income and the need to improve children's well-being by greater public investment now. (2017: 3)

None of this is lost on the contributing authors assembled here, especially when it comes to schooling and education, food insecurity, housing, the built environment and the natural environment among other socio-economic considerations that threaten resident families' standard of living widely accepted by most people in the UK. As foretold nearly ninety years ago by the Bangor city engineer responsible for social housing, Price Davies (1937), a major issue remains the geographical location of the Trem y Mynydd housing estate, which decries easy access to Bangor city's services and opportunities to work and enrol in education and training. This would sufficiently increase families' income to provide a publicly agreed-upon standard of living, but as things stand these all greatly affect the well-being and life chances afforded to children, young people and adults alike. In all my time networking with the locals, I have witnessed not only punishing hardship and unacceptable deprivation but also their grit and determination to put things right for the next generation. Despite lost opportunities in their own schooling, they showed great intelligence in devising local solutions to the problems of being poor in a rich country. These are here allied to responsive educative programmes dubbed the Not-NEET projects, which are introduced below and in the following chapters, as well as in the appendices.[21]

An 'ethnography that makes a difference'

Lewis's considerations in chapter 1 include a review of national and local government commitments to poverty reductions and a critical understanding of poverty as a social justice matter, which began with the Welsh Government's *Children First* principles to secure children's health and well-being. Her tender to win the commission had rested on proposing a close study of the locality, with an indication that evidence would be forthcoming from public data, issues arising, human services provision, gaps if any, and case stories of real-life experiences of families and multi-agency workers on the estate. She designed sessions to solicit advice and input from those professionals deployed to work on the Trem y Mynydd housing estate, and she provided draft reports as pre-reading to facilitate an interrogation of findings and preliminary analyses. This yielded valuable insights not only from the professionals but also from interview data that local residents and critical friends had contributed. Lewis identified analytic patterns in the quantitative data termed 'General population and area facts' and in the qualitative data grouped under the major headings 'Strengths and assets' and 'Barriers and threats'. Those in attendance could extrapolate what was required to ensure that children's health and well-being would not be further disadvantaged by lived experiences of child poverty, even though inequalities were even then becoming more and more explicit.

As the *Children First* needs assessment drew to a close a group decision was made to invite the civil servant in Cardiff with responsibility for *Children First* nation-wide and other local dignitaries to visit and do an 'estate walk', which provided an opportunity to relay some valuable understandings of the lived experiences of poverty to those with seemingly some authority.[22] There was also recognition that in the previous twenty years innumerable anti-poverty policies, all well funded, made very little difference to resident families' standards of living on the Trem y Mynydd housing estate.[23] With the call for further research, colleagues had no appetite for textbook research[24] and the consensus was such that Lewis's *Children First* needs assessment had capably done a first ethnographic sketch of what it is like to be poor: she identified needs, embarked on analyses, openly discussed 'theories of change' and provided local and national governments with data and directions for improvements. It was clear a critical consideration of children's needs and assets should inform requisite amendments to policies and programmes, while the disinvestment and reinvestment of regional and national government funding should influence not only adjustments in service provision but help eliminate child poverty in a rich country. The proviso was such that a focus on inequalities needed to be maintained.

This call for further research, whilst alert to residents' sentiments about irrelevant research that showed no dividend, sparked critical discussion among academic partners and the school Head about 'ethnography that makes a difference'.[25] It began with questions about definitions of child poverty, notably as need in the *Children First* needs assessment, and recognition that there are demands made of the school but also that it can be constrained in its responses to inequalities. The willingness to support the school and ongoing collaboration in the school-community is something to be harnessed, especially given the relationships established during the needs assessment, but there is an immediate sense of urgency. As the charity Children in Wales (see McFarlane, 2021) noted, its fifth annual survey findings are bleak and unacceptable, which equates with practitioners' views here that resident families are struggling to cope with financial challenges, increases in debt levels, hunger and other stresses. That said, a lot of parents on Trem y Mynydd deliberately put their children first and go without to adequately provide for their families, and all but a small minority of children present as healthy and happily engaged in school and other social activities. However, there are costs as these parents are often forced to choose between feeding themselves or their families, heating the home or slipping into rental arrears, dealing with anxieties or sometimes acting out, which all speak to the challenges that poverty poses in this school-community.

These sorts of challenges are picked up in chapter 2 by Evans, a fictitious character devised to stand in for the school Head who left at the end of the last school year after being struck down with long Covid. Before that, she had actively participated in *Children First* and our Bangor PLUS team meetings but she was obviously concerned about policy directives like 'raising attainment' and 'closing the gap' and hamstrung by welfare demands, staff burn-out and a lack of funding. This was all the more so after the pandemic during her phased return to work, but she greatly encouraged our project and academic partners have stepped in here to finish her chapter. It reflects many conversations over the years, notably her thoughts and sentiments about children's unmet needs in the Trem y Mynydd school-community. She certainly wanted it made known that a small number of resident families and their children, often numbering 4–5 at any one time, are the ones who cause inordinate disruption to school routine. This is not to demean these families and children because Evans acknowledged that their case stories are linked to a nation-wide cost-of-living crisis, pre-Covid and subsequently. She agreed that both the 2015 Well-being of Future Generations (Wales) Act and 2018–19 *Children First* needs assessment should be properly funded and operationalised at ground level – and saw this as the bedrock of a socially just school.[26]

Given ideas about 'ethnography that makes a difference', the Bangor PLUS project team likewise takes seriously Mills and Morton's (2013) conclusions about speaking truth to power, and resolved to intermittently brief politicians, power brokers and policy-makers in Cardiff and Caernarfon. Heartened by the Child Poverty Action Group's (2017) view that poverty responds quickly and effectively to policy, the task ahead was to realise the ambitions of the 2015 Well-being and Future Generations (Wales) Act and the *Children First* needs assessment. Davidson (2020) provided direction in her statement about national politics that 'Social justice and tackling poverty remain key political themes, as does the wider equality agenda including ethnicity and gender' (p. 5). Hence the need for the Bangor PLUS project as a model way of working: the design of the two seminar series took as its starting point a collaborative and cooperative approach to learning, mentoring and supporting practitioners to become research- and policy-active, reading and knowledge-building; encouraging the team to voice the practical-political realities of child poverty in terms of both children's needs, assets and strengths on this housing estate, recording the evidence for research-informed policy advocacy and lobbying for support to fund contextually sensitive and locally responsive educative work.

'The little case that can'

The first series of monthly seminars ran smoothly over a six-month period in 2019 led by academic partners. It was well attended by Caryl Elin Lewis and most of the frontline workers who participated in the *Children First* needs assessment, including Catrin Thomas, a senior policy officer in local government, who had oversight. These practitioners ordinarily work in silos given Welsh Government's ministerial appointments, policy responsibilities and government administration, so it was encouraging to see colleagues liaising across a number of portfolios and developing multi-disciplinary perspectives. They shared commitments and mutual concerns, what with Trem y Mynydd being among the 10 per cent most deprived areas in the Wales Index of Multiple Deprivation data categories.[27] The possible effect on children's learning meshed with critical discussion of the BERA Commission on Poverty and Policy Advocacy focused on poverty and multiple factors of deprivation that took issue with dominant pathologising discourses of poor people in order to develop counter-discourses and critical research. The Bangor PLUS team came to interrogate concepts of child poverty to develop the argument that the challenges are not peculiar to this school-community given globalisation and wider systemic and structural origins, but they are open to systemic and structural change. To this end, they co-designed local solutions and tied together the responsive educative potential into allied Not-NEET projects. They came to regard their collective efforts as 'the little case that can'.[28]

What it is like to live in poverty in a rich country features again in chapter 3 by Dafydd Jones, a fictitious character standing in for the local primary school Secretary, who in the end opted out of finishing this chapter after the departure of the school Head. They had worked closely together deciding on storylines, choosing case stories and sharing their corporate memories as well as their commitments to a socially just school. Luckily much of this was conveyed in professional conversations with academic partners, who again stepped up to complete the writing. Their notes are useful to showcase what it means for school staff to be confronted by extraordinary challenges in regards welfare work. This chapter details the minutiae of resident families' unmet needs that play out at the front office, but while the school Secretary insisted on an open-door policy he wanted it made known that the school's support is forever constrained by a lack of funding and resources. This can prompt parents'/carers' grievances and animosity, and the school Secretary's local solution was to ensure that the idea of a full-service school be incorporated into the mooted plans for the Youth Hall were it to become a new-build multi-agency hub. Although on another site, it is close enough to foster close ties with school staff and links to the Not-NEET project, 'Co-ordinating the future: the Youth Hall as a multi-agency hub' (see appendix 2).

A shared commitment to *Children First* and mutual concerns regarding the Welsh Index of Multiple Deprivation data categories are picked up in chapter 4 on food insecurities by Mead Silvester, writing with Joslin, who both have elaborate local knowledge of the lived experiences of poverty on Trem y Mynydd. Before they left their posts, they both worked to deliver food parcels with a team of volunteers who provide this community's tailored, local response to food insecurity. As a community development worker in a drop-in centre, Mead Silvester provided support on numerous health and welfare concerns, pre-Covid, and since its fallout, loss of employment and the cost-of-living crisis. Most importantly, she critically understands resident families' needs, all of which speaks to what it is like living in poverty in a rich country. Joslin then contributed his ideas for a local solution, given his work on secondment from Wild Elements to establish community gardens for the cultivation of food, among other initiatives. This is underpinned by the vision of the 'Incredible Edible' network across the UK to create kind, confident and connected communities. Both these authors promote the ways and means to ensure resident families' human right to food (see Lambie-Mumford, 2017), and linked their arguments to their allied Not-NEET project, 'Cultivating the estate: establishing community food gardens' (see appendix 3).

A shared commitment to *Children First* and mutual concerns about living conditions are discussed again in chapter 5 on housing and fuel poverty, with contributions by Dylan Fernley and another local resident Pete Whitby who likewise briefed academic partners. They too have elaborate local knowledge derived from living on Trem y Mynydd: Fernley is also an elected representative on Gwynedd Council and privy to resident families' housing needs and complaints, and Whitby contributes his calculations on the unbearable costs of gas, electricity and other fuel to local residents in receipt of universal credit. This is all invaluable data as together they too spotlight what it is like living in poverty in a rich country, and they are joined by Grant Peisley who does freelance consultative work on green industries and regeneration planning. He brings his professional knowledge of the comparable costs of renewable energy and how upgrading estate housing can work. Together they tie their analyses to inequalities provoked by Wales's complex large-scale economy at ground level, mindful of the problems with external companies commissioned to build and provide energy that leads to profit extraction with little or no benefits to local resident families. They then spell out their local solution allied to their Not-NEET project, 'Powering the estate: home-grown energy supply' (see appendix 4).

This first series of seminars overlapped with the release of UN Special Rapporteur Philip Alston's (2019) probe into *Extreme Poverty and Human Rights in the UK*, which featured Wales. I reached out to Alston to advise him of our work and received an encouraging reply, saying that our work showed the potential for change. This focused the mind, given that he was the John Norton Pomeroy Professor of Law at the University of New York and we were studying legislation, including the Well-being of Future Generations (Wales) Act 2015. This drew our attention to human rights and the Welsh Government's response to the report, which all culminated in our planned presentation to invited guests: Wales's then Children's Commissioner Sally Holland, and Alasdair Macdonald, an adviser to then Education Minister Kirsty Williams. This event, which showcased the Bangor PLUS team's budding project, laid out practitioners' frontline challenges and concerns about government anti-poverty policies rolled out over many years that had not the desired benefits to local resident families. Holland and Macdonald cordially received our briefings and acknowledged our project as a promising model way of working. This was a nod to the importance of recognising and acting on the perspectives and contributions of experts in the practice work setting.

Forging a notion of school-community development

The second series of monthly seminars ran smoothly over a six-month period spanning October 2019 through to March 2020. It was again well supported by Caryl Elin Lewis and Catrin Thomas, together with the small group of frontline workers who came to make up the Bangor PLUS team that included academic partners and critical friends. We agreed that our focus would be poverty and human rights for the multi-cities ethnography, and we set about developing the contours of our signature argument.[29] Being well versed with certain children's exclusion from the local primary school, our focus of attention came to be children's access to schooling and we were guided by questions about what facilitates and/or denies this; how poverty impacted on it; in what ways, if any, were there infringements/violations of human rights; and who/what should bear/share the responsibility. This interrogation was not to 'blame the victim' nor engage deficit readings, but to highlight the reality gaps between the lived experiences of poverty, Wales's various political parties' manifestos, and Welsh Government's legislation, especially anti-poverty policies rolled out in school-communities. We came to see that these gaps can be bridged by practitioners' preferred local solutions, which effectively means responding educatively to matters of basic human rights.

Gwen Thirsk, writing in chapter 6, takes issue with deficit readings of local residents by well-meaning frontline professionals when they see them as problems to be fixed. She promotes common values and principles to underpin development work in the school-community, building on an asset-based community development (ABCD) approach and links this to school development. To illustrate how this might work, she draws on case stories of parents of pre-school- and school-age children to describe the strengths and assets readily apparent on Trem y Mynydd. Key here was a group of young mums who came forward with a proposal for a place-based crèche enhanced with a vision for 0–2 education to set their children on their way, which was developed into a bid to the Welsh Government's Foundational Economy Challenge Fund. This was not successful, but it remains a popular local solution given the complexities of childcare for families engaged in round-the-clock shift work. Thirsk also draws on conversations with the school Head and another community development worker about sponsoring a family support officer: again this did not proceed because of a lack of funding, but it remains another popular local solution. These are greatly enriched by Thirsk's narrative on ABCD,[30] which is reflected in their Not-NEET project, 'Starting out for the future: 0–2 years' on-site crèche' (see appendix 5).

Maclean is another local resident writing in chapter 7 who chronicles his own difficulties in securing a positive schooling experience, which unsurprisingly resulted in his disaffection and disengagement that had its consequences in struggling to achieve GCSE results. That he stayed in school was testament to the youth workers on the estate at the time, who provided an outlet for his creative expression. After stints in various apprenticeships, he finally found success in a music technology course at Coleg Menai in Bangor as a student and tutor, then in 18-months of mentorship training with Community Music Wales to gain the qualifications to develop community music programmes. Maclean has since built up an impressive performing arts programme on Trem y Mynydd and here he showcases his collaboration with Daws on the 'Letters Grow' lyricism and hip hop project, a word play on 'let us grow'. Together they draw on Welsh oral traditions rich with song and poetry to combine with African oral traditions to develop a particular version of contemporary music. This resonates with the local children and young people, especially those at risk of disengagement and alienation from schooling yet who show great interest in such appealing approaches to language and literacy. Maclean's programme, a local solution to counter miseducation (see Reay, 2017), well informs the allied Not-NEET project, 'Acting on the future: student expression in the performing arts' (see appendix 6).

Chapter 8 is written by Graham French, who is an academic partner and who joined forces with Claudia Howard from Wild Elements, which is a local not-for-profit social enterprise organisation dedicated to engaging children and young people in learning in the outdoors. They were called on by the Bangor PLUS team to help articulate ways in which to respond educatively to some major concerns about families in need of welfare support, especially where these were concerned with the child's right to education as a matter of basic human rights. They discuss their contribution in addressing some of the many challenges facing the school, and especially the issue where a handful of young students are troubled and not reaching their potential within the traditional structures of schooling, to the point where a small number have been excluded. Their responsive co-developed Wild Elements outdoor learning programme is posited as a local solution targeted at the whole school population as an entitlement, not just for disengaged and alienated students, though it has the potential to facilitate re-entry back into primary school, transition into high school and post-school destinations. When aligned to their Not-NEET project, 'Rooting for the future: Wild Elements outdoor learning' (see appendix 7), it provides children and young people with all sorts of opportunities that will help them understand themselves and their lived experiences but also their place in the world.

At the end of the second series of seminars we had planned to work towards another presentation to invited guests, this time Bob Lingard and Philip Alston, anticipating that these briefings would provide opportunities to raise questions about practitioner voices in a social democracy and its place in Wales's future as a nation-state: especially after briefing the *Children First* national manager on an invited 'estate walk', then in my submission to Wales's Child Poverty Review. It was alarming that nothing came of these initiatives, especially given our time and effort to say the least. Regrettably this eagerly awaited conclusion to our second lot of seminars was ultimately disrupted by the first Covid-19 lockdown. This brought into sharp relief the consequences of Thatcher's de-industrialisation, Cameron's austerity and Johnson's Global Britain agenda apropos Brexit: all of which were exacerbated by Covid-19. When our Bangor PLUS project team re-grouped the task was to decide on some strategic ways forward. While frontline workers, including school staff and those in the drop-in centre, had to deal with incessant welfare demands as an upshot of social emergencies, they persevered with this edited book. However, it was ultimately left to academic partners to look to the future, take up the task of policy advocacy marked by a rationale and business case, and win support for the seven local solutions and allied Not-NEET projects devised by local residents in concert with our Bangor PLUS team.

Avoiding great mistakes in education/social policy

The report from our BERA Commission on Poverty and Policy Advocacy was another instance of an initiative being cordially received by the association's executive officer and then president Professor Gary McCulloch.[31] There was seemingly no immediate actions taken on its recommendations, which required discussion at BERA Council though, to the best of my knowledge, this did not take place.[32] The twin lesson that I learned from this was to be cognisant of different conceptual understandings of poverty and policy advocacy, and ways that key concerns like hungry children line up as research priorities seen for their utility in attracting research funding. I had to acknowledge the political calculus even in a team of co-researchers, never mind the wider professional research association. It was not enough to rely on documented knowledge of school-communities in poverty and expect a moral imperative to result in strategic action because 'poverty and schooling' is contested by those in powerful positions. The Child Poverty Action Group (2017) articulated some considerations in determining actions: concepts of poverty[33] that seek to describe and explain how (young) people are captured in poverty, such as social and economic exclusion, spatial isolation, degraded opportunity and diminished political authority, are more or less templates to help shape policy and anti-poverty strategies. As they put it, how you understand poverty – what template you choose – influences where you place the emphasis among such strategies.[34]

The Bangor PLUS project was conceived as a place-based action study, with the potential to be part of a BERA-AARE multi-cities ethnography, which is taken up again in the final chapter co-authored with fellow academic partners Graham French and Carl Hughes, and community development worker Gwen Thirsk, who has kept pace with the project since its inception and provided invaluable counsel. We draw some conclusions about the lived experiences of poverty in this local area to tell the national story of Wales, which is seen as a small European nation-state purporting to be a social democracy in or out of the UK. There remains much to be done to secure the future, and Beckett et al. also posit a co-designed local solution, this time to tap into some of the social and economic benefits from heritage tourism accrued from the slate landscape of northwest Wales being inscribed as a UNESCO World Heritage Site. They focus on Port Penrhyn with their Not-NEET project, 'Rigging the future: Welsh slate boats and World Heritage' (see appendix 8), which is a reminder that local school-communities must not be denied opportunities that come with economic regeneration, site protection and maritime heritage conservation. Like the other Not-NEET projects, it too would benefit from a facilitation fund to be managed by the Trem y Mynydd Cooperative with a board comprised of local residents and frontline workers and governed in line with cooperative models.[35]

Richard Watkins, writing an invited chapter, provides his response and advice to the Bangor PLUS project team in his capacity as lead worker on research and evaluation with the North Wales school improvement consortium or gwasanaeth gwella ysgolion rhanbarthol Gogledd Cymru known as GwE. He considered how our ideas for school-community development might interact with GwE, given its role as a more research-informed support network for schools concerned with mitigating the impact of poverty on schools' reform efforts, teachers' work and student learning outcomes. His focus is on the logistics of our work in relation to the school improvement services in Wales, which have evolved over recent years into a more collaborative model designed to offer bespoke support for schools, which includes in-service teacher education and which interlocks with pre-service programmes. In providing advice to us, Watkins draws on Thomson, Lingard and Wrigley's (2012) unifying trope, that is, ideas for practice at systemic, policy, school and pedagogic levels. He describes the efforts required of regional school improvement services to engage with our research-informed policy advocacy to promote effective teaching and learning strategies alert to child poverty, especially its extent and effects in schools serving disadvantaged communities.

Responsive and advisory statements were also sought from others keen to avoid making great mistakes in education/social policy[36] and who hold prominent roles in policy circles. Eithne Hughes, also writing an invited chapter, is a former secondary school Head, now director of the Association of School and College Leaders (ASCL) Cymru branch and fellow Visiting Professor at Bangor University. She knows fully the contours of policy emphases on meeting the needs of disadvantaged students, and she is well placed to provide critical commentary on the model Bangor PLUS project, which is ready to be scaled up across Wales. It would be best trailed in the other *Children First* areas and implemented subject to support from Welsh Government, but another needs and assets assessment should be done again in 2023, a timely five years after the last one! I also reached out to teacher education academic Sue Whatman (Griffith University) to write an invited chapter, given that she is a central figure to the BERA-AARE multi-cities ethnography project and she is struck by the significance of the 2015 Well-being of Future Generations (Wales) Act to other nation-states, which features in her work in Brisbane school-communities.

When all is said and done with this edited book, I remain haunted by meetings that I had with one of the residents on Trem y Mynydd. Alys was a very young parent at 16 years of age, encouraged by her Nain (Granny) to marry the baby's father, and they went on to have a large family. They stayed together for twenty years, separating only because he developed an addiction, but, now clean, he maintains a fatherly role. Alys to this day holds onto her dream to be a trained nurse, even though she was dissuaded by her Nain, who said 'people like us don't become people like them'. Eventually Alys went to college to study psychology, motivated by a yearning to know more about what she had been told about special needs education by the school nurse and welfare officer, her solicitor and court liaison officer. She had constantly been called up to both the primary and high schools attended by her children, some of whom had additional learning needs but also other problems within the education system. Her studies helped her to understand not only what she had been told in the past regarding her children but also informed the ways in which she could engage in ongoing conversations with school staff and other frontline workers, as well as those assigned to her case as each occasion warranted. With one son having been moved into care, she still battles the education system with her last three children in high school and she has a few grandchildren coming up to pre-school. She told me more than once, quite forcefully, she does not want any of them to grow up like her but that really nobody cares: they are numbers in the job centre, seen as NEETs, yet she says they are not NEETs, they are a family with dreams.

Notes

1   For an extended discussion, see Dorling (2018); Lupton et al. (2016); and Piketty (2014).

2   This is reflected in journalist John Harris's feature article titled 'This is a social emergency. Why is no one acting like it?', *The Guardian Journal*, Monday, 8 August 2022, and in Aditya Chakrabortty's article, 'In this Welsh town, the UK's humanitarian crisis has begun', *The Guardian Journal*, Saturday, 20 August 2022. It so happens that Shotton, like Trem y Mynydd, is located in North Wales, on the Bangor-London train line.

3   For an extended discussion, see Gannon et al. (2018).

4   Having retired to Wales after a twelve-year stint as a Professor of Teacher Education in England, which followed my work in Australia in teacher education marked by my research in what was then called disadvantaged schools, I could not in all conscience ignore the conclusions of Ivinson, Thompson and McKinney (2017) and also the findings of the Child Poverty Action Group (2017). Given my so-called voluntary redundancy I clearly had unfinished business on poverty and schooling (see Beckett, 2016; Ivinson et al., 2018), especially as I have since come to regard child poverty as a government policy choice, as for climate action. I responded to an e-mail about the 2018 policy forum in Cardiff, and as this edited book shows, I effectively continued my work in Wales albeit in a voluntary capacity.

5   Gwynedd Council located in Caernarfon has a particular structure of local government, which includes the local authority, see: *https://www.gwynedd. llyw.cymru/en/Council/Councillors-and-committees/How-the-Council-works/ Political-structure/Political-structure.aspx#:~:text=There%20are%2069%20 councillors%20on,the%20Cabinet%20and%20Scrutiny%20Committees* (accessed 14 April 2023).

6   Here I must credit the late Carey Philpott (Leeds Beckett University) and Ian Thompson (University of Oxford), who with me co-developed our initial bid for funding a multi-cities ethnography and though it did not go forward it was Thompson who coined the PLUS acronym.

7   Lingard is well known to academic partners via BERA-AARE-ECER annual conferences and through his support for our BERA commission, especially chairing our conference symposia. For an extended discussion on social democratic social imagination, see Taylor (2003). *Modern Social Imaginaries.* Durham and London: Public Planet Books; Rizvi and Lingard (2010); Whitty et al. (2016); and Saunders (2007).

8   Thanks to Alasdair Macdonald, special adviser to then Education Minister Kirsty Williams, for pointing this out.

9   Though I worked in a voluntary capacity, Graham French mocked a budget to show what would have been likely costings for two series of seminars to follow the *Children First* needs assessment: see appendix 1.

10 Years ago this situation was described as the greatest social threat of our times by Danny Dorling (2014).

11 This takes a cue from Jane Davidson (2020), the then Minister for Environment, Sustainability and Housing in Wales's devolved government, who proposed the Well-being and Future Generations (Wales) Act 2015, and who noted the importance of vision, values and narrative (see p. 27).

12 In developing this argument I draw on Mills and Morton (2013), specifically chapter 7, 'Ethnography that makes a difference'.

13 For an extended discussion see Folkes (2022).

14 I was first introduced to this position by school Head Shirley Steel at Whalan Public School in Western Sydney, given that she had signed up to the NSW Priority Action Schools Program: see Groundwater-Smith and Kemmis (2004).

15 This secretarial role takes inspiration from Apple's foreword in Gewirtz et al. (2009), and proved a successful way of my working with teachers in England: see Beckett (2016).

16 This challenge is equally pertinent to education faculties but also other faculties responsible for the accreditation of multi-agency workers, especially where teaching and research functions operate according to traditional protocols and time-limited funding and where management and staff struggle with budget cuts, staff redundancies and lack of research support.

17 A 'history in pictures' was on display in enlarged images of photos at a special community event in the youth hall, organised by Nigel Pickavance in January 2019, which was an opportunity for informal discussions about local history that plugged into *Children First* data gathering (see Lewis's chapter 1). Unfortunately, once dismantled the images were subsequently lost, which prompted archival searches with expert help from archivists and curators: see the acknowledgements at the front of this volume.

18 See *https://www.nationaltrust.org.uk/penrhyn-castle/features/a-brief-history -of-penrhyn-castle#:~:text=Only%20two%20years%20later%2C%20 Penrhyn,care%20of%20the%20National%20Trust* (accessed 14 April 2023).

19 This information was all gleaned from archival materials retrieved from Gwynedd Archives in Caernarfon and the National Library in Kew, with expert help from archivists and curators: see the acknowledgements at the front of this volume.

20 See Guderjan, Mackay and Stedman (2020) for a particularly useful commentary on Wales in regards Brexit.

21 This is akin to Moll (2019), which builds on Gonzalez et al. (2005). Also see Lingard (2013).

22 It became apparent that nothing would come of it because the civil servant responsible for overseeing *Children First* was soon redeployed.

23 Here it is important to acknowledge Gwynedd Council senior policy officer Catrin Thomas for her contributions to the Bangor PLUS team's discussions.

24 As described by Mills and Morton (2013: 130), in regards writing a research proposal and design, seeking a funding grant, and carrying out further fieldwork.

25 Again, see Mills and Morton (2013: esp. pp. 131–2) for ways of doing ethnography differently.

26 The school Head was particularly taken with the published output of scholars like Lingard, Lupton and Smyth, and took to heart Smyth (2012).

27 See the 2014 and 2019 WIMD, notably family income and employment status; health; parents'/carers' experiences/levels of education; family access to services; community safety; and physical environment and housing.

28 This took a cue from the news report of an environmentalist's story protesting against the climate crisis in Australia, headlined 'the little case that could' (*The Sun-Herald*, 17 February 2019).

29 In the planned multi-cities project academic partners had negotiated their particular foci with their home team. Bangor: poverty and human rights; Oxford: poverty and refugees; Belfast: poverty and conflict; Edinburgh: poverty and social class; Brisbane: poverty and well-being; Sydney: poverty and fairness; Geelong: poverty and de-industrialisation; Adelaide: poverty and superdiversity. This was all ultimately disrupted by Covid-19, though the Bangor and Oxford, Brisbane and Sydney teams reconvened for the 2021 virtual BERA conference, and Sue Whatman (Griffith) is contributing to this edited book.

30 This discussion is also enriched by a critical reading of a capacity-building/ capabilities approach to human rights: see Ife (2009).

31 See the final report with its recommendations (p. 31): *https://ora.ox.ac.uk/ objects/uuid:0908d3d8-afb5-42cd-8d76-f7936876b337/download_file?file_ format=pdf&safe_filename=100-160-BERA-Poverty-and-Policy-Advocacy-Final-Report.pdf&type_of_work=Report* (accessed 14 April 2023).

32 Publications followed, which were informative to the extent that our work was publicised and critical points discussed, notably the implications for policy: see Ivinson et al. (2018); and Thompson and Ivinson (2020).

33 See Townsend (1970); also Townsend (1996), which is a policy study that poses the question 'can we counter growing poverty in Britain and across the world?'

34 Terry Wrigley did much work with us on our BERA Research Commission over the years, right up to his death just after our symposium at 2021 BERA. In our last de-briefing he advised me to make contact with Ruth Lupton following the publication of her co-authored book (see Lupton and Hayes, 2021), which featured four of our teacher partners who were our students in the Leading Learning CPD programme and the MA Achievement in City Schools at Leeds Metropolitan University (see Beckett, 2016). Terry always derided individualistic perspectives and developed sophisticated structural perspectives, keen to see systemic changes in education (see Smyth and Wrigley, 2013; Thomson, Lingard and Wrigley, 2012). Ruth has contributed the foreword to this volume.

35 The Facilitation Fund was so named by one of the residents Owen MacLean (see chapter 7) and the co-operative was suggested by Pete Whitby who is another one of the residents contributing a local solution (see chapter 5), while Gwen Thirsk provided advice on the legalities: see *www.cwmpas.coop* (accessed 14 April 2023).

36 This is to borrow from the title of Lupton and Hayes (2020).

Penrhyn Castle was home to the Penrhyn family dynasty and designed to showcase its power and enormous wealth garnered in its slate quarries in North Wales but also in its sugar plantations in Jamaica. It was gifted to the National Trust in 1951 by Lady Janet Harper in lieu of death duties.

1

CHILDREN FIRST: A PLACE-BASED APPROACH TO ADDRESSING POVERTY AND INEQUALITIES

Caryl Elin Lewis (Cwmni CELyn)

Introduction

This chapter is written by the owner director of Cwmni CELyn, which was commissioned by Gwynedd Council to undertake a needs assessment of the health and well-being needs of children in Trem y Mynydd and develop a strategic plan in response to the needs identified. This came about as a result of a statement made in October 2016 by the late Carl Sargeant, Wales's then minister for communities and Children in its devolved government, inviting organisations to establish *Children First* areas in Wales.[1] This was part of the Welsh Government's ambition to create strong communities, to support children and young people in their communities and reduce the inequalities that they face when compared to their peers in more privileged areas. The idea of *Children First* that came to be developed was based on the Harlem New York Children's Zones project, which had also been replicated in England and led by Save the Children.[2]

At the time, it was emphasised that this was not a new Welsh Government programme, but a way of collaborating in a specific area for the benefit of children and young people. At the risk of repetition, the purpose, as for the aim, would entail moving towards a more expedient way of working that would bring organisations together to:

- focus on the needs of a specific area;
- work together for the benefit of children and young people within that area; and

- reduce the inequalities that those children and young people face when compared to children and young people in more privileged areas.

Gwynedd Council made known its rationale for developing a Children's Zone in Gwynedd, to be centred on a local community that consists mainly of two large areas on one housing estate, referred to here as Trem y Mynydd, given that they are geographically seamless. The community has seen a serious level of economic decline over a period of over thirty years, resulting in an increase in unemployment and decreasing local job market. This has affected the population of the estate and brought about the inherent social problems associated with unemployment, which has particularly impacted on both children and young people. What was then the most recent data from the 2014 Welsh Index of Multiple Deprivation demonstrated that the community is one of the most deprived in Gwynedd and is also included within the 10 per cent most deprived in Wales. The wards in question house 2 per cent of the whole of Gwynedd's population and the density of people in the area is very high.

The Trem y Mynydd area in Gwynedd was ultimately chosen as one of five *Children First* pilot areas in Wales, and *Children First* was launched by the Welsh Government as a new initiative and the name for children's zones in Wales. It was announced in June 2017 that the following five areas had been selected as pioneers for *Children First* in Wales:

- Trem y Mynydd, Gwynedd
- Cwm Taf
- Newport
- Caerphilly
- Carmarthenshire

Gwynedd Council, as the lead organisation who submitted the bid to be one of the pioneer areas, established a local partnership board called Trem y Mynydd Children First Board, which brought together senior leaders from key organisations working on the estate. It was this board that sought to commission an independent consultant to undertake a needs assessment and strategy for the community of Trem y Mynydd. As noted above, my company was awarded the contract, no doubt based on my earlier experience and knowledge of working in the area and past experience of working co-productively to develop an area needs assessment. I was committed to accomplish the task and to ensure that the children and families of Trem y Mynydd were able to work together with key partner organisations in an equal way to identify changes needed that would work for them all.

My work took place over an 18-month period, and in this chapter I provide the details of this work from the time it was commissioned, notably my research activities to produce interim reports then a final report and strategic plan for the Trem y Mynydd Children First Board and for Welsh Government. I draw on child poverty data for Trem y Mynydd and its school-community to explain my findings and preliminary data analyses, which lead to my chapter conclusions, which had crystallised as I had stayed on as a volunteer to work with colleagues in our Bangor PLUS team once my contract with Gwynedd Council had ended. In what follows, the *Children First* findings proved useful in building helpful understandings of child poverty, and in developing the twin ideas of a socially just school and 'school-community development' so as to engage in research-informed policy advocacy.

Winning the tender

My tender proposal to develop the place-based needs assessment was ethnographic in its orientation and proved successful. A good understanding of the local and national policy context and commitment to poverty reduction was critical, along with an understanding of the challenges faced within this particular area. It was fortuitous that I had started my career working as a local government officer, and as such I had previously spent time working within this particular community and had a good understanding of its assets, strengths and needs as well as the many organisations that work to support residents. The tender also rested on proposing a close study of the locality, with an indication that evidence would be forthcoming from public data, issues arising, human services provision, gaps if any, and case stories of real-life experiences of families and multi-agency workers on the estate.

The brief for this commission focused on two stages of work:

Stage 1 – needs assessment:

- A needs assessment would be undertaken, which would include consideration of the following:
  - health and well-being data on the community and the children and families who live in Trem y Mynydd;
  - map current issues that have been highlighted in the area, including considering community consultations that had been undertaken recently;
  - current provision of services in Trem y Mynydd;
  - gaps in service provision/issues that need to be addressed in the community.
- Identifying what should be delivered and how.

Stage 2 – long-term vision and outcomes for children and young people:

- prepare a vision for the community of the future and strategy for achieving that goal;
- outline the outcomes for children and young people in the area, and the short-term, mid-term and long-term outcomes for *Children First*.

My tender proposal was based on a thorough understanding of the brief, past experience of developing area needs assessments and strategic plans, and my deep knowledge of the area in question gained from working with this particular community as a local government officer in the past. Once the contract was awarded, the initial stages of the work involved meeting the Trem y Mynydd Children First Board to discuss the project brief and to understand what work had already been undertaken as part of the process of being chosen as one of the five *Children First* pioneer areas. I also familiarised myself with the Welsh Government support structure for this project and with the network that was formed to bring together the five areas.

In getting started, I presented a project plan to the board, which proposed in detail how I would undertake the work and the timescales for this. My aim was to ensure a 'bottom-up approach' so that the needs assessment and strategic plan were co-produced (Ersoy, 2017) and informed by the community and various other stakeholders. A stakeholder analysis was undertaken to identify who would need to be involved in this work and who else could help. Through past knowledge and experience, I was aware of the wide range of organisations working to support this community and felt that more time was needed to enable meaningful engagement and co-production every step of the way; a time extension was granted so that this could be fulfilled.

The Trem y Mynydd Children First Board agreed to form a task group in February 2018 to lead on the development and planning of the Trem y Mynydd needs assessment.[3] A mixed methodology approach was used to develop the needs assessment in order to give a comprehensive overview of the health and well-being needs of children and families in Trem y Mynydd. This consisted of:

- collection and analysis of data[4] to describe population key characteristics, health and well-being;
- qualitative information collected on the views of children, young people and their families, as well as professionals working within the area (through a mixture of focus groups, workshops, interviews and questionnaires);
- a literature review on evidence-based prevention and interventions.

A planned needs assessment document[5] would then bring together the data and information collected through various methods to create a comprehensive picture of the Trem y Mynydd community, split into twenty different key themes.[6] Under each theme, we asked two key questions:

1. What do we know about the Trem y Mynydd area?

This included quantitative data and statistics about the community.

2. What do the people and professionals tell us about the Trem y Mynydd area?

This included a mixture of qualitative and anecdotal data, gained through discussions with children, young people and their families, as well as frontline workers, including the school Head and teachers. In progressively sharing my findings with senior managers at Gwynedd

Council, who had oversight of the needs assessment, we agreed that there are many things 'known' about the area that are not quantifiable due to lack of data. For example, frontline workers and teachers told us that poor child and parental mental health was increasing but we could not find any data to evidence this. They added that the threshold for statutory services is high, and a waiting list and so many people with mental health needs were not getting any support, which was a concern.

Gathering local data

In getting underway, the focus of the needs assessment was to gain a deep understanding of what poverty and inequalities looked like in the locality, which was organised into themes that combined qualitative and quantitative data. The process, being co-produced with key stakeholders and the community, relied on the task group, a series of focus groups with frontline workers, engagement activities and events with children, young people and the community. In Wales, the *Children First* approach was to bring together organisations to improve outcomes for children and young people based around a 'place': a long-term strategic focus was to be developed with communities for that place, to reduce the inequalities faced compared with children in more socially advantaged places. *Children First* was based on seven key principles:

- clarity of place;
- long-term, shared, strategic focus;
- a focus on a community's strengths;
- local freedom and autonomy to decide the focus of activity, whilst aligning with the shared strategic vision;
- anchor organisation;
- multi-agency approach system change and effective data sharing;
- dedicated secretariat support to drive things forward.

The needs assessment identified a number of key facts about the area, which were confirmed through our many sessions on the estate engaging with families, frontline workers and key partners. An important finding was that there were a number of different agencies working on the estate, but there was a lack of early, holistic and seamless support which addressed the needs of the family as a whole. This often resulted in costly statutory intervention, high re-referral rates and the same families 'coming into the system'. Frontline workers shared that although they were working hard to help families, the families were often at 'crisis point' when they reached them, as the 'system' did not facilitate early support and intervention.

These sorts of findings were shared in periodic site-based meetings with participants, who readily identified possible root causes as well as Trem y Mynydd's strengths and assets. The needs assessment's aim was to build on this resolve, which would help determine how best to respond to the challenges faced within this community. During this process, I was soon made aware that the experiences registered were not unique to that of Trem y Mynydd. Through networking and sharing practice with other colleagues who had been commissioned in the other four areas across Wales, we identified that the conditions were a wider symptom of a 'failing system' created by national legislation and policies, and that a number of 'anti-poverty' programmes stemming back thirty years had failed to tackle the issues faced within this community and to improve conditions.

The colleagues in the five areas across Wales were clearly committed to this *Children First* project as we are passionate about co-production and working at a local level with communities. Building our understanding, co-production in research aims to put principles of empowerment into practice, working 'with' communities and offering them greater control over the research process and providing opportunities to learn and reflect from their experience (Durose et al., 2012). Co-production can enhance the effectiveness of research by making it better informed by communities' 'preferences and needs', with communities then contributing to improved outcomes and achievable solutions.[7] We also supported the Welsh Government's ambition to create strong communities, to support children and young people in their communities and reduce the inequalities that they face when compared to their peers in more privileged areas. This all informed the tender to carry out the work.

To enable change, we believe that firstly there needs to be a good understanding of an area and that this can only be achieved through listening to the community. The insights gained from quantitative data that was already in the public domain, such as the 2014 Welsh Index of Multiple Deprivation, would only ever shed light on one side of the story, but our argument was such that it is only through combining it with qualitative data from interviews, for example, that we get to fully understand and gain a more comprehensive picture of each community.

Embarking on local analyses

Back on Trem y Mynydd, and throughout the project, I was always guided by the people who have lived experiences of poverty on this housing estate. This was obviously the community – resident families and children – but the frontline workers are also confronted by the causes and effects of poverty. We encouraged active involvement every step of the way, which involved 'going to' the community and not expecting them to turn up to 'consultation events'. We identified events where the community would naturally meet or come together and decided that this would be the best way to chat to them about their lived experiences. We also held in-depth confidential conversations with families on the estate who were willing to give us their time.

Overall, we learnt that Trem y Mynydd is a very proud and resilient community that 'looks after their own'. They have a strong sense of community, anchored centrally within the estate, and a solid community voice. It was soon made known that they had been part of a number of anti-poverty initiatives over the years, and we were conscious that the community had already been 'consulted' many times and felt a sense of frustration and fatigue that this had not lead to lasting changes to their circumstances and life chances. In fact, a concern about the marginalisation of low-income areas that have been over-researched could usefully be linked with the work of Eva Elliot et al. (2020) in Wales.[8] Many of the families on the estate receive intense continuous support from agencies, such as social services, educational welfare officers, midwifery services, health visiting services, school nursing services and speech and language therapy services. As part of our work, we mapped out over eighty frontline staff working within the community, many of whom 'did not know about each other'; there was a feeling, therefore, that there was duplication at times and that resources were not being maximised to achieve seamless and holistic services which met the needs of the 'whole family'.

During our time working with the community and with local partners, such as the local primary school, we learned that the impact of poverty and wider social issues were quite widespread within the school. This included concerns about children's readiness for school, attendance, attainment, behavioural factors and parental/guardian engagement. We spent time with school staff to understand the impact that this had on their work and the school environment. It was apparent that the staff were constantly 'fire-fighting' and, due to austerity cuts, did not have the appropriate resources to respond to students' needs and to tackle problems proactively and early on. Mental health was highlighted as a concern with school staff referring to a noticeable increase in parental and child mental health needs.

As noted earlier, Gwynedd Council's rationale to the Welsh Government to include Trem y Mynydd in the nation-wide *Children First* project was based on it being one of the most deprived areas across the country. The large housing estate, with roughly 2,500 inhabitants is the third largest single housing estate in Wales. The estate has just one road entrance and exit, which adds to the local people's strong sense of community.

At the time of developing my tender in 2017, a snapshot of figures I used more or less confirmed the data from the 2014 Welsh Index of Multiple Deprivation, which demonstrated that the area was within the 10 per cent most deprived in Wales:

- in 2001 the ward was designated as a Communities First area;
- 47.6 per cent of adults on the estates have no formal qualifications;
- 32.2 per cent of all individuals aged over 16 have no qualifications whatsoever;
- free school meals data is high in the community at 45.3 per cent. This level of eligibility dwarfs the national average;
- the number of people who own their houses is below the Welsh average at 33.4 per cent, and the number of households without a car is higher than the Welsh average at 41.0 per cent;
- of those aged between 10 and 17 years old within this data area, 12.57 per cent are young offenders. The percentage of young offenders has also increased since 2007;
- the percentage of NEET[9] in Gwynedd is highest in the Communities First cluster, which includes Trem y Mynydd;
- similarly, childhood obesity rates are higher in the Trem y Mynydd area, compared to the Gwynedd and Welsh average;

- the number of Job Seeker Allowance claimants is significantly greater in this area at 7.4 per cent compared to the Gwynedd figure of 2.9 per cent

In considering some ways to respond to this, the ideas for a draft strategic plan began to emerge, which included short- and long-term outcomes for children and young people, and how these would be achieved and by whom. The participants who came to the periodic site-based meetings were then asked to commit to this draft plan in order to improve this community's quality of life and the children and young people's life chances. We readily acknowledged that the primary school would need to be the focal point to realise the intentions of this plan as this is where many of the relationships are formed with families and the teaching staff are 'trusted' by the families.

The currency of Children First

Children's Zones, first elaborated in New York and re-worked in England, was considered to have currency in Wales, and *Children First* borrowed from its concept. As Carl Sargeant, then minister for communities and children, said, the approach here must be developed in line with Welsh priorities and resources. However, in contrast with the New York and England models, Welsh Government did not provide any additional funds for its *Children First* initiative. While the ambition was to build a more collaborative approach to working with children, young people and their families around a specific place, it was expected that current resources and anti-poverty programmes such as Flying Start and Families First would be utilised to achieve this.[10]

Beyond the basic principles, the Welsh Government noted that its expectation was that an identified 'anchor organisation' and its partners should work with the community, its children and young people to develop a strategic plan based on local need.[11] This should lead to increased multi-agency delivery of support and a more collaborative approach, yet at the time Welsh Government did not provide any particular guidance on how the needs assessment and strategic plan should be produced. This gave each area the freedom to design their own process, based on their understanding of what was required. The aim of *Children First* was not to create a 'new' or 'another' Welsh Government programme; rather, it meant moving towards creating a better approach to joint working, which would enable organisations to come together to focus on the in-depth needs of a particular area.

This corresponded with Welsh Government's ambition to create more resilient communities, supporting children and young people, and reducing the inequalities that some face in comparison with peers from more socially advantaged places. The Welsh Government emphasised that *Children First* was not about replacing the anti-poverty programmes already in place, such as Flying Start and Families First; rather it was concerned with bringing together all the services and support that would effectively address the needs of children and young people in the *Children First* area. The key point about *Children First* is that it was expected to initiate change at the local level, based on the needs of the specific place, which would be identified by listening to children and young people, families and to the local community. This would enable the creation of a strategic focus, which would identify the outcomes to achieve. My commissioned task was therefore to prepare both a health and well-being needs assessment and a *Children First* strategic plan based on the Trem y Mynydd area, and this was guided by a reconsideration of the most expedient way of working in order to:

- focus on the needs of a specific area;
- work together for the benefit of children and young people within that area; and
- reduce the inequalities that those children and young people face when compared to children and young people in more privileged areas.

This resulted in wider discussions with academics from Bangor University in attendance at the site-based meetings, and then subsequently with a core group of school staff and multi-agency frontline workers coming together as the Bangor PLUS team. They were all keen to develop a research perspective on the matters identified by the needs assessment and especially the quandary about the long history of legislation and successive policies with negligible impact. This certainly provoked my further research inquiries.

According to Marmot (2010), health inequalities are the preventable, unfair and unjust differences in health status between groups, populations or individuals that arise from the unequal distribution of social, environmental and economic conditions within societies.[12] These determine the risk of people getting ill, their ability to prevent sickness or opportunities to take action and access treatment when ill-health occurs. Inequalities exist across a range of dimensions, such as socio-economic deprivation and personal characteristics like age and sex. Generally, people living in the most deprived areas can expect to spend nearly twenty fewer years in good health compared with those in the least deprived areas.

Child welfare inequalities have profound implications for the lives of children and their families. There are growing numbers of young people in the child protection and care systems across the UK, which aligns with the work of Martin Elliot (2019) who documents these data patterns.[13] This is likely to continue to feed the prison and homeless populations, teenage pregnancy and parenthood numbers, high rates of poor physical and mental health amongst young people, and premature death, with long-term human and societal consequences and costs.[14] Some qualifying figures in comparison with the wider patterns in Gwynedd[15] would be useful here as they relate to high levels of substance abuse, youth justice referrals, antisocial behaviour, domestic violence and school attendance:

- between October 2016 and September 2017, a total of 400 crimes were recorded in Trem y Mynydd, which was 161.3 crimes per 1,000 population compared to the Wales average of 104.3 crimes per 1,000 population. Out of the 400 recorded crimes, there were 124 violent crimes, 52 criminal damage incidents, 137 anti-social behaviour incidents, 15 burglaries, 6 vehicle crimes. No data was provided on comparison with the remainder of Gwynedd but it is thought that Trem y Mynydd has one of the highest recorded crime rates in the county;
- according to DWP data, 120 people were in receipt of mental-health-related benefits from Trem y Mynydd in August 2017, which is 7.3 per cent of working-age adults, compared to the Wales average of 4.2 per cent;
- school attendance in 2017 across all schools was 90.49 per cent for Trem y Mynydd students compared to the Gwynedd average of 94.01 per cent;

- between January 2017 and January 2018, there was a higher percentage of young people aged 16–24 from Trem y Mynydd (8.0 per cent) claiming benefits compared to Gwynedd (1.8 per cent) and Wales (2.8 per cent) averages.

Addressing inequalities

There is a strong economic case for investing in the early years of life. The rate of economic return on investment is significantly higher in the pre-school stage than at any other stage of the education system. Despite this, investment in services for children and young people is often at its lowest in the very early years, which are the most crucial in the development of the brain. Investment only increases at the point where development slows. Allen[16] states that there needs to be a transformational change in the way all public sector services are delivered to families, ensuring prevention and early intervention approaches are embedded in any future service change and planning.

One of the five cross-cutting themes within the Welsh Government's Prosperity for All national strategy is early years (2017): the Welsh Government want children from all backgrounds to have the best start in life. Its aim is that everyone will have the opportunity to reach their full potential and lead a healthy, prosperous and fulfilling life, enabling them to participate fully in their communities and contribute to the future economic success of Wales. This includes reducing inequalities and preventing adverse childhood experiences.

Adverse childhood experiences are traumatic events, particularly those in early childhood, that significantly affect the health and well-being of people.[17] These experiences range from suffering verbal, mental, sexual and physical abuse, to being raised in a household where domestic violence, alcohol abuse, parental separation or drug abuse is present.

The Trem y Mynydd health and well-being needs assessment report draws a comprehensive picture of the local area, presenting data and information around the area's strengths and weaknesses. This has helped to identify some of the factors responsible for holding back children, young people and their families, and the assets and opportunities that can be built upon to improve their life chances. The process of developing the health and well-being needs assessment included:

a. working with primary schoolchildren to identify what is important, good and not so good about the area;

b. working with the local youth club and young people to identify what is important, good and not so good about the area;

c. a survey for teachers to gather their views, knowledge and ideas as to how things could be improved. This was followed by a focus group to further explore the issues raised;

d. a series of five frontline staff focus groups;

e. in-depth interviews with a sample of parents/guardians;

f. a focus group with mother and baby group;

g. a workshop that brought together managers, frontline staff and community – to identify vision and outcomes;

h. a workshop with Welsh Government – develop logic model

i. a community event – history in pictures, informal discussions around the history of the area and how it has changed over time;

j. an event for school parents to gather their views around what would make Trem y Mynydd an even better place to live in.

Here it is worthwhile providing a brief summary of some facts and findings about the area:

General population/area facts

a. Total population (2016): 2,617 (0–24: 36.5%; 25–44: 25.7%; 45–64: 24.8%; 65+: 13.1%);

b. young population, high proportion of young families and lone-parent households

c. deprivation – amongst the 10 per cent most deprived areas in Wales

d. fewer people state that they are of very good/good health (76%) compared to Gwynedd (81%), 2011 census;

e. higher number of people with no qualifications (35%, compared to Gwynedd 23%);

f. household income poverty – second highest number of households in poverty

g. many parents are working, but in low-paid part-time jobs resulting in 'working poverty';

h.   high percentage are in receipt of benefits, income support, job seekers' allowance;

i.   low level of car ownership (41% of households do not have a car, compared to 21.4% in Gwynedd);

j.   higher level of social housing (56.6% compared to 16.3% in Gwynedd, 2011 census)

k.   higher levels of anti-social behaviour, crime rates, domestic violence, substance misuse;

l.   twenty-nine looked-after children from the area (total 233 in Gwynedd), thirteen on child protection register and ten children in need (in February 2018).

Strengths and assets

The people, and things to do:

a.   proud people and strong sense of community;

b.   close-knit and resilient community, everyone looks out for each other, especially during hard times;

c.   children and young people see their future in Trem y Mynydd and are proud of their roots;

d.   active children, who like to play outdoors;

e.   three play parks, two football pitches, allotments;

f.   two shops, newsagents, post office, fish and chip shop, laundrette, florist, hairdressers;

g.   range of community activities: Rainbows, Brownies, karate, gymnastics, Majorettes, boxing, etc.

h.   proactive and respected elected members;

i.   community partnership office in a central location;

j.   health centre: hosts flying start staff and 30-hour childcare scheme staff (Gwynedd Council owned);

k.   youth centre building (Gwynedd Council owned);

l.   youth workers who have gained trust and respect;

m.   older people residential home (Gwynedd Council owned);

n.   church.

Barriers and threats

The area:

a. lack of local amenities for such a large population;
b. play areas 'boring', nothing for teenagers to do 'we want a skate park!';
c. lack of play schemes during school holidays for primary and secondary age;
d. transport links are difficult: two buses needed to get to anywhere, 'return bus tickets have been stopped';
e. litter a problem in some areas;
f. recent closure of Communities' First, youth club and social club.

Housing:

a. high level of social housing is bringing people into the area, but they do not necessarily stay; and some families are placed in flats where there are substance misuse problems.

Health and social care:

a. high level of missed children health appointments: speech therapy and paediatric based in local hospital (which is two bus rides from the estate);
b. energy drinks are popular, cheap and cool (sold in local shops);
c. CAMHS:[18] long waiting list, bad experiences, intimidating and traumatic, case closed after three missed appointments (two buses to get there);
d. high levels of substance misuse and parental mental-health problems.

Crime and disorder:

a. youth justice service: numbers have reduced but still higher number of referrals compared to other areas in Gwynedd;
b. high level of antisocial behaviour, crime levels and domestic violence;

    c.   drugs are a worry 'Get the druggies out'. Feeling unsafe and needles around certain areas. Drugs brought into the area bring associated violence, prey on vulnerable young people to deliver drugs.

Early years, education and skills:

    a.   no childcare provision (no school holiday club, local crèches too expensive, far and hard to reach). Missed opportunity for early intervention, stimulation for young children;

    b.   high number of young children not 'ready' for school, lack of basic skills and abilities (communication, speech, toileting);

    c.   increase in younger children with difficult and challenging behaviour outside the norm for their age;

    d.   low school attendance rates for primary and secondary (without permission);

    e.   stigma at secondary school: 'you're from …', resulting in young people feeling that others do not expect them to achieve;

    f.   school expulsion rates: higher compared to Gwynedd and Wales average;

    g.   unique trend in the area: increase in home schooling at secondary school age. Parents taking children out of school before expulsion;

    h.   traditional methods to stop young people from leaving school not working, problems are not picked up early enough;

    i.   some parents with lack of basic skills (reading and writing);

    j.   high number of families do not attend school attendance/ behavioural appointments – two buses to reach secondary schools, lack of trust, confidence and intimidating experience;

    k.   barriers to engaging back with education: lack of confidence and additional learning needs.

Jobs and income:

    a.   high level of NEET young people: 16–24-year-olds not in education, training or employment. Young people want to work and would like apprenticeships but there is a lack of local opportunities;

b. many parents want to work but are unable due to lack of childcare (which is available all year and affordable);

c. good take up of free 30-hour childcare scheme for 3–4-year-olds, many parents want to work;

d. high debt rates, money problems and loan sharks used, and reduced Citizen's Advice Bureau hours on estate impacting on families;

How services are delivered:

a. valuable services for families in the health centre, but lack of space for further key agencies and community activities;

b. many different agencies working on the estate, but workers are unaware of each other, and families report that they are confused regarding what is available and how to access;

c. families want someone to help them access services, they lack confidence, trust, can feel intimidated;

d. good relationships between individual families and workers but general feeling and perception of agencies and organisations not being supportive listening (Gwynedd Council, social services, CAMHS);

e. many families with low-level needs not addressed early enough resulting in costly statutory intervention;

f. re-referral rates for statutory services high, same families coming into the system;

g. need seamless support, too much referring on, case closed, 'not our problem anymore';

h. staff work hard but feel that they no longer make any difference, families are at crisis point when they get to them.

Likewise, it is also worthwhile providing some data that informed the Trem y Mynydd Children First strategic plan, which followed extensive work with the community, children, young people, families, frontline workers and participants who came to the periodic site-based meetings and who contributed much to a strategic vision and sense of the outcomes to be achieved.

Vision in the Trem y Mynydd strategic plan:

Our overall vision for Trem y Mynydd is that children and young people, and their families, are free from disadvantage and are supported to reach their full potential.

Outcomes in the Trem y Mynydd strategic plan:

- families have easy access to the right services at the right time;
- young children are ready for school and are supported with their early learning;
- children and young people are supported and encouraged to reach their potential;
- children and young people are safe, happy, healthy, resilient and emotionally healthy;
- a safe, prosperous and skilled community.

Conclusion

Once the Trem y Mynydd health and well-being needs assessment and the Trem y Mynydd Children First strategic plan were submitted, my commissioned work finished. I was quite satisfied that I had fulfilled my obligations and my company did the groundwork as required, advocated for it being co-produced as much as possible, and equipped the end products with a series of recommendations. The implementation of the strategic plan was down to the Trem y Mynydd Children First Board, but there were no additional resources from Welsh Government forthcoming into local communities to support children and young people and reduce the inequalities present. To reiterate, as Carl Sargeant had put it, the approach here must be developed in line with Welsh priorities and resources. It was not within my remit to be concerned with what happened next, and I was not party to any negotiations. Reflecting back on the commission, my company had spent a lot of time in the area getting to know the community, frontline workers, the local schoolchildren and teaching staff, and key partners. The work over an 18-month period involved working with the Trem y Mynydd Children First Board, established to guide this project, and I learned much about the lived experiences of poverty and gained such valuable insight.

I remained greatly inspired by the *Children First* principles and joined colleagues to take the experience forward into the two series of seminars sponsored by Bangor University. I was encouraged by academic partners to embark on doctoral studies, and I went so far as to submit an application with a proposal to focus on a policy study of *Children First* as an anti-poverty programme in regards the options and possibilities for professional practice on Trem y Mynydd. I was interested in the holistic 'whole family approach' and early support as part of a suite of policy solutions to address the effects of poverty on children's capacity to learn, given that local primary school staff work alongside frontline multi-agency staff frequently. A lack of KESS[19] funding for a PhD scholarship prevented my going down this path, and so I remain working as the owner director of Cwmni CELyn but also part of the Bangor PLUS team. In this capacity, numerous research questions about *Children First* gnaw away: to what extent was real change expected? What are local and national governments' preferred 'theories of change?' And how will real change be realised?

Notes

1   See *https://gov.wales/written-statement-children-first* (accessed 4 September 2022).
2   *https://www.savethechildren.org.uk/content/dam/global/reports/advocacy/developing-childrens-zones-summary.pdf* (accessed 4 September 2022).
3   Task group: a working group of officers with specific responsibility over data collection and analysis within each partner organisation. The group was formed to assist with the work of producing the needs assessment and to ensure up-to-date, relevant data from each organisation.
4   Quantitative and qualitative data which gave a picture of the health and well-being of the Trem y Mynydd population.
5   A health and well-being needs assessment on the Trem y Mynydd population.
6   Themes relating to health, well-being, poverty, education, crime and disorder, employment, transport.
7   E. Ostrom (1996). 'Crossing the Great Divide: Co-production, Synergy and Development', *World Development*, 24/6, 1073–88.
8   For an extended discussion, see E. Elliott, G. M. Thomas and E. Byrne (2020). 'Stigma, class, and "respect": Young people's articulation and management of place in a post-industrial estate in south Wales'. *People, Place and Policy*, 14/2, 157–72.
9   NEET: an acronym for young people not in education, employment or training.

10 *https://gov.wales/flying-start-health-programme-guidance; https://gov.wales/sites/ default/files/publications/2019-07/families-first-guidance-for-local-authorities_0. pdf* (accessed 4 September 2022).

11 In this case, Gwynedd Council was the lead 'anchor organisation'.

12 M. Marmot (2010). *F` air Society Healthy Lives*, available at *http://www. instituteofhealthequity.org/* (accessed 4 September 2022).

13 See M. Elliot (2019). 'Charting the rise of children and young people looked after in Wales', in D. Mannay, A. Rees and L. Roberts (eds), *Children and young people 'looked after'? Education, intervention and the everyday culture of care in Wales*. Cardiff: University of Wales Press, pp. 210–24.

14 E. Murray et al. (2020). 'Association of childhood out-of-home care status with all-cause mortality up to 42-years later'. Office of National Statistics Longitudinal Study. *BMC Public Health, https://doi.org/10.1186/ s12889-020-08867-3.*

15 See *https://hact.org.uk/tools-and-services/community-insight/* (accessed 4 September 2022).

16 G. Allen (2011). 'Early intervention: the next steps', available at *https://www. gov.uk/government/publications/early-intervention-the-next-steps--2* (accessed 4 September 2022).

17 *https://phw.nhs.wales/topics/adverse-childhood-experiences/* (accessed 4 September 2022).

18 CAMHS: child and adolescence mental health services.

19 This is the acronym for the Knowledge Economy Skills Scholarship, at the time awarded to residents located in the north-east of Wales, not the north-west where I live.

This posed photo of a quarryman, positioned at a slate rock face and harnessed by a rope secured cliff top in the Snowdonia mountains, shows the working conditions at the heart of the lengthy and bitter 1900–3 Penrhyn Quarry dispute that also included trade union rights and pay.

2

A BALANCING ACT: JUGGLING SCHOOL POLICIES IN A COMMUNITY WITH UNMET NEEDS

Angharad Evans

Introduction

This chapter is written by a school Head with over ten years' experience in the position and another two as deputy, here in the guise of a fictitious character given voice by academic partners following the departure of the one in post because of long Covid. The years spent at the school called Ysgol Trem y Mynydd, to use its pseudonym, point to a corporate memory of some of the challenges facing the primary school on the Trem y Mynydd housing estate. These range from statutory requirements in regards the implementation of policy directives, which feature school performance and accountability, and the welfare demands on staff time, including my own. These might sound routine, but the challenges and demands can be relentless in the face of the causes and effects of child poverty on the school's work. My knowledge is frequently shared in conversations on the phone, in meetings and during site visits with the school's assigned supporting improvement adviser, and also with academic partners. At the very least we are agreed that the school is located in a community where we can improve children's life chances by homing in on, and honing, school improvement in a context of disadvantage. This is invaluable because it means credence is given to my desire to shape a socially just school.[1]

The extent of the disadvantage was brought home to all of us in the 2018–19 *Children First* needs assessment data presented by Lewis in a series of multi-agency meetings (see Lewis's chapter 1). The scrutiny of publicly available data on child poverty along with the comparisons made between the high levels registered in our school-community and that experienced in Gwynedd and further afield across Wales provided me with some deep insights into our educational setting. The same can be said about the study of the ethnographic data collected by Lewis: it shed light on the messy realities of our school life. This was complimented by my early participation in the practitioner research activities of the Bangor PLUS team, and I learned much from the study of related concepts such as unmet needs, inequality, powerlessness and degraded life chances (see Child Poverty Action Group, 2017). This gave me more of a critical understanding of the ways poverty impacts on children and their parents/carers, which is acknowledgement of what we are confronted with locally in the school. That this is all linked to the moral and political imperatives to tackle regional and national concerns with child poverty in Wales pre-Covid and subsequently gives me hope.

Data from the *Children First* needs assessment and the research perspectives certainly provided me with directions on what we might do to address unmet needs in an effort to counter the effects of poverty on children's schooling and education. This thinking and theorising came to better inform the school development plan, and my work with my allocated supporting improvement adviser: we discussed work that was made possible by the deprivation grant and the regional school improvement service called GwE. Together we then purposefully co-developed responsive strategies and structures that are tailored to this community's school. However, it should be noted that there are still significant challenges in the overlap of the unmet needs that impact the children, and hence school outcomes. These complex interactions are difficult to account for in a school development plan, which is by its nature school-based. Also, while outside agencies are key to the strategies for improvement outlined in it, their funding cycles and accountability measures are not always in alignment with those of the school. This highlights the need for synergy in the approaches to both the educational and social needs of our school community.

I have my own views on the ways our joint work is constrained by the terms of school inspections, which potentially deny professional autonomy and innovation because of requirements to focus on particular criteria that frame the judgement of teaching and leadership practices. This is where my school leadership comes under scrutiny, and I am held accountable for educational outcomes on two levels: local 'school improvement' and national education standards. But this glosses over the complexities and the particularities of the situation in the Trem y Mynydd school-community, and the ways any combination of factors intertwine to impact on children's learning and our professional practices. Be that as it may, in my capacity as school leader I strive to find the fine balance to deal with the unmet needs of the school-community, and at the same time provide a safe, nurturing environment for the children in my care. I subscribe to Lingard's ideas about 'leading learning', building a socially just school, and intelligent accountability (see Lingard et al, 2003; Lingard, 2009). This then bumps up against Lupton and Hayes's work, *Great Mistakes in Education Policy* (2020), which was presented in a BERA online seminar that I watched with my academic partners. I am inspired by all these works and their authors' stance on the Global Education Reform Movement, known as the GERM (see Sahlberg, 2011).

A subscription to this sort of internationally renowned work is not enough, however, because the school is limited by national and local policy decisions and some systems in place that work against us developing research-informed practical interventions. With more considered systemic support, time and resources, we would embark on our university-school-community partnership with enthusiasm, but we are currently inhibited. The best we can do under the circumstances is to lend in-principle support to the Bangor PLUS team, and endorse their responsive educative work on local solutions with resident families, adults, young people and children. Their so-called allied Not-NEET projects can in fact work with the *Curriculum for Wales*, which makes provision for outreach into this school-community. The school could then re-orient its school development plan to resonate with their notion of school-community development, which is values-driven and assets-based. In my view this is all worthy of public investment, especially after discussing the Not-NEET project proposals put forward in this edited book: they are exactly what is required to improve children's prospects. As the Child Poverty Action Group (2017) put it, it is vital to invest in early childhood education and care, family support, education, skills and training, housing, health and mental health, and so on. This was echoed in our *Children First* needs assessment (again see Lewis's chapter 1).

In this chapter, I provide an overview of some professional concerns about policy requirements and welfare demands on my time as a school leader but also on my staff's time, then I lay out the extent of the challenges that confront me given the causes and effects of child poverty on the school's work. I then focus on the worth of practitioner research activity to a school Head, and describe ways to use official school data, child poverty data and the Welsh Index of Multiple Deprivation data to compliment professional reading, case stories and analyses that facilitate developing critical understandings of poverty and inequalities to infuse the school's work. I bring these critical understandings to my conversations with my supporting school improvement adviser, with particular attention to ensuring our work echoes a contextualised version of school improvement to take into consideration the stark social and educational disadvantages experienced locally, regionally and nationally. I share my thoughts on the experience of school inspections and draw on our last one to critically reflect on my professional aspirations and the inspection areas and judgements, especially where staff are seemingly told that they have it wrong. I finally explain what it means to be juggling school policies such as Estyn inspections in a school-community already troubled by Covid-19, austerity, cost-of-living crisis and the fallout from welfare cuts. I remain concerned about school budget cuts at the expense of local solutions that are of paramount importance to eliminating child poverty.

Reading the runes

As school Head, my role is a complex balance of leading my organisation, adhering to national and local education policies, training and motivating my staff including fellow school leaders in the senior leadership team (SLT). There are many resources and training in existence to support this function and while these are invaluable, they must all be applied to a complex challenging local situation so that my staff and I can be both appropriately responsive and work to ensure what Ysgol Trem y Mynydd can offer. Essentially my role has three important interfaces which in turn governs my time and my workload day-to-day. I must manage my staff team, ensuring their health and well-being, attend to recruitment where necessary, and ensure professional development opportunities so that my team can grow and remain effective. I must interface with the local authority, school improvement service and to a lesser extent directly with Welsh Government. This is to ensure that I fulfil statutory responsibilities, confirm delivery of the *Curriculum for Wales* in an effective manner, and meet the inspection/outcome standards required. Finally, I must work with the wider school-community, ranging from parents/carers and resident families with children to the many multi-agencies on this housing estate, which is not to ignore the number of visitors to the school including academic partners.

The statutory requirements with which a school Head must ensure compliance are mostly concerned with the safety, health and well-being, and education of the children in our care. In practical terms this means delivering the *Curriculum for Wales*, which at the time of writing is undergoing significant change, moving from a centrally prescribed content base to a more locally designed, responsive learning experience for children. Philosophically, this is a positive move for school leaders in responding to the unmet needs of their community, but the process of developing my staff team with capacity to design curriculum takes time and resources. Frequently, my time spent in statutory reporting on curriculum initiatives and policy directives is greater than the time spent delivering those things. This presents a restrictive, upward-reporting-focus view on my work which is only partly true because so much of my time is spent recruiting and developing colleagues as competent practitioners, future school leaders and members of SLT to meet the challenges in this school-community. It all requires strong leadership to ensure that things get done, and all in the face of myriad other more immediate demands on staff time, which all plays out across the school, especially as they impact on teachers' work.

The most persistent demands on my time come when I must support my staff dealing with challenging behaviour from children, either in class or in common areas of the school. The school's behaviour policy decrees that staff have both authority and autonomy, but more serious incidents are referred to me and many require urgent action. When children's behaviour becomes boisterous, my time is given over to dealing with the incidents and to supporting my staff. There are many of these serious behaviour incidents, which can be closely linked with challenging home lives. For example, what we need to manage includes inappropriate language, which is more than simply swearing because it involves concepts and actions that are not normally expected of young children. It calls into question their awareness or understanding or both, but mostly the language is simply repeated or copied from what they observe at home or elsewhere. There are also threats of physical violence to other children, which sometimes involves the use of items to hand to reinforce the threat, for example, where household tools like a screwdriver or chisel have been brought to school. Beyond an immediate response, more time is spent in the aftermath of the incident and follow-up with parents/carers and sometimes outside support agencies.

Then there are instances when these sorts of incidents can escalate to become even more serious, especially when some children's behaviour is triggered by what might be happening elsewhere. Again, these demand my immediate attention, and it is important that we read the signs in disturbing behaviour, language, attendance patterns and so on. This helps to ensure that things do not reach the levels that we have seen, for instance with a child trashing the classroom and assaulting other children and staff. These critical incidents require my immediate intervention and often outside agency support, and while I often have an overview of these situations the number of critical incidents can frequently appear overwhelming. I must also ensure that my staff are provided with a safe working environment, which highlights another one of my major concerns about the demands on my time in regards upward reporting and inspection. These can pale not so much into insignificance because they are crucial when it comes to judgements made about our school, but my priority is to maintain a safe working and learning environment. In essence these are all the things that need to be in place first before we can attempt to engage with the most obvious of our statutory responsibilities, namely delivering the *Curriculum for Wales*.

Reading the runes and understanding the fundamental needs of the children at Ysgol Trem y Mynydd is a necessary first step in being a safe, happy and effective school. This can seem much removed from a school development plan focused on educational outcomes, school improvement, national standards and competence in curriculum. Indeed, much of our work is devoted to meeting unmet needs in our school-community and our students' home lives, being aware of parents'/carers' circumstances and, ultimately, being alert to the causes and effects of child poverty. With an understanding of this complex and challenging context, school improvement can then appear distinctly attractive. Frequently it is because of these challenges that teachers are drawn to work in schools like ours, and here we take inspiration from Lupton and, more recently, Beckett as one of our academic partners. They both point to supporting teachers to be both active in their professional development and part of networks such as the Bangor PLUS team that includes outside agencies. This all helps teachers to move beyond surviving to thriving: making significant contributions to our school-community and the school improvement process as a whole. It is crucial to be part of the team and to have the team working with us so that the needs of our school-community can be addressed to provide a coherent and connected approach that can truly change lives.

Looking deeper into unmet needs

The *Children First* needs assessment provided a significant insight into many of the issues facing resident families that we see acted out through the lives of children at Ysgol Trem y Mynydd. I was already aware of some of these issues in my daily interaction with parents, families and children from the estate, but the details of the needs assessment highlighted both the interconnectedness of so many of these and the complex nature of those interactions. Lewis's report on the needs assessment and the most recent Welsh Index of Multiple Deprivation initially paints a bleak picture for children living on the estate. With our school in one of the 10 per cent most deprived areas in Wales, it is unsurprising that many parent/carers work several jobs just to keep the lights on and provide some food for their family, even if this is at the expense of spending time parenting their children that other families can offer. This gives pause for thought in developing a school development plan that is focused on school improvement, and calls into question our values and principles (see Thirsk's chapter 6). This perhaps only serves to illustrate the calling to serve in this school-community in the hope that we can address unmet needs and improve the lives and life chances of the children in our care.

Working with partners in the Bangor PLUS team I have been drawn to look further into the experiences of other systems and the impact of poverty experienced elsewhere, along with school-community-led solutions to some of those issues (see Whatman's chapter 11). While it is nigh-on impossible to factor in time for reading something academic into my day-to-day work schedule, I made time on the urging of academic partners to deepen my understanding of the issues I see every day when children growing up in poverty walk through the school gates. I have been particularly taken by Prof. Danny Dorling's *Peak Inequality* (2018), which highlights poverty and inequalities and their effects on children. I have learned much from the ways he connects a lot of this to Brexit and a broader neo-liberal agenda, and from his innovative use of phase portrait graphs to visually show many of the trends that he discusses. His recent comments on why, in the UK, more poor people have died from the Covid-19 pandemic resonate with my experience of working in this school-community. Likewise, the other authors in this volume have mentioned how poverty is not just a problem for resident families, but a bigger systemic and structural problem across Wales, the rest of the UK and beyond.

It is really important that we all do some professional reading about child poverty, exploring its causes and effects, because it helps develop our understanding of the challenges that we face. One important step in seeing how I can be more effective in my role as a school leader in this school-community became apparent through the series of seminars that were the first stage of the Bangor PLUS project. Initially, I found the idea of becoming research- and policy-active perplexing and the recommended reading to be demanding, but I appreciated the opportunity to discuss the issues openly because we were able to come to a shared understanding of the lived experiences of resident families and children on the Trem y Mynydd housing estate. The report and findings from the United Nation Special Rapporteur Philip Alston (2019) garnered my attention because he specifically talked about what it means to be in receipt of universal credit in Wales and the impact that this has on the lives of children. In further seminars we examined ideas from the Child Poverty Action Group (2017), and this further crystallised my thinking on the unmet needs I see in our school-community every day, and how this situation is the result of policy decisions – and is probably a breach of their human rights, as Alston highlights.

This literature underlines inequalities, but it also in many cases presents a hopeful argument: these situations can change if we maintain a wider school-community focus. Reading more about how families experience poverty from Smyth and Wrigley's book, *Living on the Edge* (2018), I have been inspired to put some of their suggestions and philosophical counter-arguments into actions that we can put in place in our school development plan. It became clear that there are some specific areas that require direct investment to allow the school to address a wider range of needs. The concept of Full Service Schools (see Beckett's Editor's Introduction and Jones's chapter 3) rings true as an appropriate responsive local solution that would no doubt be effective on Trem y Mynydd. There are some children who are so seriously affected by poverty and the problems it causes that they need 1:1 support, but this requires attendant funding. This would allow the children most troubled by their experiences of poverty to receive the specialist support needed and allow my staff to spend more time with those children who, though still impacted by poverty, do not manifest its influence so explicitly in their behaviours.

A deeper look into the way that child poverty impacts on school gives us an enhanced understanding of what goes on beyond our 6-hour daily contact with the children. I have a positive relationship with my school improvement adviser, whose focus is on school improvement. This includes brief acknowledgement of what goes on outside the school gates, much like the tide that ebbs and flows twice a day. In more concrete terms, we can see it in very young children because poverty prompts some delays in their development: for example, in their hesitancy talking and engaging in conversations about all the things that they might ordinarily be doing, which flags up their speech and language. We see it in their capacity for reading and comprehension, which suggests that perhaps books and puzzles are not available to them in the home. We can also see it in hungry children, especially coming in without breakfast, which flags up how many nutritious meals they might get each day, or in the clothes and shoes they are wearing. None of this is to blame the parents/carers because they may be working two or more jobs to provide for their families, and many stepped up to be essential workers during the Covid-19 pandemic, which is truly something to be admired. Gannon et al. (2018) captured the situation perfectly:

> Taken together, these [challenges] hint at worsening children's experiences of the compounding effects of disadvantage that are felt before they begin school and shape their futures beyond school and through their life course. (p. 1)

We've got your back, almost

By the simple acknowledgement of the role that poverty plays in the lives of the children of Ysgol Trem y Mynydd, and of where this fits in the larger picture of UK politics and policy decisions, we improve the ways that our school-community can work to support those children and resident families. We are already well supported by our regional school improvement service, GwE, but ultimately much of my work is confined within the current policy framework. It is therefore important to be pragmatic and realistic about what can be achieved in our school with the resources available, and about what can be made available in circumstances such as these. An example of this is the funding available through the deprivation grant that has allowed us to establish a nurture group for particularly vulnerable children. This is staffed by two trained adults, and before Covid-19 I recruited an outside business partner to work with us on parent engagement to strengthen the relationship between resident families and the school. The ideal is to invite parents to get involved, become partners and help us read the runes a little more quickly.

The regional school improvement service, GwE, already mentioned many times, is a key partner in both strategic and more practical terms in supporting children at Ysgol Trem y Mynydd. Our school improvement adviser's role is to connect our school with wider support networks, sometimes with other school Heads experiencing similar issues so that we can gain peer support, but also to provide that support directly. Many GwE staff are seconded from schools so they have relevant recent experience of challenging situations in school-communities. While there are challenges working within a policy framework, there is often much that can be done to ensure school improvement[2] can be yoked to bigger and broader issues that point to the impact we may yet have in the wider school-community. This can take the form of the school improvement adviser making site visits to discuss progress and support needs, as well as in working though documentation such as the school development plan to ensure that it is both appropriate and achievable. They are often able to link us with specific project funding or research projects that are appropriate for our children, which is something that a busy school Head would not be able to do alone.

Sometimes the logistics of responding to the unmet needs of children and resident families in our school-community can fall outside the auspices of GwE and what they provide in terms of school improvement support, and we are frequently bound into systems that do not offer the flexibility needed to deal with situations as they arise. For instance, teaching staff will identify that a child has a particular additional learning need, which may or may not have been identified during their nursery or pre-school years. This is often the case if parents/carers were unaware of the developmental delays or they were unable to access the assessment process for a variety of reasons, not least local council-funding decisions in regards assessments but also special school provision. The window of opportunity for the school to apply for additional support for children with additional learning needs is open between October to March, which does not help children with needs identified in April and the following months. In some cases, it may be that even if a need is identified there is no funding available, and so we must work with the resources we have.

Yet it is often apparent that these children may be better supported in facilities with specific resources and specially trained staff. Ordinarily when circumstances reach this level, a recommendation is made to move the child to a special school that has the capacity to deal with these issues. Consequently, when this is not possible, because the local authority's special school Pendalar has no room on its roll, for example, the child stays with us but this results in a significant postponement in the delivery of support for their specific need. This in turn can have a negative effect not only on the child's progress but also on our ability to serve the children and resident families who are already struggling in our school-community. One upshot is that it stretches staff contact time in two directions: towards the child with additional needs, and away from the other children who also have educational and social needs. This is not to decry the sort of support we already receive because it does allow us to put in place responsive strategies and structures: fortunately we have a nurture group and much else in place from early years' entry to support literacy and numeracy, bilingual language learning, programmes to develop physical and motor skills, homework clubs, sport and recreation clubs, and both in-school and after-school activities like the music group, community food garden group (see Silvester and Joslin's chapter 4) and the hip hop (rap) group (see Maclean and Daw's chapter 7).

With appropriate funding, I envisage that we could do much more in the Trem y Mynydd school-community and go past band-aid solutions and other compensatory education programmes for children in poverty. As things stand, I would suggest that many school Heads cannot afford to allocate scarce funding and resources to projects that could be considered extracurricular and then showcase their achievements. The strain on resources becomes most apparent when inspections loom, because although we are providing substantial support on a local level, this may be at the expense of what is deemed the national standard, educational outcomes being the main concern with little proper contextual consideration. On these occasions there is little recognition that some local authority funding decisions, in turn tied to UK politics and policy decisions, can sometimes exacerbate the difficulties faced by children at Ysgol Trem y Mynydd. Any wonder school Heads hesitate to use their own professional judgement on what is needed due to being hamstrung by the emphasis placed on inspections by politicians and the misrepresentation of the inspection process by the populist media, especially when there are mistakes made valuing and understanding inspection reports by the general public.

Hitting a brick wall

School inspections by Estyn, the Welsh equivalent of Ofsted in England, are viewed by many school Heads as being an ambivalent experience. On the one hand, it is always beneficial to engage with fellow professionals in conversation, but frequently the inspectors come with student attainment data to judge the school and they look for evidence to prove/ disprove their conclusions. On the other hand, their report does not always adequately celebrate the work a school is doing, which could provide a boost in reputation and perhaps enrolment – and therefore funding. More often than not, it may make an already challenging job in a challenging environment almost untenable, except the teaching staff in our school are absolutely dedicated to their calling. Many authors have written of the ineffectiveness of school inspections to judge a school's performance, both because the criteria used for judgement are too narrow and performative, and because schools prepare for the inspection ahead of time and many run special 'inspection showcase' events throughout the period (again see Whatman's chapter 11). It is the case that we simply do not have this sort of time, which undermines the value of an inspection and the few days' prior warning is truly hard to digest.

Parents/carers have an opportunity to contribute to the inspection process and there are usually meetings with inspectors as part of the process, but this can be a double-edged sword. The meetings can be frequently divisive, which was the case when a few parents made complaints that remarkably contrasted with students' responses to the inspectors. I would wager that these parents do not necessarily understand the work that modern schools do, especially in challenging circumstances. They likely relate their children's schooling experiences to their own, often unhappy, experiences but this has changed much in the last twenty years, all the more so since devolution of education policy away from the UK governments in Westminster to Welsh government in Cardiff and local councils. Also, sometimes parents' expectations of what a school can do are unrealistic, which was the case when I suggested a child take some home respite from school with a view to coming back in a more stable frame of mind. The family reacted with anger and frustration because they saw it as our job to take the child during school time. We were then 'caught between a rock and a hard place' because of expectations that we 'deal with children' in all circumstances, yet here we had a child whose mental health was of serious concern.

These sorts of scenarios are ones that are not necessarily captured in inspection reports; although luckily they do contain written commentary. Some of the complexities can be included in the front-end section that provides background, but the short word limit and, indeed, the short time period of an inspection make it difficult to convey, much less insightfully understand, the context in which our school-community functions. Sadly, it is often only the judgements that are reported in the media, and these by their very nature are given in standardised language without contextual qualification. Schools, and in turn school staff, are judged by outcomes recorded in data based on educational attainment. There is no room for more nuanced, fine-grained understanding in our soundbite, headline-hungry culture. For example, a child who is in the junior part of the school, so in the 7–11 age bracket, struggled with incontinence. Our staff needed to care for the child who was suffering physical discomfort but also psychological stress, and this would be on the good days. On the bad days this same child used inappropriate language and draw attention to it in unsightly ways, but the inspection criteria does not accommodate these sorts of challenges so they simply do not get recognised.

Against this backdrop of challenging behaviour, unmet needs and a performative culture of data heavy evaluation, I too am the subject of a judgement on my school's improvement and effectiveness. Specifically, my leadership of the school is considered in terms of how I develop my colleagues in the senior leadership team and how I provide direction for the school. I aspire to the premises of Lingard et al.'s (2003) idea of 'leading learning', now twenty years old, and I have demonstrated my commitment to working with the Bangor PLUS team as part of my professional learning and development to become research- and policy-active. However, from both a personal perspective and from the point of view of my staff team, we are so caught up in managing the day-to-day immediacies of the needs of our children, that we rarely have the time or energy to pursue more than what seems necessary to get through the day, never mind next week. This is a simple reflection of our reality in the moment, and the amount and regularity of critical incidents that we deal with on a day-by-day basis. These are far beyond the educational objectives to which we are held accountable given the inspection criteria, which really need to be pulled more into line with some acknowledgement of the whole gamut of the work we do.

I have read enough to know that many academic authors remain critical of education systems (see Lupton and Hayes, 2021; also Harris and Jones, 2020), especially where punitive inspection regimes that purport to ensure high standards across all schools still pay homage to the GERM. This effectively undermines trust and drives schools to showcase the ultimate in performativity, producing inspection performance lessons and meetings that are far from everyday activity and operation. So much weight is given to the judgements and decisions made by inspectors that school Heads are almost duty bound to ensure that their performance is as good, or better, than their last inspection. Inspection criteria, almost always devoid of contextual understanding, inevitably adds further pressure on a school Head. We are caught between trying to avoid a poor inspection report and its consequences in terms of funding and reputation, and meeting the real needs of staff, children and the school-community. Thankfully there are sympathetic and supportive colleagues, notably the school improvement adviser, but they too are subject to a work brief on school improvement. As it stands, I continue to strive to achieve Lingard's ideas of leading learning, building a socially just school, and engaging in intelligent accountability.

Credit where credit is due

In this final section I revisit some of my initial concerns and try to identify the fine line that needs to be walked between the services and support that our school staff provide to this school-community, and the oft-expressed frustrations of resident families that the school is an icon of authority. This needs some insightful understanding because in the *Children First* needs assessment (again see Lewis's chapter 1) we were briefed on the importance of hearing their voice, especially when it came to the suite of anti-poverty policies that had little or no effect on alleviating our school-community's experiences of poverty. I turned to Dorling's *Peak Inequalities* (2018), which raised the issue of the creeping neo-liberal agenda, including Brexit, mindful that the GERM is a detrimental force which can hamper this school-community's true realisation of children's human right to education. As a school leader it is my duty to ensure the teaching and learning of the children in our care, and in doing so I must ensure their health and well-being. But I must juggle multiple and sometimes opposing challenges in a sensitive yet sensible and realistic manner, and in what follows I will try to elucidate the ways in which I have sought to address them.

The causes and effects of child poverty are often reported in deficit terms by those who observe from the outside and are quick to judge some of the children's challenging behaviour and their home lives. To be sure, there is often a build-up of critical incidents that can and do boil over that then requires intervention by the school Head. Even some parents/carers regularly associate children's behaviours with the school's failure to meet unmet additional learning needs, but this is not the full story. Indeed, many of these stories 'break us all' as we hear about the troubled lives of these children growing up in poverty, and in some cases, this becomes overwhelming. I have had numerous staff develop stress-related health concerns and I too share this emotional toll. We are human after all. One of the most effective ways to cope with the external pressures is to stick together tightly as a professional team, share the burdens with colleagues and acknowledge and celebrate the good things that we do. In this we are strong: there is great collaboration with staff who are so adept at dealing with classroom disturbances that it is easy to forget that these challenges and demands are way beyond what should be within their work remit.

The point being is that people in this school-community are crying out for help, and yet all we encounter are government policy decisions such as the emphasis on 'raising achievement' and 'closing the gap' with a school inspection system that does not permit us the professional autonomy to put useful innovative systems in place. A pertinent example is the student SEN assessments to avert parents and children waiting six months. There is no doubt that this is tied to budget cuts and under-investment in service provision, which seemingly suggests that local government has no funding: we have already mentioned the special school Pendalar, which is full and over capacity, but there was also Felinheli behaviour unit, which closed ten years ago; likewise Brynffynnon closed (a special school for children with emotional and behavioural difficulties), and there are no pupil referral units (PRUs) in Gwynedd. This makes both tactical and strategic planning difficult. If assessments for support for those children we see with additional learning take six months, how are we to manage what is often a deteriorating situation in terms of their behaviours and our relationships with resident families? In the meantime, all we can do is encourage parents'/carers' engagement in schooling, but it comes as no surprise that they remain reluctant and then make complaints.

A further challenge to our ability to support our children and resident families can be seen in the school budget cuts and changes to the additional learning needs (ALN) code of practice and safeguarding policies. This means that there is less specialist support for the school, and it is much harder and more time-consuming to arrange to have multi-agency workers on the school site, despite the fact that they are there to help the children with the greatest need. Waiting lists for the child and adolescent mental health service (CAMHS) assessments can be as long as two years, lengthened by the backlog from the Covid-19 pandemic over the last three years, which can be linked with wider reporting of this issue.[3] The school building is a relatively new build, but during the redesign we specifically requested office space to make the site a one-stop-shop for families. This was not forthcoming. I can only applaud my colleague in the school's front office and his concerns that we are linked into a model for Full Service Schools (see Jones's chapter 3). There must be policies in place and inspection visits that make allowances for our professional judgements and decision-making to ensure the needs of each individual child and his/her family can be met rather than remain as unmet needs.

This all brings me to my closing statement, which effectively is a call for public investment and now is an opportune time. Welsh Government's Covid-19 recovery policies could come with funding to effect change in local school-communities in the interests of schoolchildren who are the future generation. This requires determined action on the 2015 Well-being of Future Generations (Wales) Act, in concert with 2018–19 *Children First*, both an expression of Wales's Labour government's suite of progressive policies. Here we have it on site with the Bangor PLUS team developing a model way of working in this school-community, alert to multi-agencies' multi-disciplinary perspectives, developing local solutions with their allied Not-NEET projects, forging a notion of school-community development that lends itself to research-informed practical interventions. Without hesitation, I wish them well as they present it to school staff meetings and our Board of Governors, teacher union meetings, and further afield to teacher professional associations, school Heads' networks, the Association of School and College Leaders, and meetings with personnel in local and national governments. There is no better way to build a more prosperous local school-community integrated into Welsh society.

Notes

1   This was certainly the intention of working with the Bangor PLUS project team, attending a number of their seminars in the two series as time permitted, and re-grouping to work towards the publication of this edited book. I will always be grateful for the introduction to Lingard et al.'s (2003) *Leading Learning* and Smyth's article on a socially just school in a special issue of *Critical Studies in Education* (Thomson, Lingard and Wrigley, 2012) and other research publications. These research insights sat well with me.

2   There is a large area of professional literature on debates over the nature of school improvement and school effectiveness, and I particularly like the approach taken by Profs Bob Lingard, Terry Wigley, Ruth Lupton and Lori Beckett on it (see their work in the references).

3   See W. Crenna-Jennings and J. Hutchinson (2020). *Access to child and adolescent mental health services in 2019.* London: Educational Policy Institute; also Welsh Government (2022). *Specialist Children and Adolescent Mental Health Service first appointment waiting times: November 2021.* Available at: *https://gov.wales/specialist-children-and-adolescent-mental-health-service-scamhs -first-appointment-waiting-times-november-2021* (accessed 27 April 2023).

23-12 1.7.59

This slate workshop shows the mechanisation introduced in the nineteenth century to speed up the production of roofing slates during the Industrial Revolution, which came to dominate not only the landscape of Gwynedd but its way of life given the employment of 20,000 people in industries prior to the First World War.

3

AN 'OPEN DOOR' SCHOOL POLICY FOR RESIDENT FAMILIES: CROESO/ WELCOME!

Dafydd Jones (Ysgol Trem y Mynydd)

Introduction

This chapter is based on professional conversations with a primary school Secretary in the front office who also clerks for the Board of Governors, here in the guise of a fictitious character brought to life by academic partners who completed the writing after the departure of the school Head because of long Covid. It recounts insights into what is required to keep the school day humming for the school staff along with visitors like student teachers and their supervisors, multi-agency workers, consultants, academic partners, but most importantly for students and parents/carers on the Trem y Mynydd housing estate. This might all sound straightforward but it belies the complexities of the administrative roles required to exercise the school's support for resident families, especially where parents/carers have had varied daily experiences before the start of the school day and come in to share all sorts of concerns. I will describe the frontline efforts required to support these parents/carers, share some of my knowledge and show why there must be sensitivity and respect going both ways between school staff, governors and parents/ carers under duress. I also point to what is required to meet the needs of these parents who are 'living on the edge' so that they can work with the school.

Working in these two administrative roles for such a long time has provided me with some very rewarding work experiences but also some grief. I count myself lucky to have come to know generations of resident families, students, parents/carers and grandparents as well as the staff coming and going. In many respects I feel privileged, especially where so many have taken me into their confidence in the front office and on the phone, and I have come to know them through letters and on social media. These accounts of the strains and stresses of living in poverty readily show some of the challenges and tensions for resident families, some testing home-school relationships, but also what needs to be done for those dealing with emergency situations. The point here is that this school's challenges are so different from other local/county schools because they are deeply rooted in resident families' socio-economic circumstances: we hear of troubles regarding family circumstances, benefit payments, low paid work, Covid-19 and the cost-of-living crisis that bite hard on this housing estate. It is important to think about what support comes into the school from Welsh Government via the local authority and other sources, especially given the constraints on funding and resources.

I am always struck by the demands on my time, especially that devoted to repetitive non-core tasks in school administration. This invariably happens when the school day gets underway and a number of parents/carers present with a wide range of complex welfare issues related to health, capacity to work and earn a living, family finances, emotional strains and sometimes anti-social behaviours. They often require my urgent attention, assistance and very often advice not only to themselves, but also to the school Head, school staff, and on quite a few occasions to multi-agency workers. These parents/carers certainly require empathy, respect and insight, and reciprocal trusting relationships, which is not easy when trust with agencies here is low. Three case stories stand out, all with different welfare needs: Carys, a young mum and sole parent who requested a letter of support to the social housing agency; Cadi and Aled, two parents who struggled with the expulsion of their son from three primary schools; and Alys, another sole parent who was faced with the consequences of a son consistently absent from high school. The first one was easily supported; the second illustrates the constraints with current school policies and funding arrangements; and the third nearly ended up in court. Then there are case stories of teen mums, grieving families, refugee families and rainbow families that require support often beyond the school's remit.

The most effective strategy to date has been an 'open door' school policy, which means that everyone is welcome to come and visit this community's school, and which is one way to counter the perception of the school as an icon of authority (see Evans's chapter 2). This is not to endorse the idea of community schools being bandied about because its 'one size fits all' does not acknowledge and accommodate the fragile situations we confront. I pause on Wales's Education Minister Jeremy Miles's intention to send in family engagement officers and community managers to tackle the impact of poverty on young people's attainment.[1] I am not sure if this is meant to supplant our frontline school and multi-agency team already working with parents/carers who are at their wits end and are now having to deal with the cost-of-living crisis. Because we all have the requisite deep, granular understandings of resident families' unmet needs, it would be more expedient to address the lack of school-community funding that leaves us inadequately resourced to deal with family hardships. Poverty leaves teaching staff hamstrung in their efforts to concentrate on their routine work of teaching and learning, worried if not haunted by policy pressures on students' performance, Estyn inspections and school accountability. They often have no option but to relegate welfare matters, but this raises questions about schools' responsibilities and school doors not always being open. This is evident in the knock-on effects of child poverty drawn out in my case stories.

There are arguments for and against all these parties in conflict, and there are serious human rights considerations, like the child's right to education and schooling. That said, questions remain about what can be done differently to secure a productive role for the school in this community; to consolidate productive relationships between resident families, parents/carers, students, school and multi-agency staff; and to guarantee the integrity of the school-community-university partnership. It is a testament to the work of our Bangor PLUS project team that some critical understandings of these concerns are coming to the fore, especially as the team have worked to explore the underlying systemic and structural causes of inter-generational poverty and its effects and to forge a notion of school-community development. In doing so they have worked to foster local solutions like tapping the potential of the mooted new-build multi-agency hub with recreation facilities to provide education, training and employment opportunities for adults, young people and children on the estate. The hub also provides potential with school staff coming together with local council and multi-agency staff to bring into effect a full-service schools model way of working collaboratively and cooperatively.

In this chapter I provide an overview of my two administrative roles to maintain the smooth running of the school, which requires some critical understanding, especially when some parents make their grievances and animosity known. I share my knowledge of the Trem y Mynydd school-community and the ways it has evolved and changed, noting the strains and stresses of living in poverty experienced by parents and made known to me on a daily basis through conversations, letters and via social media. I also share some of the challenges presented to the school staff. I then provide details about the work I do in regards a wide range of complex welfare demands and illustrate these with three case stories. If these are not handled carefully, there can be serious repercussions like legal proceedings and court appearances. I then come to describe my open door policy, which for the most part works well, although there are tensions in the ways the school has to manage different and difficult situations and there are more challenges when it comes to the provision of additional support. Finally, I present my chapter conclusions, which call for a critical understanding of the daily challenges faced by the school that are not education focused; the additional work required by frontline school and multi-agency staff to support resident families and children in poverty; and the proposed local solutions to ease these burdens.

Keeping it sweet

In this job, I have seen quite a few school Heads come and go, but I have always been fortunate to be able to build a solid working relationship with 'the boss'. I was certainly sorry to see the last one leave because of her battles with long Covid, which started to take a toll after her phased return to work when she had to stand up to the constant welfare demands peculiar to a school like ours. We worked well together, and I know that she greatly valued my corporate memory and my ideas about the school felt respected. This was no doubt because of my years of experience and because I know 'my stuff'. I am competent in running the school IT systems to do with school data and finances, keeping all the paper and electronic records up-to-date, and being the 'front face' of the school. I like to keep it humming and keep a cheery smile to welcome the children, parents/carers, and all the other visitors to the school, and keep it sweet on the phone and in my e-mail replies. This part of the job is fairly routine, but there is another side to it that is quite demanding as we are often stretched to the limits and are in dire need of more school funding and resources.

I do not want to gloss over my administrative roles and my multi-tasking. These include responding to teaching staff and teaching assistants, looking after sick and/or traumatised children, liaising with parents/carers and others in our school team, like the welfare officer, librarians, kitchen staff, cleaners, bus drivers and vendors. I also spend some time making appointments and setting up schedules for those coming in to run activities, including musicians, resident artists, sports coaches and the outdoor learning team taking children for classes in the forest. This is not to forget school improvement advisers, consultants, Estyn inspectors when they come into the school, and likewise student teachers, supervisors and academic partners, as well as different multi-agency workers including the police when we need them. This is typically the point when we need back-up on top of specialist professional help to deal with all the 'top end' health and welfare issues, which requires an army of school nurses who take care of mental health, dental health, sexual health and, more recently, trans issues; we also rely on the school counsellor and educational psychologist, who are usually allied to the child and adolescent mental health services. I often feel like a triage nurse in the local hospital's accident and emergency department, pointing people in all sorts of directions.

I have to make decisions in emergencies and other chaotic situations, which mostly involve calling in parents/carers when we have critical incidents, and then directing them to service providers as needs be. This happens frequently enough, but not as often as when parents/carers who have had varied daily experiences before school starts want to share all sorts of concerns with me. These conversations often reveal that there have been some changes in the household or in the family's circumstances, such as relationship breakdowns, or there are added caring responsibilities, or there are concerns about health or health vulnerabilities among different family members. With Covid-19 there was always the need for one or more family members to self-isolate, which could mean a whole family being in lockdown. There might also have been loss of work, loss of access to children, loss of childcare, a need to move house or relocate away from the housing estate. There could have been arguments, domestic violence, family court matters, divorce or separation, alcohol and drug abuse, a death, prison sentence, and other legalities including debt collection and neighbourhood disputes. There could have been changes to benefits or universal credit, delayed payments or waiting times, slow data-sharing with the local authority's benefits department, disruptions due to digital inaccessibility, or incorrect information processed (for example, children not counted correctly).

It is crucial that I maintain the confidence and trust placed in me – which is not easily won – and show sensitivity and respect towards these parents/carers who have shown a good deal of courage to disclose their families' circumstances of living in poverty. It cannot be easy to share their personal details, even if it is only to let off some steam and garner some sympathy. Most times they want to make it known that they are under duress and need help to make ends meet, especially as they are caught in the trap of either being unemployed or the working poor, battling low or stagnant wages and zero-hours contracts. Without exception, all our resident families are confronted by the rising cost-of-living crisis, and some of these pressure situations are constant, while others might be triggered by sudden changes in personal circumstances. These can be time-limited, or constant thereafter. It is always necessary for me to use my better judgement when it comes to providing advice in all directions, and while there is wraparound support on Trem y Mynydd more needs to be said about this, especially in regards the current social emergency and what the future might hold.

Our academic partners captured the situation when they showed us the book called *Living on the Edge* (see Smyth and Wrigley, 2013), and I can only agree with their findings because life for large numbers of our resident families is precarious, and many of their children's schooling experiences are fragile to the extent that quite a few come to feel disaffection and alienation. However, it is important not to make hasty judgements or, worse, make assumptions about the children's family lives, but instead develop critical understanding about their circumstances, even in the face of shredded emotions. One of the reasons I have stayed in this job is because of the children, whom I believe deserve a better chance in life, and because I see the school Head, the teaching staff and the rest of our team, including the Board of Governors, all working so hard to provide so many opportunities for them. I enjoy my standing with my colleagues, and I sense that they like my approach to the job, where it is crucial to show empathy, respect and insight, and in turn share this with our team, visitors and resident families across the generations.

The apple doesn't fall far

Some of these resident families are 'early settlers', descended from the working men employed in the Penrhyn slate quarries and dockside at Port Penrhyn, now with three to four generations on Trem y Mynydd. Other resident families are 'blow-ins', to use a local phrase, and have been allocated social housing here because of a variety of reasons to do with their own family circumstances. Some can be itinerant, which causes problems for our school numbers, funding formulas and staffing, but others stay for the long term. There are even great-grandparents who have stayed but, were they ever able to afford the purchase of real estate, would have liked to move off the estate and into more upmarket areas. Then there are resident families who remain because of a commitment to the school-community and its way of life that includes security of tenure, family and friendship networks, the church, social club and sports clubs as well as the old people's home and other amenities. There are certainly many resident families who are content to stay on this housing estate and make a life for themselves, their children and grandchildren. Security is one thing, but we need to be mindful that this place is geographically defined, which brings limited local employment, education and training opportunities, consequent unemployment and intergenerational poverty.

This is not to say that it has not changed over time: I have seen each generation with their own sets of problems. Looking back, there were industries that readily employed a workforce and there was seemingly work around to the point where it was not socially acceptable to be unemployed. As the industries declined, work opportunities became more and more piece-meal and some resident families had to rely on benefits.[2] Then came the UK's Blair-Brown New Labour governments, whose policy orientation was more towards technology and the service industries, which left so many of our resident families behind: this led to a growing acceptance of being unemployed and in receipt of benefits. Then came the Cameron-Clegg Coalition government's policy choices on austerity, with punitive sanctions continued by a string of Conservative governments led by Prime Ministers Cameron, May, Johnson, then Truss and now Sunak. Consequently, I am seeing more and more families – including those in work – in poverty, what with spiralling housing costs, cuts to benefits and the cost-of-living crisis, with reliance on food parcels, evictions by private landlords, a shortage of smaller social housing and child-benefit capped at two children. All this causes disruptions to children's schooling.

These problems have been made known to me over the years by parents/carers in face-to-face conversations or on the phone, but sometimes this has gone further than just venting to me. With the decline in living standards, I witnessed resident families going without disposable income that enabled the purchase of household goods, a family car, money for holidays, sporting events, bus fares into the city to go to the cinema or shopping for items like children's school uniform and trainers. With a further fall in standards, families suffered the indignity of a lack of income for basic needs and, more recently, there is a major cost-of-living crisis and resident families require emergency support now that there are unmet needs in regards to food and fuel to heat their homes. From my conversations with parents/carers, it appeared that the school had become a target to make things better, likely because they were angry, frustrated, hungry and cold. It is important to remember that this school-community is confronted with long-standing inequalities and does not operate on a level playing field, especially considering that our children come from households going without basics like food and fuel, but also because their parents are focused on survival, are under enormous stress and are worried.

I have also been made aware of these problems via social media, which comes with its own set of problems with parents/carers posting comments and making public complaints about the school but remaining anonymous, and school staff therefore unable to engage in an intelligent exchange about what is at issue. Often the social media posts can be vehicles for grievances about the school, seen as an icon of authority, and these can range from minor grumbles – for instance about staff responses to children's unruly behaviour – that can then escalate to major concerns with teachers' work. These posts attract comments, and in next to no time these virtual conversations can drum up animosity towards the school. It takes skill to handle these tricky situations, but the main thing is to try to avoid pitting the school against parents/carers whose criticisms need to be properly addressed. It is often part of my job to open up channels of communication and invite the different parties in for an informal chat, maybe an interview or mediation session, or to meet other multi-agency workers who can provide specialist support and/or emergency support. More often than not, parents/carers expect the school staff to be there in a supporting role and help them through their situation or simply to fix it.

We often get criticised if we do not meet expectations, but a realistic response to resident families' lived experiences of poverty should be taken into consideration. First, there is the question of what may or may not be done by the school, keeping in mind that there is a great need for more school-community funding and resources. This comes down to the UK Conservative government's allocation of funds to the devolved Welsh Labour government; its allocation to the local authority, and then what funding and resources comes to this school, and how we manage the budget. These considerations unwittingly underpin some of the tensions revealed in conversations and social media posts, and in some testing home-school relationships. Secondly, we need a good sense of who/what is responsible, what the issue is and what it is that has led to the concentration of poverty in this postcode: the decline of industry and manufacturing, job losses and the role of the gig economy, in tandem with an increase in family and social problems, marked by a lack of social infrastructure. This all gives rise to resident families' unmet needs (again see Evans's chapter 2), which come into the school as parents/carers and children present with a wide range of complex welfare demands that require a good deal of thought and time.

Some brutally honest records

The welfare demands that come into the school, a result of the causes and effects of poverty, are experienced by both children and parents/carers, but also school staff. This affects my job – providing clerical support to the school – which I like to call the 'day job' part, where I ensure that my colleagues can do their own jobs. Then there is the additional job that comes with being the first point of contact for parents/carers and children, where I am at the frontline, fielding welfare demands and consequently doing repetitive non-core tasks. These are above and beyond my job description, and remain constant and recurring.[3] This is because resident families' deep needs remain, and were possibly skimmed over in the pandemic despite the fact that our school-community rallied to provide kind and humane emergency support. This was especially so with our school kitchen providing free school meals to the children of key workers, and the local drop-in centre providing resident families with food parcels and more direct help with emergency cash for fuel top-ups, baby items, sanitary items, household items and the like. We brought in a full-time mental health and well-being worker, signposting or advocating for more accessible family support. The school also provides family support, as my three case stories show.

Carys is a young, sole parent of two pre-school children, a girl aged four and a boy aged two, and a trained nursery nurse on universal credit. Following a change in the family's circumstances, when the children's father moved out of their allocated flat in a social housing block on Trem y Mynydd, Carys had to pay the rental arrears, which she did. But now the family needs to move, and for good reason. They are bothered by constant disturbances, including police visits to other residents, banging on doors at all times of the day and night, and fighting in the shared public spaces. The pre-school raised concerns regarding the little girl acting out, and Carys approached me for a letter to be sent to Gwynedd Council's housing options department in support of her request for a transfer to a three-bedroom home, preferably on the estate. Our school's welfare officer obliged and noted her concerns about the anti-social behaviour, the harm and distress it caused the family and the need to prioritise the children's welfare. Carys also secured a letter from her health visitor, though she reneged on paying a £60 fee to the local GP for a third support letter: it is a huge sum to come out of her limited income.

Cadi and Aled co-parent a son aged seven, and the mum is one of our school-community's key workers who does shift work cleaning in the local hospital. The boy had been expelled from our school and another two local primary schools; Cadi was advised to withdraw the boy from his last school so as to avoid another expulsion. Having sought support from the local drop-in centre, she then wrote a letter to our school Head to say that this was clearly a problem for each school, Gwynedd Council, her son and the family. She stated that the boy needed to be in school, especially as he was not learning his basics, could barely write his name and had effectively missed out on years of schooling. She said that she had worked with numerous professionals, from school staff through to the local authority education welfare officer, the school nurse, nursery nurse, an occupational therapist and a school psychologist, and the boy was on a waiting list to be assessed in the hospital neurology department. The burden to place him in a school fell on Cadi and she was clearly at her wits' end, but our school Head negotiated a compromise with the local authority to accommodate the boy.

Alys is yet another sole parent, introduced in an earlier chapter (see Beckett's Editor's Introduction). I remember her as a teen mum and she was determined that her little children would get something out of primary school. This came as no surprise because she readily acknowledged that she had fluffed her opportunities at education, and though she still harbours dreams to be a registered nurse, she devoted herself to mothering her eight children. The last three are in high school, but she continues to battle the education system having been charged with non-cooperation on the matter of her 12-year-old son's lax attendance at high school and a threat of court action. She sought support from the local drop-in centre, then wrote a letter to the high school Head to say this was all grossly unfair, especially as she had made every effort to make an appointment for a meeting and she had not had her calls returned. When she pestered the school Secretary, she finally secured an appointment, sent the letter again by registered mail, but then the appointment was cancelled. The matter escalated and it was Alys who negotiated a compromise solution with the local authority to accommodate the boy.

These three case stories show the ongoing need for family support, but this all needs to be sensitively handled because of frayed nerves with all parties upset, annoyed, angry and worried. It takes inordinate skill to handle these very tricky situations, but the focus of course should be on the children: the grievances in each one of the case stories do not augur well for their future. Yet again we need to be mindful of the great need for more school-community funding and resources, and who/what is responsible and what is at issue with regards to the underlying causes and effects of poverty and the ways it plays out. The case stories also show that family support is a crucial part of the work undertaken by frontline school and multi-agency workers in the local drop-in centre. This shows that rather than send in family engagement officers and community managers, that funding by Welsh Government would be better spent on a family support officer who could collaborate and coordinate with our school's welfare officer and other frontline workers as well as with local authority staff. Plus we would all do well to remember the school's main business is teaching and learning.

Opportunities lost

I am truly proud of our open door school policy, which means that everyone is welcome to come and visit this community's school. This is one way to counter the perception of the school as an icon of authority and to promote cooperative and collaborative partnerships in schooling and education. But there is a proviso here: this does not mean that our school on Trem y Mynydd has capacity to be a community-focused school mooted by Wales's Education Minister, Jeremy Miles:

> A community focused school is one that provides a range of services and activities, often beyond the school day, to help meet the needs of its pupils, their families and the wider community. Across Wales many schools already provide some community services including adult education, study support, ICT facilities and community sports programmes.[4]

If this were to happen and a business manager were appointed to oversee the practicalities and legalities, it would surely have implications for my 'day job'. They would require clerical and administrative assistance in regards school property, site-management, the adult workforce, after-hours usage, supervision, health and safety, DBS checks, responsibility for keys, lock-up, alarms, burdens on school finances for any damage, lost or stolen items, rental and recompense, as well as insurance and public liability.

This suggests an extra burden on our school Head, taking the focus away from primary school teaching and learning, sharing our stretched resources, and bringing in a whole new set of logistical challenges. This is a long way from our community's school on Trem y Mynydd, already burdened with a set of repeat challenges and welfare demands that come with the causes and effects of poverty, which now include social emergencies. This requires a shared understanding of the work of this community's school but, again, there is another proviso because this is not the same as those community schools already bandied about in

Wales. One iteration is community partnership schools, which is an idea worth considering but not in any meaningful way to inform our call for family support.[5] Another iteration is the community schools already being rolled out in Wales with school Heads' visits to the USA funded by the British Council.[6] The work in the USA is worth reading about because it covers pertinent matters:[7] school leadership, teacher leaders, teacher preparation, family engagement, youth leadership, and so forth. But then it buys into the dominant GERM agenda to tout improvements in student outcomes, attendance, achievement, graduation, and reducing racial and economic achievement gaps, which make for great sound bites but they are all such a long way from the work that needs to be done here.

Instead of our school Head and teaching staff having to attend to parents'/carers' complex welfare demands, including emergency support, a family support officer in our community's school could handle fragile situations; seeing it from the parents' point of view, sympathising because they are at their wits' end having to deal with all sorts of worries. Take Carys, for example, firing off letters in the hope that they will be read and responded to, although we are all well aware of the constraints on the local authority having its funding shredded by austerity, and the consequent dire situation with the lack of supply of social housing (see Fernley et al.'s chapter 5). Carys understands the points system of allocation, waiting lists, priority cases and her band 2 place, but said she needed empathetic understanding. Most importantly, she needs a safe and secure place to live with her children where they are not exposed to strangers, a noisy police presence, alcohol- or drug-fuelled night binges, and violence. As a nursery nurse, she also knows what it takes to meet their social and educational learning needs, and she has great aspirations for her children in regards their pre-schooling, primary schooling and beyond.

The same thing could be said of the other two mums. Cadi put it into writing that she saw value in schooling and education, including play and outdoor education, and she wanted her son to benefit from his re-enrolment, settle into a routine, learn and achieve, gain qualifications and make something of himself. Alys said much the same in her letter: she wanted her son to settle and do well so that he makes something of himself, and she understood the importance of him attending school and finding a route into further education, employment and training. They shared commonalities in that both these mums had been advised that they were breaking the law, which was frightening, if not threatening. Yet Cadi had self-reported to social services on a number of occasions, and Alys had made great attempts to arrange meetings with the high school Head, the school's welfare officer, her son and his form teacher. Both mums opted to work with multi-agency workers in the drop-in centre and were prepared to take a nominated support person to meetings to help protect against demeaning resident families and demonising their children. Beckett (2016) had pointed out such negativity is a sad reflection on the teachers and students whose experience of social and education disadvantage finds expression in the urban school classroom (p. 3). These two mums also both came to learn how the system works – or not, as the case may be.

At the risk of repeating myself, the situation is pressurised with the school Head and teaching staff having to juggle Welsh Government's policy expectations of teachers and students meeting national standards, and having to facilitate frontline efforts required to support parents/carers in our community's school. We need more funding and resources, especially for a Family Support Officer who has critical insight into the causes and effects of poverty and wraparound community welfare support. We also need to fund and resource school staff and the multi-agency team who have intimate knowledge of resident families' unmet needs and ways to support parents/carers so that they can work with the school. This is not to endorse the import of external managers, especially a business manager to run the school as a community-focused franchise; it is to warn against any potential educational damage that comes from children being locked out of schools, on waiting lists of 18 months to be medically assessed with lengthy delays for risk assessments, and unable to access the limited special education facilities in Gwynedd (because of austerity and the withdrawal of services). This brings me to my endorsement of the Bangor PLUS team's work on asset-based school-community development.

Conclusion: breaking the cycle

Alys spoke for all the parents/carers on Trem y Mynydd when she said that she most definitely did not want her son to squander his opportunity for schooling and to forfeit his chances for qualifications as she did when she was a teenager. Cadi put it more bluntly: when confronted by the prospect that no school was prepared to take her son, he was effectively being denied access to primary education, which could be considered an infringement of his human rights. Thankfully their requests to work cooperatively, with courtesy and respect, and their preparedness to compromise meant that resolutions could be found that saved everyone from further grief. We were all grateful for a fresh start with a 'clean slate', no pun intended on Wales's history of education. This history and human rights, like the child's right to education and schooling, demand serious consideration, and this is something we have done from the get-go in our *Children First* needs assessment meetings and again when academic partners ran their series of seminars (again see Beckett's Editor's Introduction).

In fact, Wales's history of education and human rights in relation to a string of ineffectual anti-poverty policies were discussed at a large group meeting where a presentation was given to share some of the data from the *Children First* needs assessment (see Lewis's chapter 1). In the group discussion that followed exploring the causes and effects of child poverty, the mooted new-build multi-agency hub was considered as were ways to streamline services in response to welfare demands, disadvantage and deprivation on Trem y Mynydd. Beckett, who was there in her capacity as academic partner, said that the means of improving the circumstances and opportunities for families on the estate were hidden in plain sight. She suggested that the team eventually working on planning for the hub, notably commissioning architectural design, securing building approval, overseeing demolition of the old building on site, construction and landscape gardening, could simultaneously coordinate with local education institutions to provide opportunities for resident families' education, employment and training. This was barely acknowledged at the time, probably considered too radical a suggestion, never mind a policy option, but it was a worthy idea.

Our local solution to appoint a Family Support Officer to collaborate and coordinate with our school welfare officer and other frontline workers would work that much better in a multi-agency hub providing family support. Though not on the school site, there is potential for school staff to network with colleagues and institute the idea of a full service school, albeit in the hub, and bring together a range of education, health and community services for resident families. The community development workers' vision for a one-stop shop to meet the complex welfare demands on Trem y Mynydd would be a focal point for cooperation, and it meets a professional need for adequate work space (see Silvester and Joslin's chapter 4 and Thirsk's chapter 6). While the health service has its own on-site centre next to the mooted new-build site, other multi-agency officers are currently working out of their cars if not in the drop-in centre, which is an old shop front recently converted into office space. It is a designated space that allows them to 'hot desk', but there are issues regarding privacy and constraints on timetabling because of the need to plan, then limit the days on site.

A full service school model for the hub would certainly make my extra job triaging that much easier and provide easy access to those who can readily respond to the complex welfare demands that come to my attention. Back to our local solution to secure a family support officer, allied to the Not-NEET project, 'Co-ordinating the future: the Youth Hall as a multi-agency hub' (see appendix 2). This taps into the potential of the mooted new-build multi-agency hub to provide education, training and employment opportunities for adults, teenagers and children on the estate. This is one way to harness the assets and potential of those inevitably growing up in poverty and facing the prospect of unemployment or becoming the working poor, considering the current set of circumstances and the growing social emergency. Carys, Cadi, Aled and Alys would certainly jump at the opportunities for their children to learn about the demolition and building industries, but also the multi-agency professions, and about the sports and recreation industries subject to the plans for the attached recreation facilities getting the funding to proceed.[8] This too will take a good deal of time and thought to bring to fruition because collaboration in a network of service providers and also the coordination of the welfare work of schools and multi-agencies, not to forget the Not-NEET project, is a complex process.

All this is at the root of our efforts in lobbying Gwynedd Council given its part-funding for the hub,[9] but also in convincing educational institutions responsible for the certification of school staff, multi-agency workers and others that responsive planning and our educative strategy is consistent with their focus on working in Wales's national interest. By encouraging productive relationships between resident families, parents/carers, students, school staff and multi-agency workers as well as academic partners and critical friends, our focus is on pushing back against child poverty, just as the Child Poverty Action Group (2017) put it:[10]

> More than anything, as a nation we need to commit to ending poverty, as a national priority. We especially need to end the narrative that has demonised people in poverty and instead see that we all have the same positive interest in bringing people out of persistent poverty and into full participation in society and the economy. Our investment will, in the long run, be rewarded with greater productivity, high tax receipts and lower social costs, enriching everyone financially, socially and morally.

Notes

1 See *https://media.service.gov.wales/news/gbp-25m-investment-in-community-focused-schools-to-tackle-the-impact-of-poverty* (accessed 1 April 2023).

2 See David Gwynn (2015). *Gwynedd Inheriting a Revolution. The Archaeology of Industrialisation in North-West Wales*. Stroud: Phillimore Press.

3 Look up school secretary at *nationalcareers.service.gov.uk*; and school secretaries at *ucas.com* (accessed 1 April 2023).

4 See this extract in the statement found online: *https://gov.wales/sites/default/files/publications/2018-03/27-community-focused-schools.pdf* (accessed 1 April 2023).

5 This is promoted by David Egan, 'Poverty and education in Wales: enabling a national mission', in Thompson and Ivinson (2020).

6 See British Council Wales's International Education Programme team, which hosted the British Council Wales Digital Event on Community Schools in Wales on 27 April 2021: see *http://wales.britishcouncil.org//* (accessed 1 April 2023).

7 See Ferrara and Jacobson (2019). *Community Schools. People & Places Transforming Education and Communities*. London: Rowman & Littlefield.

8 This was to be inspired by the discussion in the section subtitled 'It does not have to be like this' in the introduction to Marsh et al. (2017). *Poverty: The Facts* (6th edition). London: CPAG.

9 This is jointly funded by Invest Local and the local council with further matched funding sought (see Thirsk's chapter 6) but plans are in flux at the time of this book going into print.

10 This quote is taken from the section subtitled 'It does not have to be like this' in the introduction to Marsh et al. (2017).

This train engine was named after Linda Blanche Douglas-Pennant (1889–1965), granddaughter of the second Lord Penrhyn, George Sholto Gordon Douglas-Pennant (1836–1907), who was a protagonist in the Penrhyn Quarry dispute in 1900–3.

4

HUNGRY KIDS: FAMILIES' FOOD INSECURITY FURTHER EXPOSED BY THE PANDEMIC

Jess Mead Silvester (Mantell Gwynedd) and Paul Joslin (Wild Elements)

Introduction

This chapter is was written by a community development worker, who prior to leaving post had multiple responsibilities for different programmes and projects in the local drop-in centre here called by its pseudonym, Mynydd Ni.[1] A few of these related to the culture of food, especially as I worked with a team of volunteers who do some catering and run the Hive Café, which draws on supplies from our community kitchen gardens. Prior to the pandemic I had some awareness of some resident families' reliance on food banks, but this increased during the pandemic when an ongoing need for food crates and parcel deliveries became apparent. The response was firmly led by resident volunteers and supported by elected representatives for Trem y Mynydd on Gwynedd Council and Mynydd Ni workers, Welsh Government, Gwynedd Council and the Betsi Cadwaladr University Health Board. Here I should note my joint work with Paul Joslin prior to his leaving post and his contribution to this chapter, who is was then on secondment from Wild Elements to oversee our community gardens. Paul helped in delivering food crates and parcels, and had first-hand experience of resident families' needs in regards to health and welfare.

We both share concerns regarding the political principle that while the right to adequate food is a universal human right, consecutive UK

Conservative governments under prime ministers Cameron, May and Johnson have seemingly assumed limited responsibility for food insecurity. This is in line with their 'Big Society' agenda for a voluntary/third sector in welfare, though some responsibility is taken by Welsh national and local governments.[2] At the time of writing, it remains to be seen what the latest Conservative replacement Prime Minister Rishi Sunak does following Liz Truss's short premiership given that we are witness to a good deal of hardship, families in distress and a school-community with unmet needs. These link to those included in the *Children First* needs assessment (see chapter 1) and by the school Head (see chapter 2), though this chapter focuses on emergency food provision as one response to the unmet needs of resident families. Their reliance on food banks was re-confirmed in a survey we conducted a few months into the first Covid-19 lockdown in August/September 2020, which provided insights into the circumstances that left households and individuals exposed during the pandemic both temporarily and longer term.

This all raises questions about the affordability of food and the necessity that led this local community to devise an immediate practical local solution to meet food needs during the pandemic and subsequently, as we are now seemingly freefalling into a deepening, widely recognised and normalised cost-of-living crisis. This too requires careful analysis, and we begin by asking who/what is responsible for our community's vulnerability and sensitivity to these economic shocks, undoubtedly felt across the UK and beyond. These point to Cameron's austerity programme, then May's and Johnson's handling of Brexit, but also Johnson's handling of Covid-19 and its fallout; however, our concern is with the frequency and depth with which food security shows up for individuals, families and households on this housing estate. This highlights the ways in which this community not only assumes its responsibilities but organises itself to care for one another in the face of common hardship. Later in the pandemic, after lockdown, multi-agency workers returned to the estate as part of a 'support hub' in the model of volunteers' support. Looking to the future, our vision was always to develop a more permanent local solution where food is grown in community gardens, to supply the Hive Café, but also to start a venture in market gardening on Trem y Mynydd.[3]

Joslin's contribution to this chapter draws on his work on community gardening and 'greening' the Trem y Mynydd housing estate. His plan was to establish plots on any available piece of land identified as being appropriate; these include grass verges, lawns, overgrown patches and perimeters of parks and playing fields, especially brownfield sites now disused. He reported that discussions have been held with Gwynedd Council and the two local housing associations known as ADRA and North Wales Housing, all as the principal public landowners. This has proved to be anything but straightforward, but ADRA have been open to negotiation and some 'guerrilla' planting has been carried out. There is quiet satisfaction in seeing children and young people so protective of growing food plants that might otherwise be vandalised and trashed, but hunger has got the better of them. Joslin advised us that the concept of edible landscapes evolved from a community gardening/greening project that started in 2008 in Todmorden in the Calder Valley in Yorkshire. This has since become a model for our community gardening group, who has done much towards greening the estate but also encouraging residents to get involved in growing fresh food, which would then be available to purchase at reasonable prices from a small shop on the estate as part of a small local social enterprise.

Though our emergency food supply on Trem y Mynydd was born of our community response to an immediate need during the pandemic, this local solution was subsequently tailored to meet more complex community, household and individual needs. More recently, we are taking a degree of statutory responsibility not previously seen for food security, having received funding from Gwynedd Council, Welsh Government and the Betsi Cadwaladr University Health Board that has enabled us to continue funding emergency food support. Our community group and our community gardening group came to provide a space for meaningful care, connection and kindness, and played a role in accessing other care and support. It all worked on the basis of trust and self-referral, and accommodated the need to change directions depending on the ways that resident families' food insecurity unfolded over time. In working with the Bangor PLUS team, we harnessed these community/local actions on Trem y Mynydd to tie into our Not-NEET project, 'Cultivating the estate: establishing community food gardens' (see appendix 3). This opened a space for partnership work with local networks of schools and educational institutions on cross-curriculum food projects with the potential to scale-up regionally and nationally; which demonstrates that there are clear advantages to localised, community-led responses to food insecurity if they are well resourced by Wales's national and local governments.

Feeding the family

Access to a good food supply can be difficult on Trem y Mynydd, which is situated outside a city and is isolated topographically from the city on one side and bounded by a busy road and railway on the other. It supports two local/corner shops, neither of which sell fresh fruit or vegetables, a chip shop and, more recently, a deli. It is a bus ride into the city to access a supermarket, with the most used being Aldi, though there is also Lidl, Asda and M&S in the same vicinity; yet, the bus company has recently increased fare prices and withdrawn the return service. Given the distance some residents cite physical access, the impracticality and cost of transport, and ill-health as barriers to reaching the supermarket.

Prior to the pandemic, food insecurity on the estate existed, yet access to emergency food was a somewhat unseen issue, addressed – to my knowledge – only through the provision of Public Health Wales's School Health Enrichment Programme (approx. forty primary pupils). This ran over the summer holidays to provide support for children's holiday hunger, and families could draw on other agencies with a presence on the estate such as the local authority family and early years' support services, and Citizen's Advice Bureau for referrals to the local cathedral food bank. Also, families could go on a drop-in basis to a local councillor's supermarket surplus scheme (both approx. 3 miles away). Beyond these initiatives, food insecurity was not something residents had either raised with me or, to my knowledge, addressed collectively.

Before the pandemic, food-based community initiatives centred on food as a means of bringing people together, sharing and socialising. From bring-a-dish events to the buzzing weekly community at Hive Café where residents cooked and ate together and served up to sixty warm meals, with many often unaccompanied children coming in for food. Then, early on in the pandemic, the Hive Café volunteers shifted to preparing and delivering warm meals to residents who were over seventy and isolating, mostly as a means of offering comfort and care. These were prepared using mobile catering equipment set up in an office space (the only organisation willing to open) and was dubbed the 'Soup Squad'.

During the course of the first lockdown, the provision of food came to be a means of connecting with elderly residents across the community, tackling isolation and boredom, but also building resilience. The weekly food deliveries became a natural vehicle for checking-in on residents' welfare, providing jigsaw puzzles and book swaps, delivering Easter eggs, plants or other retail surplus stock donations and making referrals to other volunteers for prescriptions to be collected or to other support services. To volunteers and other residents who baked cakes for the Soup Squad, food was a way of sharing generosity and care towards neighbours, their community and a way of getting through a difficult time by helping others.

These same volunteers were also informally providing emergency food to those at crisis point, which includes those who had run out of food and/or the means to procure it either because of physical isolation, inaccessibility through public transport or finances. They became volunteer food shoppers, and they delivered home-made ready-meals or food crates for anyone unable to afford food. They also set up a fruit-and-veg buyers' cooperative to help access fresh fruit and vegetables. During this period, a fifth of households on the estate received support with food; over a tenth of households received regular support with food security.

These local solutions regarding food response in this emergency evolved naturally as residents communicated what they needed and the volunteers responded, and they came to operate as a community group and worked increasingly closely with Mynydd Ni workers and their local elected representatives on Gwynedd Council, also Penrhyn House and, more recently, Bwyd Da Bangor in the city centre.[4] Together we endeavoured to meet the needs of different groups as practically as possible, and it should be noted that many funded and sponsored services were initially unavailable, and then became remote off-site as the pandemic took hold. This included support services, social care, Flying Start, family support services, the cathedral food bank and food distribution by the homeless hostel. Of necessity our community group stepped into the space vacated by professionals though we were soon receiving referrals from them.

Digging into the roots of food insecurity

Remarkably, we found that we all shared set principles that worked in a state of emergency, and we came to rely on an open system of self-referral that was trust-based and our emergency food provision needed no personal data or justification of need. We soon came to learn that, in this context, food insecurity was one of the ways poverty is experienced by families and individuals: their first request for emergency food support was often urgent and immediate, mainly because they had run out of options. Though nobody is asked to justify their need, they were invited to share a little about the circumstances they found themselves in to help us understand and refine our provision, and we could share what might not be working with colleagues further afield.

It soon became apparent that money ran out after paying for 'unavoidables', like gas/electricity, paying an outstanding or threatening bill or debt, needing to purchase a school uniform or new shoes for children and school bus passes. Food can be the last on the list of things to buy and the only one with any 'give' or elasticity within a tight budget. This reinforced our pre-Covid-19 concerns regarding resident families' circumstances and incomes, which were registered in the *Children First* needs assessment on Trem y Mynydd (again see Lewis's chapter 1) and noted by the school Head (again see Evans's chapter 2). This all highlighted causes and effects, like the physical access to adequate food including fruit and vegetables (encompassing shops, transport), precarious income security (e.g. zero-hour contracts), income level (e.g. low wages), benefits disruptions (e.g. universal credit waiting times, sanctions) and the rising cost of living (e.g. food, housing, fuel).

Perhaps it is helpful to share a conversation with Alys, who has already been introduced in the opening chapter (see Beckett's Editor's Introduction) and who has expressed a desire that her story is told. In receipt of universal credit[5] and unable to hold down a job because of ill-health, she shares her house with three teenagers, two with special educational needs, and she had older children and grandchildren who would come to stay. Alys was often at her wits' end trying to make ends meet, which came to light in our survey of sixty-one households on Trem y Mynydd in August/September 2020. We found that the pandemic amplified economic insecurity as household income dropped (50 per cent households) and living costs increased (30 per cent), which is acknowledged in UN Special Rapporteur Philip Alston's (2019) report after his probe into *Extreme Poverty and Human Rights in the UK*, which featured life on universal credit.

Alys came to rely on our food crates, which were assembled from supermarket surplus food via Fareshare, and other as-and-when arrangements that facilitated donations with local retailers to be packed and delivered by volunteers.[6] Surplus food more suited to batch-cooking was cooked by resident volunteers in the certified kitchen at Penrhyn House and distributed to vulnerable individuals who were without facilities or unlikely to cook themselves. This settled into a more regular pattern of deliveries to over ninety households each week at its height, and extended to the more vulnerable or excluded residents. Any new requests for support tended to be at the point of crisis and urgent boxes were sourced from a local councillor who had long been distributing supermarket surplus in the nearby city.

In August 2020, an assessment of £1,000 funding towards food insecurity on Trem y Mynydd found a social return on investment of £1.47 for each £1 spent.[7] The deliveries by volunteers from the fruit and vegetable buyers' cooperative grew to forty-five per week, collected from a central point and providing access to fresh fruit and vegetables for those without vehicles. At the time most residents were nervous about using buses, even when they could afford the fare, because of the risk of exposure to Covid-19; the distance plus carrying heavy fruit and vegetables meant that nearby shops were more likely to be used. The deliveries ensured a more even supply of fruit and vegetables, and at £3.70 for a mixed bag were good value.

One of the toughest challenges we faced in the delivery of our emergency food provision was how to negotiate the ways different individuals made us aware that maintaining their self-respect, pride and dignity was a sensitive issue. Sometimes we had to adjust our ways of working where possible; for instance, making home deliveries during school hours, but these were technical solutions to resident families' deep feelings. We were also aware of the wider Bangor communities' judgements about the Trem y Mynydd housing, especially given tendencies to demean resident families and demonise the children, as noted elsewhere in this volume. This sits well with Beckett's (2016) work on so-called 'failing schools' and Jones's (2011) analysis of the demonisation of the working classes that has given way to the term feral underclass or CHAVS in a deeply unequal society, a myth at the heart of British society. This all plays out in regards the acceptability of emergency food support, and again we made every effort to make the situation more comfortable in the following ways. We had conversations with resident families about inviting grandparents to share their experiences of budget cooking over the years and shopping tips; but also discussions about challenging media reporting on unemployment, as well as employment terms, wages, food prices, public transport, living income and universal basic income. These conversations prepared the way as we planned to have more inviting spaces to share in the Hive community cafe and our community gardens.

As we went in and out of lockdowns, the informality of our community group's work and the partnerships we had formed – sharing organisational constitutions, bank accounts, funding, kitchens, volunteers, vehicles, staff time and so on – came under strain as our previous workloads resumed and we faced other mounting challenges. We struggled to meet fluctuating demand with unpredictable surplus food supplies until the local authority offered to 'support, not take over' and supply staple foods using their supply chains and equipment (fridges, freezers, shelving). We struggled for space as the enterprise grew, which prompted us to move the operation into the local church hall on Trem y Mynydd, then into Bwyd Da Bangor's premises. This was collaboration between our community group and Penrhyn House, with support from Gwynedd Council, Welsh Government and our regional Betsi Cadwaladr University Health Board.

As volunteers returned to work, those of us available to work out of our drop-in centre took on the deliveries, which proved to be a vital way of staying connected with resident families during this time. Funding was initially easy and quick to access through Invest Local,[8] but as food costs increased, we had to accommodate increasing demand, which exceeded the surplus food on offer. We also wanted to include fresh food, and fortunately we were able to apply relatively successfully for Covid-19 relief and later Covid Recovery Funding. But by March 2021, much of this funding was withdrawn or excluded; not only for food relief but also for community groups that had been set up since March 2020. Likewise, our emergency food relief was de-funded, which would have caused some anxieties for resident families as well as for volunteers who were still trying to meet needs.

Who/what is responsible for this?

Fortuitously, by the time the funding was withdrawn in March 2021, we had settled on a workable, more sustainable, local solution to food insecurity, which delivers thirty to forty-five food crates to resident families on Trem y Mynydd, and thirty-five frozen ready-meals each week to households in the wider Bangor city area. This enshrines the ethos we started within our community group: anyone who asks for help will get it; it is a self-referral, trust-based, open model where there are no questions asked about affordability. Our community group secures the funding for emergency food, while some in another community group source and pack surplus food for delivery and those of us in paid work deliver the food crates weekly using our private vehicles. Our way of working within this partnership of community groups requires the equivalent of a full-time salaried worker, currently alternating between several different jobs: one who collects and packs the crates, three who deliver in their own local areas, one who does the paperwork to secure funding and another to monitor and share quantitative evaluation. If we are to be consistent and reliable in the long term, then this requires more than colleagues working in voluntary roles.

At the same time, those of us then back in our paid positions as community workers were also playing an increasing role in signposting residents in need of emergency food to other financial, family and mental health support services, and providing emergency relief where services fell short. This included practical necessities like fuel for those who had a car or access to one, and other household essentials, baby food, nappies and sanitary products. This all ties into affordability and the ways the Covid-19 pandemic further exposed insecure work, low wages that lag behind the cost of living and universal credit delays (see Calder, Gass and Merrill-Glover, 2012). These are the key drivers of the need for emergency food provision – even for those who stepped up to be key workers – which is telling about what it means to be poor in a rich country that came to rely on this section of the population. It was especially galling when governments and industry leaders then ignored public calls for reward and recompense of these key workers.

A worsening cost-of-living crisis provoked us to begin reconfiguring how services were delivered or accessed, which involved building connections with trusted workers like Paul Joslin then from Wild Elements, whom we welcomed into our work space along with those from the Citizen's Advice Bureau, Department of Work and Pensions, and the ICAN mental health and well-being service.[9] It then came as something of a surprise to learn that Gwynedd Council, our regional Betsi Cadwaladr University Health Board and Welsh Government offered to fund what we were doing as the only community-led 'Covid support hub', and one among six such hubs.[10] This was part of the 'protect' stream of Track Trace Protect, supporting communities more likely to be impacted by Covid-19, until March 2023.[11]

This enabled us, for the first time, to build in sustainability, envision a future that could be consistent and reliable, and move beyond simply reacting to needs. We could take the initiative to better identify needs and assets, respond better and build more effective support around resident families given their lived experiences of poverty. We also took this support to be a crucial acknowledgement of our community group's emergency food provision, as well as the responsibilities assumed by Wales's national government, the regional Betsi Cadwaladr University Health Board and Gwynedd Council. Recipients of emergency food tell us that they valued the food crates and ready-meals and that our way of operating to guarantee accessibility with the no-referral/self-referral and as-often-as-you-need policies were important; the same was true for the delivery element. We were aware that some depend on the crates entirely for their weekly food, others as part of a complex assembly for getting by, and some needed it for longer or shorter periods of time.

Our work in this 'Covid support hub' has required some critical reflections, as we have received some negative feedback, which is worth laying out below:

- there is inconsistency in the crates' contents;
- the experience of planning on a budget is taken away;
- there are difficulties in using what is provided to make into meals;
- this can deny opportunities to come together to eat as a family;
- there are challenges that come with not choosing your food;
- this can be tiring and disempowering;
- this can lead to a lack of confidence in cooking to shop around it to make meals;
- crate contents are not always enough and in tough weeks it is all a family might have for food;
- it isn't tailored enough to family size and age of children; and
- most importantly, it can hurt the family's pride.

At the time we were spending £3,120 per month on emergency food provision, and there is little financial scope to respond to the feedback we have received. While the ready-meals work for more vulnerable individuals, they are costly in terms of time, fuel and top-up ingredients (£8 per week). The majority of families who needed emergency food chose the food crates, which are free to recipients but cost us £5 each, plus £3 to include fresh fruit and vegetables. The quality was variable given the standard of surplus food, and though we have worked with Public Health Wales's dieticians to find a compromise, they are not adequate to live on. We complemented our emergency food provision with other food projects' research that have included Flying Start's advice on slow cooking with store-cupboard ingredients and Public Health Wales's 'Eat Smart Save Better' online cookery class, which came with weekly recipes and shopping list,12 which we supported with an initial £10 voucher. There remained complexities to negotiate, however; not least resident families in maintaining their pride and dignity. This was recognised from the outset and we all set out to provide caring, kind, hopeful support for one another, and we even won a 'Supporting communities in Wales' award!

An incredible local solution

We began streamlining a more joined-up approach to community food beyond the pandemic and necessary emergency provision, and set about developing more wide-reaching responsive planning and an educative strategy. This not only addressed food insecurity but made families' experiences of food provision better, which came to our attention when the Soup Squad stopped after the first lockdown. When the community Hive Café reopened in March 2022 the emphasis was on getting together as a community, facilitating participation, a shared food experience and inclusion. It also served as an informal forum for refining our local solution given that the community café caters for fifty to sixty people, free of charge. A significant proportion are children and young people, though increasingly we were seeing the whole family come to eat and, in return, new people volunteer to help with cooking and clearing. Some of the Hive Café volunteers who were adept at feeding for £1 per head per meal planned a session to share hints and tips around shopping, budgeting and batch-cooking for parents.

At the time of writing, six months later, volunteers were considering opening an additional night to support anyone struggling with food during the cost-of-living crisis and are planning batch-cooking sessions, where people can cook together at an economy of scale and take home meals. Our overall impression was that while a free meal and the opportunity to reciprocate was becoming increasingly important as the cost-of-living crisis deepened, what mattered most was belonging and showing up to support one another. The community kitchen garden supplied fresh seasonal produce to the Hive Café, which was an opportunity to try new foods in new ways and share the produce grown by volunteers. Outside the church hall, children planted potatoes to be eaten at the cafe later in the season, learning about growing food and developing skills for food resilience.

It is notable that the houses on Trem y Mynydd under the jurisdiction of the ADRA housing association have reasonable gardens with good prospects for growing food plants. Sadly, the same cannot be said for the blocks of flats on the estate, but this should not preclude residents from getting involved in our community food project. We are guided by the concept of asset-based school-community development (see Thirsk's chapter 6), and our ideas for community gardens are intended to engender local empowerment and responsibility alongside the recreation of community spirit and values. As Julia Dobson (2014) reported in *The Ecologist*:

> It goes beyond just growing food, but serves as a practical, real way of giving agency, power and meaning to local people being able to respond to 'big' issues through their own actions.13

Our project took inspiration from the Incredible Edible project, started small and grew slowly – one might say 'organically'.[14] It has been called 'urban acupuncture' by Jaime Lerner, mayor of Curitiba in Brazil, and is a way of making small, targeted, but visible interventions that began to be noticed and make a difference. For example, we have erected herb planters on the street with edible plants and herbs that everyone can share. The Incredible Edible group say that 'people responded to simple shared ideas, rather than heavy handed persuasion'. Their motto is 'If you eat, then you are in'. They are more concerned with community development, unencumbered by the rigidity of imposed timescales that come with specific funding programmes. They proceed conversation-by-conversation, engaging with people when they wanted to join and making them feel welcome.

This approach guided our work on Trem y Mynydd, where we encouraged active participation in our community food project from a very young age. The school Head was certainly open to a proposal to involve the local school in planting our community garden spaces. This included one located out of public view behind the community health centre, which then became known as our 'secret garden'. It is an enchanting space, no longer vandalised but cherished for its worth, which our community gardening group came together in building multiple raised beds and planting seeds for growing seasonal fruit and vegetables, herbs and flowers. The children and young people who joined us learned much about their food sources, and we also invited older people to join in and contribute their knowledge and expertise from years of tending their own gardens. This is significant because it is a way for all ages to be able to do something real about food shortages and come to feel in control of a worrisome situation.

There is certainly the potential for everyone to improve their health and well-being through participation, sharing, being outdoors and engaging in physical activity (see French and Howard's chapter 8). We also ensured some benefits for wildlife by constructing a pond for frogs and water insects, and talked at length about pollinator plants that attract insects, food plants that do the same, and the 'wilded' areas that provide habitat homes for birds and small mammals. The funding for these mini projects was provided by Wild Elements and Gwynedd Council, which allowed our community gardening group to build a further seven raised garden beds for food crops, clear paths through the woodlands, plant trees, hedgerows and wild flower meadows. These take time and effort, but there is always a good return on the funding, especially as we are encouraging a more acceptable engagement with food support through care and social inclusion and fostering community empowerment and climate action.

Our community gardening group came to emulate the Incredible Edible group's ideas about slowly working towards a 'self-sustaining community by engaging with people and the planet'. We set out to create a kind, confident and connected community, and we agreed on a shared responsibility for the future well-being of our planet and ourselves: working together, reaching out to potential partners/stakeholders, promoting and supporting social enterprises, local food businesses and industries. We also did much to enhance the local built environment, with parts of it aesthetically pleasing but we had to get past the initial resistance to wild areas being seen as 'untidy'. Mown grass is not the best way to manage green spaces in a community; in some places, yes, but so much more can be achieved by gradually introducing a new look to the streets and if you can eat some of it as well, even better!

The logistics

Our local solution to the problem of food insecurity on Trem y Mynydd and our efforts to hone more wide-reaching responsive planning and an educative strategy readily lent itself to co-developing a Not-NEET project with our Bangor PLUS team titled, 'Cultivating the estate: establishing community food gardens' (see appendix 3). We could all see the wisdom in working towards the provision of education, training and employment opportunities that derived from our community food and garden projects, both ripe to inspire children and young people looking to gain qualifications in food production and supply. These opportunities are best coordinated with other local schools, Bangor University, Coleg Menai and other course providers, as well as the stakeholders in our ventures. Coincidentally, Paul Gordon, who is a colleague in Penrhyn House, had also set in train his plans for a large-scale social enterprise titled 'Growing for Change', which involved growing food to provide education, training and employment opportunities for his recovery community and to supply local seasonal food to Bwyd Da Bangor: they provided 30 kg of lettuce last summer!

There was merit in joining forces again in a productive partnership with Penrhyn House, due to there being an overlap between its project and our Not-NEET project, especially the intention to coordinate with local schools and education institutions. Our relationship with Penrhyn House was solid to the extent that I was involved in the development of Gordon's application to Gwynedd Council in regards the use of a brownfield site on Trem y Mynydd.[15] This had the potential to involve the community in the cultivation of a market garden with polytunnels, and as Penrhyn House had already received Heritage Lottery funding, Gwynedd Council agreed to an assets transfer. As such we were in a good position to configure our Not-NEET project spearheading the educative component and we invited Penrhyn House to work with us on our proposed curriculum committee. Joslin and I were both prepared to join specialists including horticulturalists, landscape gardeners, food business and industry, third-sector partners, and representatives from our regional Betsi Cadwaladr University Health Board working with education representatives from Undeb Cenedlaethol Athrawon Cymru (UCAC), NASUWT Cymru, NEU Cymru, ASCL Cymru, Gwynedd Council, GwE and Bangor University.

We all need to develop a depth of understanding through working with schools on Wales's national curriculum and the 14–16 qualifications framework, which will provide support for teachers involved in cross-curriculum food projects in schools and reaching out to their local communities. Subsequently, students in networks of school-communities are actively engaged in learning about horticulture, agriculture, the economy of food production, food supply chains, as well as the practicalities of growing food, running social enterprises, businesses and industries – and they may even find their vocation. They also participate in learning about local and global food supply crises compounded by Brexit, Covid-19 and the war in Ukraine, and the public concerns with shortages, rising prices and the environmental impact of 'food miles' what with major conglomerates transporting food all around the world.

Consolidating these sorts of productive relationships with Penrhyn House, Gwynedd Council and local partner organisations is the basis for regional and national scale-up, not only across Gwynedd but also in the other areas that were earmarked for a *Children First* needs assessment (see chapter 1). Our local solution may not reach the point where all our local food needs are met, but when allied with our Not-NEET project, it has the potential to ensure that the human right to food is enshrined and encompassed in education, training and employment opportunities for future generations. In turn they will then be equipped to tackle the systemic determinants of food insecurity, which prominently feature in the lived experiences of poverty. This not only requires responding to rising inequalities, re-writing modern welfare policies and reframing statutory responsibilities but also having the political will to make this happen.

Notes

1   It should be noted that a number of multi-agency workers usually come and go, using hot-desks in my office in the course of any one week.

2   See Alcock (2010) who describes what it takes to realise the conservative 'Big Society' agenda.

3   I should acknowledge the work of Pete Gardner, who was seconded from Wild Elements and who established some of our community gardens before he left this post and was replaced by Paul Joslin.

4   Penrhyn House is home to the North Wales Recovery Community (NWRC), founded in 2014 to provide services to people with drug and alcohol addictions, which includes delivering a programme of meetings and recovery activities for its social groups; Bwyd Da Bangor is a food enterprise on the high street, connected to Penrhyn House who operates as a third-sector partner.

5   See *https://www.gov.uk/universal-credit/what-youll-get* (accessed 17 April 2023).

6   See *https://fareshare.cymru/about-us/* (accessed 17 April 2023).

7   See *https://www.mantellgwynedd.com/eng/svc/social-value-cymru.html* (accessed 30 August 2022).

8   See *https://www.bct.wales/about?locale=en* (accessed 17 April 2023).

9   See *https://bcuhb.nhs.wales/health-advice/mental-health-hub/i-can/* (accessed 17 April 2023).

10 Our Trem y Mynydd community-led 'Covid support hub' team was approached by the local authority to be recognised as modelling a way of working because of our respected community response to supporting one another through Covid-19, and our model has now been rolled out across Gwynedd and the pilot rolled out across Wales. It must be acknowledged, however, that there are five other such hubs.

11 It remains to be seen if this timeline is extended given the rise in Covid-19 cases taking hold at the time of writing, and in view of the cost-of-living crisis across the UK.

12 See *https://phw.nhs.wales/topics/latest-information-on-novel-coronavirus -covid-19/how-are-you-doing/keeping-physically-well/eating-well-at-home/* (accessed 17 April 2023).

13 See *https://theecologist.org/2014/jan/01/incredible-edible-todmorden* (accessed 17 April 2023).

14 See *https://www.incredibleedible.org.uk/* (accessed 17 April 2023).

15 This was an unused designated play site (for football) that had been relocated elsewhere on the estate.

These train waggons were a feature of the pioneering rail/port arrangement carrying dressed slate tiles from the Penrhyn Quarry on a 6-mile journey to Port Penrhyn, where they were then loaded onto a fleet of sail/steamboats destined for domestic and overseas markets.

5

PRIDE IS KEY: THE BUILT ENVIRONMENT, SOCIAL HOUSING AND FUEL POVERTY

Dylan Fernley (Gwynedd councillor), Pete Whitby (local resident) and Grant Peisley (Datblygiadau Egni Gwledig – DEG)

Introduction

This chapter is written in part by academic partners in light of conversations with two local residents with long experience of living on the Trem y Mynydd housing estate, who are both extremely proud of its social housing. They share a commitment to the political principle of large-scale, state-funded provision of stock at low rents, though both remain concerned about the ageing and dilapidated conditions of the built environment. Dylan Fernley is an elected council representative whose role is to highlight the views of the community. These mostly involve concerns regarding immediate needs such as inadequate housing, and in most cases the common response is helping residents to simply understand their predicament and encourage negotiation should they want to take their concerns further, and making sure that they are alert to how the system works and the legalities involved. There are also instances of major concern, such as anti-social problems, evictions, homelessness, temporary housing and re-housing, including sole parents recently separated, those with disabilities, addictions or recently released from prison on parole. This may require Fernley to field and filter complaints from residents regarding the provision of services, especially social housing, and either act on their behalf or direct them to the appropriate multi-agency workers on the estate, or further afield should they need to meet with Gwynedd Council housing officers.

Conversations were also had with local resident Pete Whitby, who has first-hand experience of housing needs, being a family man on a limited income with lived experiences of fuel poverty. As he puts it, there is simply not enough income to meet needs, especially living in old housing stock built just before the Second World War that were never designed to be energy efficient. Whitby describes the nightmare of having to juggle the costs of home energy, which was made worse during the Covid-19 lockdowns with all the family at home, and made worse again by the cost-of-living crisis. Some resident families can pay bills by direct debit but others have to rely on pre-paid meters, which requires minute weekly calculations on what is affordable. For instance, with a weekly £20 allocation for energy, there is a standing daily charge of 30p and 50p per gas and electricity utility, which means 80p a day, £5.60 a week, before any energy is used. This means that only £14.40 worth of energy is actually supplied, which plays no small part in the 'heat or eat' decisions being made. With financial assistance, Whitby had solar panels installed on his house and he brings a detailed understanding of electrical infrastructure, energy resources and power supplies, which in turn provoked him to devise the 'Greener than Green' local solution in regards the energy needs of resident families.

Fuel poverty adds to resident families' suffering and punishing hardship, and both Fernley and Whitby share concerns about resident families on universal credit, ranked as the working poor or unemployed on low incomes.[1] This was well reflected in reports from former UN Special Rapporteur Professor Philip Alston's probe into *Extreme Poverty and Human Rights in the UK*, which included commentary on Wales.[2] Fernley and Whitby pick up on these concerns, and drive home some points about poverty that come as a result of job losses and the rise of the GIG economy, in tandem with the decline in manufacturing and a lack of local and regional infrastructure. Fernley's work is not always straightforward because of the limited supply of social housing and a complicated system in Wales still reeling from the UK Conservative government's policy choices, such as former Prime Minister Thatcher's right-to-buy scheme.[3] Whitby's efforts stem from difficulties with the UK Conservative governments' policy choices in regards the privatisation of energy supply and reliance on multi-national companies to produce and supply fuel and energy. This is made explicit in news that 'Energy firms have paid out £200bn to shareholders since Tories took power'.[4]

Fernley's and Whitby's contributions to this chapter were reinforced by Grant Peisley, a consultant who added his professional knowledge regarding the 'Greener than Green' local solution and shares some lessons learned from working on sustainable communities. As he put it, community groups have for the past decade been drawn to the idea of community-owned renewable energy generation that can provide cheap electricity to local residents as a means of addressing fuel poverty and the rising costs of electricity from suppliers. Ofgem rules do not, in practice, allow for this.[5] It is possible for an individual to live off-grid (self-sufficient in energy generation) but it is very difficult, if not economically impossible, to get a group of existing houses or an entire community off-grid. For a decade, community activists across Wales and indeed the UK have been trying to solve this issue. In almost all cases they have failed. When they have been successful in finding a local solution, as in Bethesda with Energy Local (a virtual grid utilising smart meters), it has then been very difficult to replicate in other communities. This does not mean that a local solution to the problem of fuel poverty cannot be found, but it does mean that there needs to be the political will.

Whitby's 'Greener than Green' local solution on Trem y Mynydd is responsive to myriad problems, not least meeting unmet needs. The immediate response to welfare demands in the present is met by frontline workers, including school staff and multi-agency workers. The local drop-in centre staff handle resident families' requests for emergency £15 top-ups for energy supply, which are funded by a system of charity donations. As they collectively put it, this local solution is more medium-to-long term – 5–10–20 years hence. The intention is to set up and support a local community of 'prosumers' to facilitate social action on fuel poverty. This term refers to those who produce and then consume their own energy, and it is often confined to households who fit solar panels, install batteries to generate/store renewable electricity and heating, and often supported by enhanced insulation with specially designed windows, doors, walls, roofing and sometimes floors. A co-operative would oversee/manage rolling out this local solution on the Trem y Mynydd housing estate, and we would make good use of a facilitation fund to get work underway.[6] We want it allied to a

Not-NEET project, 'Powering the estate: a home-grown energy supply' (see appendix 4), co-developed with our Bangor PLUS team to ensure that everyone involved in these initiatives not only learn about green energy but secure the necessary qualifications.

In the chapter sections that follow, Fernley and Whitby begin by sharing the experience of what living on Trem y Mynydd is like. We thrash out some arguments about affordability, and discuss the cost-of-living crisis as it relates to fuel poverty. We then share some thoughts on the problems that have been caused by policy choices regarding universal credit, and the privatisation of social housing stock and energy supply. Then Whitby and Peisley provide some detail of the 'Greener than Green' local solution to fuel poverty. Finally, they come to the logistics where this local solution allied to a suggested Not-NEET project is tied to the strengths and assets readily identified in this school-community. The project has potential for regional and national expansion, not only across Gwynedd but also in the other areas that were earmarked for a *Children First* needs assessment (see chapter 1).

Proud of ourselves

There is certainly a sense of security living in social housing on Trem y Mynydd, and one grandmother boasts that she has had 'the best landlord in the world' with the local council! There is a good sense of community, where everyone looks out for each other: we are all in this together, despite former UK Conservative government Prime Minister Cameron's pronouncements. There are family and friendship networks, which are really important in good times and bad, and the amenities are good although we lost our social club, which was sold out from under us, and the youth hall is dilapidated and ready for demolition. There is reasonably good provision of social services, although the public transport links are tenuous at best, so we tend to stay close to home. This might sound fairly normal but it is all on the condition that none of us fall into rental arrears and become laden with debt, which is widespread given the pressures on family incomes with the cost-of-living crisis. It was bad enough when Covid-19 hit because quite a few families on the estate were struck down with sickness. For some it meant having to endure lockdown with children at home, household costs escalated, and now they are skyrocketing.

This is a far cry from stories of family history on Trem y Mynydd, especially for those resident families who are descendants of the men who worked in Penrhyn's quarries and Port Penrhyn. Just before the Second World War they had been relocated from the Bangor Port area, which was part of the plans for poverty relief and regeneration of Bangor city. This was something we learned whilst doing archival work with the Bangor PLUS team and is noted in the images that appear in this book. Historically social housing won prizes for its design in providing accommodation for those on low incomes (see the image preceding chapter 9). This is often unknown or taken for granted these days and even denigrated by those outside the system because social housing is provided at lower cost than the commercial property market. But it should not be considered less valuable by resident families because it still provides a place that can be called 'home'. This is something that is common to everyone, whether people own their own home, pay a private landlord or live in social housing. The value of a safe place to live and care for your family is a source of pride, no matter what circumstances resident families find themselves in, this is felt even if it is rented accommodation. Those 'early settlers' would not know the place eighty years later: being considered for accommodation here can be incredibly complicated given vetting, waiting lists, affordability and the system of ranking into bands, matching tenants to housing, not to forget property maintenance.

These experiences cannot be underestimated. Take repairs, for example, and who bears the responsibility for these: in Wales it is complicated because housing is a devolved matter with housing law the responsibility of Senedd Cymru and Welsh Government. Ministers therefore regulate the social housing sector in Wales, whether that housing is provided by local authorities or registered social landlords, such as housing associations. It is Welsh ministers who are responsible for deciding who is eligible for social housing and for the quality standards that social housing must satisfy.[7] This may well be the case according to the law, but at local level the perception is different. Ostensibly, only the most urgent of repairs get attention, which is hard for those residents who are the least likely to be able to afford the maintenance for which private landlords have legal obligations. Take the example of Carys, introduced earlier in this book as a young mum with two young children living in a two-bedroom flat that became her responsibility after her partner left them in rental arrears (see the introduction). She had a leak coming from the flat above that was staining her bathroom ceiling, but it took the housing association weeks to respond to the issue. This was somewhat distressing because she did not know whether it was a water pipe leak or toilet waste.

These sorts of situations add to the feelings of frustration for some local residents, especially as we take personal pride in our family home, but we have little control over how often, when or what happens in terms of its upkeep. Though of huge importance to the families concerned, these problems are the least of Fernley's worries because he has urgent welfare demands that he must respond to. One distressing case stands out: a sole parent with a terminal illness, who needed some stability for herself but also for her two children with additional needs, was evicted by a private landlord who wanted to sell the house. This was formerly social housing stock, bought as an investment and sold for profit. Thankfully Fernley was able to arrange temporary accommodation, but there was always the fear that this family would be relocated somewhere else and further away. This would have meant upheaval in regards family support and schooling opportunities for the children but, in this case, there was more at stake. There was great urgency to get them re-housed on Trem y Mynydd, where the family had their support network and the mum could put in place her plans for the children's future. It is a case story that highlights matters taken up by elected representatives, and shows the folly of consecutive UK Conservative governments that relish populist policy choices that drive social housing into individual ownership with seemingly little thought for the consequences.

It is more than eighty years since the housing was built on Trem y Mynydd, and we are confronted with another set of problems. This is a result of the policy choices of the UK Conservative government under Johnson – or not, as the case may be – in regards the cost-of-living crisis. His Conservative replacement, Prime Minister Liz Truss, showed no indication of plans to address the problems and alleviate energy costs, which contrasts so markedly with what is happening in other European countries.[8] Should her successor Rishi Sunak follow suit, then the lack of action by the Westminster government is shocking; their soundbite platitudes only promise sticking plasters to a problem that requires replenishment of the housing stock, with an adaptation towards energy efficiency. Back on the estate, costs are increasing across the board with rent, overheads and household necessities, and none of it is keeping up with inflation, all of which indicate what life is like for residents on the Trem y Mynydd housing estate. This is critical with rising energy prices, especially when it comes to trying to heat old stock social housing that is not energy efficient on an ageing estate with inflexible energy supply infrastructure. The worry about rising energy prices and fuel poverty causes so much suffering and punishing hardship in our school-community.

Affordability

Whitby's own story about the affordability of his family's housing needs began some years ago when he and his wife found themselves homeless in the city. The two of them were allocated temporary accommodation in an old three-storey terrace house, which was a private rental. The space was far too big for them and they could not afford to heat the house, and resorted to placing blankets over doors to try to keep it warm. They needed a one-bedroom flat or house, but none was available. This is a situation that needs rectifying, because this many years later the same need stands but consecutive Conservative Westminster governments are seemingly committed to right-wing neo-liberalism, tax cuts and a 'small state'. This means that no funding flows into Wales to re-stock social housing. We are lucky that on Trem y Mynydd there is a good supply of two- to three-bedroom houses, but there are not enough one- or four-bedroom houses for families composed of multiple generations. Those people in need of single room occupancy are then pushed into multi-bedroom multi-occupancy tenancies off-site in the private rental market that charges £200 per week, often with shared bathroom and laundry facilities but no living areas. Set against this background, the social housing system is in need of an overhaul with new builds on a scale to meet demand but this requires a groundswell of public support.[9]

So much of the social housing stock that was purpose built by Bangor City Council all those years ago, which won significant recognition and prizes, has now entered the private market. Here we include housing associations' ownership, even though they are called social landlords, because they are not replacing housing stock in the public realm. We are left with a serious decline of supply, increasing unmet needs and huge gaps between 'affordable' and 'out of reach' accommodation. There is a demand for housing to provide resident families with a suitable space for children to grow and develop, and while it may be unrealistic to have single bedrooms for every child, the number of bedrooms should reflect the size of the family. Children and adults need separate spaces for some of the time they are together at home, and it is unrealistic for families with four, five or six children to be accommodated in two- to three-bedroom houses. Another distressing case stands out: a young mum, Delyth, with a new baby had no choice other than to move out of her family home as it was not adequate for multi-generational occupancy, which meant that they were then homeless. They were provided with temporary accommodation for months on end whilst awaiting permanent accommodation, and fearful they would be relocated away from family, but luckily they were re-housed on Trem y Mynydd.

Whilst social housing under the direct management of the local authority is in decline, there are multiple housing associations that attempt to fill the void. This policy choice, which resulted in a 55/45 per cent split between social housing and housing associations on Trem y Mynydd, may have initially had some success in cost-saving by taking housing stock out of the public realm in the short term. But the demand for social housing, coupled with the diminishing supply of stock, was only ever going to get worse, and we have already witnessed welfare demands become social emergencies throughout Covid-19. The full effects of the cost-of-living crisis felt over the last winter amounted to a humanitarian disaster, which sounds unthinkable in such a supposedly rich country, but it brought yet more suffering and punishing hardship. This has meant further challenges in keeping our homes warm in a way that is appropriate for a family residence, and it sounds petty to be raising concerns over the quality of accommodation. It hardly seems fair with waiting lists for social housing so long and suitable housing stock so scarce, and no one wants to be seen as a 'difficult' tenant. This has all sorts of consequences, not least when it comes to requests for maintenance and repairs to be carried out. This can lead to major problems, especially with plumbing, radiators, badly fitting doors and windows, insulation and worn double glazing, with major delays in repairs posing both health risks and other worries. It can make the property look shabby, presenting a picture of someone who does not value their home, when in fact the opposite is true.

Whilst the 55/45 per cent split appears to have resulted in the cost of house maintenance being passed on, and therefore kept local council taxes lower, this was at the expense of the local authority's control over how the housing association stock is utilised. With the housing associations also affected by the cost-of-living crisis, they no doubt needed to generate capital to finance their work, which could be off-set by outsourcing, if not reducing, services, negotiating mortgage deals with the banks, or selling housing stock on the commercial market. And so social housing seemingly becomes a cash cow, a quick way to generate funds, no doubt to meet budget deficits. In the face of the unravelling of the safety net of social housing and the practice of putting affordable homes up for sale, is there any wonder that there are now campaigns against private landlords or property developers looking to purchase these homes for investment returns, to rent them out short term or as holiday lets, or selling them for profit?[10] The focus on investment returns highlights the lack of incentives for property owners to improve the quality and efficiency of their housing. Such improvements can improve the lives of tenants, but that improvement is not reflected in returns; therefore, no improvement is made.

This situation creates a problem for the future, especially given the scope of the issue on Trem y Mynydd with its old housing stock and the need to retrofit energy inefficient homes. Surely it is the responsibility of Welsh Government, local authorities and housing associations to operate in a strategically responsible manner and either model or anticipate the need for quality social housing here, across North Wales and beyond? Thankfully we are able to work cooperatively with the local authority and the housing associations and we take direction from work already underway. Here Peisley shares an example, Project Sero Net Gwynedd (SNG) is an innovative partnership piloting a local solution to help Gwynedd households use energy more efficiently while providing employment and training opportunities for local people.[11] Similarly, the Freedom Project in Bridgend is a cross-sector collaboration project seeking to understand the potential role of smart solutions to support the delivery of low-cost, low-carbon domestic heating.[12] There is also the developing community-based responses highlighted by Community Energy Wales that saw 22,453 people helped in 2022 through energy efficiency activities, with £256,574 saved for individuals and communities and £134,524 spent providing building improvements to 11628 recipients.[13]

A conundrum

Here Fernley and Whitby share some thoughts on the policy choices surrounding universal credit, which impacts so decisively on resident families on the Trem y Mynydd housing estate, as it does across the nation. It is heart-warming to hear that there are plans underway for Wales to claim devolved responsibility for its administration (see Beckett et al.'s chapter 12). In the meantime, the UK system, with its inhumane bureaucratic processes, has repeatedly failed while its punitive sanctions have caused untold harm. The principal complaint is with the inconsistencies, discrepancies and errors made by job centre officers, including logging inaccurate computer entries. An extreme example stands out: a local resident, Twm, broke his leg and was shipped by ambulance to Ysbyty Gwynedd (hospital) for treatment. Understandably, he was pre-occupied with hospital administration and medical procedures, and had no way of contacting the job centre because he did not have enough credit on his mobile phone. Because he did not alert the job centre about his pending appointment that would need re-scheduling, staff simply registered him as a no-show and put a stop to his benefits, which had a punishing impact on his family, including his school-aged children.

This is a good illustration of resident families' circumstances. So many simply do not know what next the month will bring, and they are a pay cheque away from losing everything, falling into increased debt, which will result in not being able to feed the family and keep them warm. This all adds up to so many worries and stresses, and there are a lot who find a salve in prescription medications. The effects of all this on residents' mental health and feelings of self-worth can be difficult to measure – but they do have an impact. Academic partners shared stories of research on psycho-geography – a title that is somewhat off-putting – but it comes down to an attachment to place and the ways it influences health and well-being. It helps us understand the feelings of frustration, especially when people have little control over when, what or how often something happens. There is so much at stake here, not least pride and dignity, and what is left is a sense of hopelessness from trying to find a way forward and bring about a change in circumstances. It stands to reason that resident families want to improve the status quo for their children so that they will not have experience what their parents and grandparents have had to endure.

Whitby recognises the historical problems of privatising the energy system. In the three decades since privatisation started, under Prime Minister Thatcher's Conservative government, energy costs have grown for consumers alongside the level of profit in the sector. Ofgem says that the current rate of profit of 4 per cent for suppliers has grown from about 1 per cent in 2009.[14] The Competition and Markets Authority's 2016 report on the sector suggested a 1.25 per cent margin should be expected, and it estimated that customers paid £1.4bn a year more than they would in a fully competitive market.[15] The UK Labour Party promised to nationalise energy in 2017 but, recently, their leader Sir Keir Starmer reversed that decision,[16] despite the support of 75 per cent of Labour voters (even 62 per cent of Conservative voters favour bringing the energy market into public ownership[17]). The TUC has highlighted that taking the Big Five energy retail firms into public ownership would cost £2.85bn;[18] recent energy retail company bailouts have so far cost £2.7bn suggesting that nationalisation would provide value for taxpayers' money. All this highlights the continued failure of government policy to make the energy sector serve people and not-for-profit.

Peisley's advice here is helpful: the main infrastructure for generating and distributing energy, both nationally and locally, are owned by distant, multi-national organisations with a main focus on extracting profit for the benefit of their shareholders. There is no obligation to provide any benefit to the people of the UK, and Wales does not have the power to change the system. The Welsh Government, for example, have policies to promote 'local ownership' of electricity generation but these policies sit within the privatised system overseen by the UK Government's non-ministerial department and 'independent' national regulatory authority, Ofgem. This is a revolving door providing opportunities for high-level employees of energy organisations, regulated by Ofgem, to take positions within the regulator and vice versa. Ofgem rules are often cited as creating high barriers to entry for new, innovative energy organisations that are trying to change the system to be fairer, more transparent and fit for the decentralised, zero-carbon future required. When the revolving door is combined with the highly resourced fossil-fuel and nuclear lobby, it is clear why fracking and nuclear remain a focus of UK energy policy despite mature, renewable energy technologies being far cheaper.[19]

This hardly demonstrates a possible alternative for Wales and its sources of potential energy for the future; there needs to be the political will, which displays the purported commitment to social democracy, to push for Wales to retool its economy. Peisley's consultancy work sits at the intersection of economic regeneration, social justice, environmental activism and resident-led community development, with an emphasis on community and co-operative owned energy, such as the generation of renewable energy. We are keen to heed his advice and improve the design of a local solution to overcome the challenges of rising fuel costs and improve homes' energy efficiency. As things have changed more towards self-sustainability it makes more sense to self-produce and self-consume energy; this means every house needs to be retrofitted and the priority should be that the power generated goes straight to occupants at a price that respects the people it serves rather than the fill the pockets of distant owners. Guided by the success of projects such as Repowering London, Egni Coop and, locally, Ynni Ogwen's Energy Local project, an innovative combination of these examples would bring local ownership of renewable energy infrastructure, training youth for green jobs, fighting fuel poverty and supplying locally generated renewable electricity for local people.[20]

Greener than green

The detail of Whitby's 'Greener than Green' local solution to fuel poverty on Trem y Mynydd is such that its community of prosumers would learn about and benefit from a system that combines domestic solar PV, battery storage, heat pumps, electric vehicles (EV) and EV charging. These can be combined on a scale to optimise residents' use of locally generated renewable energy at prices far lower than what the market presently provides. This sympathetic retrofit programme will require significant public investment, which echoes Bangor City Council's social housing initiatives prior to the Second World War, and we are certainly alert to the realities of the current system of privatised energy. As Peisley counsels, we are reliant on connections to the national electricity grid, which are used to sell locally generated electricity not consumed locally, and to buy electricity when local generation does not meet local demand. This approach meets the requirements of many government policies and is expected to accelerate the transition to net-zero, which holds promise for relieving fuel poverty.[21] This is not to say that there is no room for systemic change towards a Smart Local Energy System, which is a technological solution to a multitude of challenges presented by the transition from a centralised, fossil-fuel-based electricity system to a distributed, decentralised, decarbonised system.[22]

Whitby wants to see his idea of a cooperative set up on Trem y Mynydd come to fruition, and we can learn from other ventures because cooperatives already exist locally at Ynni Ogwen and Ynni Anafon; however, they are based on a single locally owned generating asset selling the electricity to the national grid. The income from these sales provides the local benefit in terms of money for other community actions, such as energy efficiency or electric transport projects. Our cooperative of prosumers would be a further development of their approach, building on lessons learnt from their exemplary projects about governance: for example, who would serve on the board and how would they be run to ensure maximum local benefit? This tried-and-tested approach allows local people to become members of the Trem y Mynydd cooperative, to elect representative to the board to raise capital and run the organisation. Other local organisations, such as Mynydd Ni, can also be members with the rules of the cooperative providing a space for such important local organisations. This approach has been used by YnNi Teg, who have two places on their board reserved for Community Energy Wales. All this knowledge and experience exists locally: Datblygiadau Egni Gwledig (DEG) have supported dozens of communities along this route and the GwyrddNi movement, consisting of six Gwynedd-based social enterprises, are trialling emerging social democracy approaches to community engagement and empowerment.

It is envisaged that in setting up the Trem y Mynydd cooperative community of prosumers there will be a need for support in bringing in knowledge, expertise and time, both on legal and technical matters. Collaboration will be required by many stakeholders, including social housing organisations, town and county councils, and the District Network Operator (SP Energy Networks). Getting assistance from these stakeholders may be problematic due to a clash of values and existing patronising relationships towards community action. Furthermore, although we believe in the ability of communities to take ownership of such important infrastructure we are also cognisant of other models of public ownership. However, we remain alert to residents' needs for social housing and the alleviation of fuel poverty, but this means a turnaround in Welsh Government policy choices to be underpinned by a social democratic ethos. This requires convincing the electorate that the responsibility for the care of those most in need should be re-situated back to the public realm. None of this is easy because social housing has been identified as property with commodity value, with old stock transformed into another 'market' to generate individual wealth. We cannot ignore the fact that while commercial market pressures are still in force to drive what should be a social concern, the cost-of-living crisis is widespread. We are, however, prepared to play the long game.

In looking to the future, we are keen to identify some place-based local resources to be tapped. Trem y Mynydd boasts a large array of south-facing roofs for solar panels, a river with potential hydro capacity (albeit limited), and a wind resource that could be exploited. To build electricity-generating infrastructure to take advantage of these natural resources will require agreements with the owners of the homes that are to have solar panels or the land that banks the river or will house the wind turbine. This is complicated by the sale of social housing to private owners, some distant landlords and landowners seeking to maximise the return on their land. Obtaining agreement from these disperse asset owners and the cost of those agreements could increase the price to the point of limiting the benefit of any infrastructure installed. There will also be planning consent and permissions to connect to the local electricity network; there may be the need for environmental or archaeological assessments and permissions. None of this should be insurmountable but there needs to be recognition of barriers and the time and cost associated with dealing with such complexities.

Whitby's 'Greener than Green' local solution is educative insofar as it dovetails with Peisley's suggestions for an allied Not-NEET project, 'Powering the estate: a home-grown energy supply' (see appendix 4). This is a place-based education, employment and training programme that contributes to the re-energising of Bangor and Gwynedd through the reconstruction of fuel and electricity sources, their use and efficiency. This is responsive to the extent that it promotes poverty relief in that it addresses resident families' struggles not only with soaring energy bills, old and inefficient appliances and whitegoods, but also the unaffordability of heating aged, inefficient housing. As we have shown in a critical discussion of their lived experiences, low incomes result in judgement calls on 'eating or heating' – feeding the family or staying warm – both greatly impacting on health and well-being. The intention in setting up and supporting a local community of prosumers to facilitate social action on fuel poverty is to promote a move away from fossil-fuels towards developing local community-based energy sources, run by a cooperative on this housing estate that advances local ownership of energy production and supply.

The logistics

Whitby's 'Greener than Green' local solution and its suggested allied Not-NEET project are tied to the strengths and assets readily identified in this school-community, and there are people on this estate willing to commit their time and expertise. We are also alert to the need to work with academic partners in the Bangor PLUS team who put together a briefing for a business case to go to Bangor University, and we took direction from Community Energy Wales to provide some input.[23] This connected with work undertaken by Bangor University academic Dr Sioned Hâf and environmentalist Angharad Penrhyn Jones, who together developed and trailed a brand new educative resource about community energy as part of an initiative to raise awareness of the community energy sector in Wales.[24] It was also heartening to read of Hâf's doctoral work in an online report entitled 'How local authorities can encourage citizen participation in energy transitions'.[25] This focus on ways European citizens could become co-designers and leaders of renewable and sustainable projects alerted us to a new European Union (EU) Clean Energy for All Europeans package.[26] Her advice was particularly pertinent to our Not-NEET project:

> The recommendations include the need to adopt more open and inclusive structural procedures that allow for the input of citizens, deliberative democracy measures that seek out public voices to co-lead and design developments, use of creative collaborations and to bridge connected issues such as wellbeing, health, local economies, social issues with energy transition.

We are happy to incorporate these recommendations into discussions about the 'Greener than Green' local solution, and we are open to some lessons. As well as the legalities, we were mindful of potential pitfalls, notably in regards our vision for the cooperative's ownership of the green energy sources/renewables, and also the hardware subject to using the facilitation fund to install solar panels. Then there were questions about the operation and maintenance matters like upkeep, charging local residents, smart meters, yearly services, defaulting on payments and debt collectors, for instance: all the nuts and bolts of the project, if only hypothetically.

Peisley posed these questions that needed consideration to deliver our vision:

1. Who will pay for the infrastructure and where will this money come from? Will the money need to be repaid?
2. Who will own the solar panels, batteries, heat pumps, etc.?
3. Who will be paying for operation and maintenance costs? Where will this money come from year after year for the next twenty to twenty-five years?
4. Is there an expectation that residents will pay for any of this? If so, who will be collecting their payments and how will this be managed? What happens if someone can't/won't pay? What equity will there be in the system if one doesn't pay, why should others?

An off-grid community sounds ideal but what happens on days when there is little sun or wind to generate electricity? Batteries at present do not allow for long-term storage of electricity. The community will need to remain connected to the grid to buy-in electricity on days when local supply isn't possible; this will mean that residents will still need to pay bills made up of standing charges, even for days when they do not use energy from outside the local system. There are also questions of equity for nearby communities. If Trem y Mynydd produces more energy than needed, can they share with neighbouring estates? What infrastructure exists for this? Or do they let it go to waste?

These are critical questions that lend themselves to learning in our Not-NEET project; they are easily incorporated into teaching and learning programmes that best meet resident families' specific needs and circumstances and reflect the school's ethos (see chapter 2). Whitby's 'Greener than Green' local solution certainly shows potential as a school-community initiative underpinned by the four purposes of the *Curriculum for Wales*:[27]

- ambitious, capable learners, ready to learn throughout their lives;
- enterprising, creative contributors, ready to play a full part in life and work;
- ethical, informed citizens of Wales and the world;
- healthy, confident individuals, ready to lead fulfilling lives as valued members of society.

In keeping with the aims of the Bangor PLUS project and its vision to broaden into the other four *Children First* needs assessment areas, we come back full-circle to the political will needed to make this happen. We are alert to the need for a feasibility study, and we took directions from the community energy projects underway across Wales, with the potential to coordinate nationally via the member-led organisation Community Energy Wales. Peisley's organisation, Datblygiadau Egni Gwledig, has provided support to dozens of communities seeking to start an energy project. Its network of local energy experts is well placed to provide practical support, feasibility studies and ideas testing. Furthermore, its work with partners in the GwyrddNi movement, funded by the National Lottery's Climate Action Fund, provides exemplary practices that augurs well for putting different school-communities across Wales in the forefront of this type of work.

Notes

1 For an indication of their income, see *https://www.gov.uk/universal-credit*.
2 See Alston's report, dated 23 April 2019: *https://digitallibrary.un.org/record/ 3806308?ln=en* (accessed 19 April 2023).
3 See Harvey (2005) and Keegan (1984) to inform debates about consecutive UK governments' penchant for neo-liberalism.
4 See Phillip Inman, 'Energy firms have paid out £200bn to shareholders since Tories took power', *The Observer*, 16 January 2022, *https://www.theguardian. com/business/2022/jan/16/energy-firms-seeking-whitehall-loans-paid-200bn-to-shareholders-since-2010* (accessed 20 August 2022).
5 See *https://www.ofgem.gov.uk/about-us/our-role-and-responsibilities* (accessed 25 August 2022).
6 This idea of a facilitation fund is credited to Owen Maclean (see chapter 8 elsewhere in this book), and discussed at length in the introduction and again in other chapters by authors reporting on their concerns about child poverty and respective local solutions tied to their specific Not-NEET project.

7   See *https://law.gov.wales/public-services/housing* (accessed 23 April 2023).

8   See *https://www.theguardian.com/environment/2022/sep/03/energy-citizenship -europes-communities-forging-a-low-carbon-future?CMP=Share_AndroidApp_ Other* (accessed 9 April 2023).

9   See Spratt (2023). For an online discussion event with the author, see *https:// www.youtube.com/watch?v=cJWoKZvH7_U* (accessed 20 August 2022).

10 See the article by Sirin Kale on the situation for residents of North Wales pushing back against available properties being converted into short-term rentals and holiday lets: 'I wanted my children to grow up here', *The Guardian G2*, Wednesday, 10 August 2022, *https://www.theguardian.com/technol- ogy/2022/aug/10/i-wanted-my-children-to-grow-up-here-how-airbnb-is-ruining- local-communities-in-north-wales* (accessed 12 August 2022), which features a teacher and her family having to fall back on social housing.

11 See *https://www.adra.co.uk/en/sero-net-partnership-secures-record-uk-community -renewal-funding-for-gwynedd/*; *https://www.deg.wales/project-sero-net-gwynedd -providing-employment-and-helping-gwynedd-households-become-more-energy -efficient/?lang=en* (accessed 25 August 2022).

12 See *https://www.wwutilities.co.uk/media/3861/freedom-project-interim-findings -2018.pdf* (accessed 25 August 2022). This is a package for clean energy developed by the European Union, an official website noted on this website: Clean energy for all Europeans package (europa.eu) (accessed 25 August 2022).

13 See *http://www.communityenergywales.org.uk/ycc-login/resources/welsh-report- draft-8.pdf* (accessed 21 May 2023).

14 See *https://www.bbc.co.uk/news/business-48284802*; also *https://www.ofgem.gov. uk/sites/default/files/docs/2013/11/css_2012_summary_document_0.pdf* (accessed 25 August 2022).

15 See *https://assets.publishing.service.gov.uk/media/5773de34e5274a0da3000113/ final-report-energy-market-investigation.pdf#page=634* (accessed 25 August 2022).

16 See *https://inews.co.uk/news/politics/labour-axes-pledge-nationalise-energy-water- keir-starmer-vows-pragmatic-plan-rail-networks-1761359* (accessed 25 August 2022).

17 See *https://weownit.org.uk/blog/biggest-ever-poll-shows-hug e-support-nationalisation* (accessed 25 August 2022).

18 See *https://www.tuc.org.uk/news/tuc-publishes-plan-cut-bills-through-public- ownership-energy-retail* (accessed 25 August 2022).

19 See *https://www.gov.uk/government/publications/contracts-for-difference-cfd- allocation-round-4-results*; also *https://www.theguardian.com/news/2017/ dec/21/hinkley-point-c-dreadful-deal-behind-worlds-most-expensive-power-plant* (accessed 25 August 2022).

20 See *https://www.repowering.org.uk/*; *https://egni.coop/*; and *https://www.ogwen. wales/en/community-projects/ynni-lleol/* (accessed 25 August 2022).

21 See *https://gov.wales/renewable-energy-deep-dive-recommendations- html*; *https://gov.wales/sites/default/files/publications/2021-11/*

regional-energy-strategy-north-wales.pdf; https://www.nea.org.uk/news/new-report-highlights-uk-wont-reach-net-zero-without-support-for-poorer-households/; https://es.catapult.org.uk/report/fuel-poverty-in-a-smart-energy-world/ (accessed 25 August 2022).

22 See *https://es.catapult.org.uk/news/what-are-smart-local-energy-systems-sles-how-can-they-support-the-uks-transition-to-net-zero/* (accessed 25 August 2022).

23 See *http://www.communityenergywales.org.uk/en/about-us* (accessed 25 August 2022).

24 See *https://www.bangor.ac.uk/news/archive/an-innovative-project-to-create-an-educative-package-about-community-energy-in-wales-32730* (accessed 25 August 2022).

25 See *https://www.bangor.ac.uk/doctoral-school/news/how-local-authorities-can-encourage-citizen-participation-in-energy-transitions-43667* (accessed 25 August 2022).

26 Clean energy for all Europeans package (europa.eu).

27 See *https://hwb.gov.wales/curriculum-for-wales/designing-your-curriculum/developing-a-vision-for-curriculum-design/#curriculum-design-and-the-four-purposes* (accessed 25 August 2022).

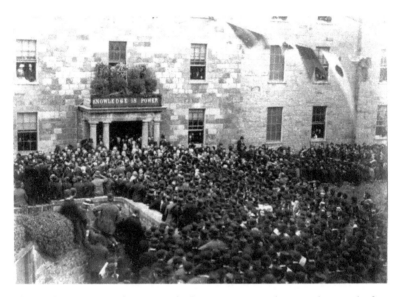

The Penrhyn Arms Hotel in Bangor, built in 1799 as a coaching inn, became the first site of the University College of North Wales, which opened on 18 October 1884. Funds were raised by quarrymen among the 8,000 workers who subscribed to the university. Note the 'knowledge is power' motto.

6

'IT TAKES A VILLAGE' TO REALISE SCHOOL-COMMUNITY DEVELOPMENT

Gwen Thirsk (Swyddog Buddsoddi Lleol)

Introduction

This chapter is authored by a community development worker whose work covers three areas of North Wales that are considered socio-economically disadvantaged, one of which is the Trem y Mynydd housing estate, to use its pseudonym. My contribution to this book is done in a voluntary capacity, in my own time, and the ideas expressed here are not necessarily representative of my employer. That said, a commonality is the community development approach to supporting and working with local residents, which is a way to ameliorate some of the child poverty effects by improving health and well-being in the community. Ideally this should start with a mapping of local assets, which can sit well with a needs assessment. As it happened, I was a member of the data task group of frontline workers that came together for the *Children First* needs assessment on the Trem y Mynydd housing estate (see Lewis's chapter 1). In these meetings I was struck by how some well-intentioned professionals viewed the residents on the estate as the problem, and not as people who are an invaluable and essential asset in joining forces to do something practical, constructive and productive.

Sadly, this deficit view comes as no surprise because most statutory services are designed from the point of view of needs definition; these are mostly defined by those in positions of authority making policy and resource decisions but who very often rely on a needs assessment and who claim to know the needs of a community better than that community knows its own needs.[1] This is not to discount the expertise of these professionals but the community itself must be involved in the process of defining its needs, which connects with a more ethnographic approach and the co-production of local knowledge.[2] This corresponds well with the school-community development perspective being forged by the Bangor PLUS team and further elaborated on in this chapter, which begins with problematising the idea of need.[3] First, the idea that 'we know what Trem y Mynydd needs' is challenged, then facilitating efforts in co-designing and co-producing the services available is discussed. This means engaging with resident families who would identify as the recipients of these services, exemplified in a case story about Carys, already introduced in earlier chapters as a sole parent currently in receipt of universal credit with two pre-school children (see Beckett's Editor's Introduction and Jones's chapter 3). In this way, local residents are recognised not as passive recipients but as active participants and valued members of the school-community with much to contribute.

Through my experience as a community development worker I registered that school staff not involving the local community of residents, community groups, third sector and voluntary organisations was a missed opportunity on two counts. A huge array of assets that could support the school are simply not acknowledged and the benefits of building relationships with the local community are likewise ignored, which is unfortunate because these can positively impact on children's experience of schooling and education. An anecdote about a colleague and I offering to work with the school Head serves to illustrate the point. Specifically, in a fruitful conversation about meaningful and substantial engagement with multi-agency workers and local residents, we committed to look and apply for funding to pay for additional support to help address some of the challenges faced by the school. We had in mind a family support officer and, despite a good deal of enthusiasm shown by the school Head, as the months passed it became apparent that she did not have the time to invest in our offer. We soon realised that she was in relentless crisis-management mode, constantly responding to parents' and students' unmet needs, dealing with many difficult situations and firefighting to the detriment of working on some solutions (see Evans's chapter 2 and Jones's chapter 3).

The second case story presented here provides a way forward. A group of young mums came together on the Trem y Mynydd housing estate before Covid-19 to seek support from the community nurse and a community development worker to establish a community crèche – on the proviso that they could train in early childcare to deliver the service. In doing so, they identified a local solution to the problem with childcare, which coincidentally was one of the findings from the *Children First* needs assessment and which had no follow-through (see Beckett's Editor's Introduction and Lewis's chapter 1). The mums' group reported the difficulties that families face with having only one registered childminder on the estate, their geographical isolation and distant proximity to private providers in the Bangor city area, along with prohibitive costs and the sheer impracticability and costs of public transport. These young women pointed out that they were either doing shift work as care workers, hospital cleaners or shop assistants, for example, or they wanted to be employed as such; the market was not providing the required services, especially as the regular hours of childcare simply do not work around shift work.

These two case stories – of Carys and the young mums – are classic examples of local residents being invaluable and essential assets in joining forces to do something practical, constructive and productive. A small team of multi-agency workers including Melanie Jones, an officer who works for the Department of Work and Pensions, developed the young mums' application for funding from Wales's Foundational Economy Challenge Fund.[4] Their bid was not successful but Jones was able to source further education funding and secure four places in early childhood education at Coleg Menai. In this chapter, I provide an overview of what I do to promote an asset-based community development (ABCD) approach to empower local residents to make the positive changes that they want to see in their school-community. I describe a systemic co-designed and co-produced approach to community development synchronised with school development,[5] and the importance of building relationships with school staff. I provide the details of the young mums' proposal to address this school-community's apparent lack of social infrastructure. I then come to my chapter conclusions to demonstrate the logistics of their exemplary local solution and our allied Not-NEET project: this was the impetus for the idea of school-community development.

Asset-based community development

As a community development worker using an ABCD approach to work with residents and frontline workers on the Trem y Mynydd estate, but also as a parent with a child in primary school, I can see the worth of common shared values and principles that would readily inform our Bangor PLUS team efforts in forging a notion of school-community development. I have long been guided by Community Development Cymru, an organisation set up in 2003 as a company limited by guarantee to support the development and promotion of community development in Wales; sadly it was dissolved in 2018 when Welsh Government funding came to and end. Here are its principles:

- Social justice: building an equal and fair society where all community and human rights are promoted and oppression in any form is challenged.
- Self-determination: individuals and groups identifying shared issues and concerns to enable them to take collective action.
- Working and learning together: valuing, sharing and using the skills, knowledge, experience and diversity within communities to collectively bring about desired changes.
- Sustainable communities: supporting communities to develop their strengths, resources and independence whilst making and maintaining links to the wider society.
- Participation: the right for all to be active participants in the processes that affect their communities and lives.
- Reflective practice: people learning from their collective and individual experiences to inform their future action.

More recently I have come across another set of standards developed by a professional organisation called Nurture Development,[6] which promotes ABCD and suggests that they should act like a compass:

1. Citizen-led;
2. Relationship-oriented;
3. Asset-based;
4. Place-based;
5. Inclusion focused.

All these values and principles can be challenging to fulfil in practice but they are vital to implementing an assets-based approach, beginning with the assets that already exist in a place, working with them and building on them. Sustainability is one reason for doing so: if we want initiatives that last in a school-community like Trem y Mynydd, we need to identify its existing strengths and assets in local people and involve them in co-design and co-production. In this way, we engage with people from a positive standpoint rather than a negative one, which comes from understanding the community in terms of its deficits/problems/challenges. The aim of any school-community development should be to support/facilitate/ empower people to then identify their needs with a view to any necessary changes. Though some of this will need to be done with support, it is crucial not to start this conversation from a negative standpoint, which is hardly empowering. An initial asset map of the area is a key strategy in beginning this work, which is underpinned by the recognition that the people living on the estate are its greatest asset. It follows that trusting in what they know and what they need is a good foundation for co-designing and co-producing what it is that needs to be developed and/or changed.

Asset mapping relies on building trusting relationships: residents must be made to feel confident and safe enough to engage in open conversation, talk about themselves and their families, and what they have to offer, especially when it comes to addressing matters of concern, and this includes discussing more difficult personal matters. This comes with a bottom-up approach to school-community development, which is different to a needs-based approach – particularly when it is commissioned by the local council at the behest of Welsh Government. The *Children First* needs assessment on Trem y Mynydd was guided by a worthy set of values and principles. Lewis, who had been commissioned to do the needs assessment (see Lewis's chapter 1), took her obligation seriously to develop an ethnographic approach that teased out residents' strengths and assets along with their needs. It was lamentable that the set of recommendations in her final report and strategic plan were not adequately resourced to develop local solutions; without Welsh Government providing resources to follow-through, the needs assessment is likely to be seen as a map of the deficits on the housing estate. It should come as no surprise, therefore, that despite numerous 'anti-poverty' policies rolled out over the years, how little anything changes in terms of ameliorating child poverty.

Another issue that struck me whilst working with the data task group was the lack of connectivity among the frontline workers on the estate, both with each other and, at times, with local residents. This surely informs the lack of policy impact on child poverty, which is currently escalating in Wales, as it is across the UK. It comes as no surprise to read statements such as 'Child poverty levels have remained alarmingly high over the last decade', no doubt compounded by Covid-19 and the current cost-of-living crisis.[7] Likewise, a top-down approach replicated across portfolios, government departments and multi-agencies should also be open to question. Despite a considerable amount of money paid to numerous well-meaning people in professional roles, we have witnessed another missed opportunity in terms of using these resources to affect change; which is to acknowledge Welsh Government's intentions for *Children First* as a place-based collaborative venture, but without any resources or guidance to operationalise more expedient ways of working, it adds to the culture it perpetuates in that residents are the problem to be fixed. This also supports the rhetoric of poverty being an individual problem, rather than a policy choice as the Child Poverty Action Group (2017) has shown, which influences the attitude of some paid professionals towards residents or clients as passive recipients of the services that they provide. In turn, this can affect how residents or clients see themselves as people who need to be helped/rescued.

The strategy of 'being done to' has proven to be ineffective, and certainly in the long term. Lewis's sets of recommendations at the conclusion of the *Children First* needs assessment on Trem y Mynydd are most welcome, and any suggested interventions are likely necessary. However, there needs to be a shift of focus – or rather foci – in the ways the local council approaches problem-solving. For example, in the OB3 'Place-Based Funding: A Scoping Report', civil servants seemingly know what the Trem y Mynydd estate needs:

> There are different perspectives as to what needs to be done in the area with local residents frequently highlighting the need for a new football field and a boxing gym – while local agencies feel that improving access to basic services, encouraging employment and facilitating new business creation is the way forward to get to grips with tackling poverty.[8]

Putting to one side poverty and its effects, including suffering and punishing hardship, and the undertone of denigrating residents, the logic is almost convincing but the principle of residents having their say in identifying need is put at risk. As it happens, football and boxing are strategically organised activities, and are there not only to attract children and young people to join clubs. In the positive direction of their energy, and engagement in healthy relationships with positive role models, these activities can deter children and young people from getting involved in negative behaviours and experiences, such as vandalism, anti-social behaviour, and at its most extreme county-lines drug trafficking. The county-lines issue is a grave matter of concern for resident families, especially where some young people have simply vanished, presumably recruited to work across transnational borders.

Moving towards co-production

A belief in equality/equity is helpful in preventing a culture of 'us and them', but it must be recognised that we are operating in a society that is structured unequally and inequitably. History has certainly played its part: the sight of Penrhyn castle casts a long shadow over Bangor and reminds us of the valuable lessons to be learnt. We should be conscious of this contextual understanding – an upshot of the Bangor PLUS team's archival work – and consider this history of disadvantage because it speaks to the ways wealth and power still operate. This includes the paid professionals providing the services in this area: they assume more power in their meetings with resident families, and they hold sway in conversations and in decision-making. It is therefore important that those on low incomes are encouraged and supported to believe in their own power and agency in these situations. This starts with more equitable conversations that identify assets and strengths before needs, and encourage positive experiences affecting some changes in their circumstances. It follows that opportunities must be created for this to happen, which means doing things differently.

This all points towards finding the commonalities in the values and principles that are held by frontline workers, whether school staff or multi-agency workers on Trem y Mynydd: from social justice to empowering children, young people and adults, to encouraging their leadership roles and seeing them as fellow citizens. These types of values and principles easily sit with the practice of co-production, which is when professionals work in partnership with people who have lived experience, to develop (local) solutions to challenges in public services and communities.[9] A question to be explored by frontline workers is whether or not there is a likely chance of forging a notion of school-community development, which would not only depend on the synchronicity between school development and community development but also on policy directions. As it stands, a school development plan is a statutory requirement,[10] drawn up by the school's governing body in consultation with the school Head, for a period of three years, drawing on guidance from the schools' inspectorate for Wales, Estyn. It must contain school improvement priorities, along with expected outcomes, and a professional development strategy. And within is a section with the subheading 'Working with the community', but only one paragraph is allocated to this in the guidance document, which is twenty-three pages long.

A first reading of the requirements for a school development plan suggests a preferred way of working for teaching staff, based on Welsh Government's school policy choices (see Watkins's chapter 9 and Hughes's chapter 10). But this is not to ignore further advice from the Co-production Network for Wales on co-production as an asset-based approach to public services, which enables people providing and people receiving services to share power and responsibility, and to work together in equal, reciprocal and caring relationships. This is best exemplified in the case story of Carys, the trained nursery nurse out of paid work, on universal credit with two pre-school children being put in harm's way because of other tenants in her block of flats arguing, which has escalated into displays of violence. In her dealings with staff at the pre-school, Carys readily acknowledges these influences on the children's behaviour but here the focus is on her little boy, who is not yet two years old. Having received support from the school Secretary (see Jones's chapter 3), she is open to the idea that her son would benefit from a crèche given her optimistic views about what should be provided with this sort of childminding.

This knowledge from a young mum is certainly a recognised asset to be valued, and allows those of us working with her to approach her concerns in a far more holistic and comprehensive way. For example, her worry that the little boy might be affected by seeing violence requires the local agencies concerned about child poverty effects to pull together and draw on local residents' lived experiences in their school-community, particularly their knowledge and critical understandings of violence and anti-violence initiatives. This ABCD approach lends itself to finding a sustainable long-term local solution that readily finds expression in the notion of school-community development. As the young mums' support team noted in their funding bid for a crèche, their bottom-up approach starts with their knowledge of resident families' challenges/needs, which includes the intricacies and subtleties. They also have knowledge of local assets, including what each of the mums in their group can bring to their project. They have already mapped out what is needed in terms of childcare oriented to early years' education that shows promise for the children's progression into pre-school, primary school and beyond. In addition, they have mapped out what is needed in terms of their own further education and training to equip them to run the crèche and shore up family support services.

This demonstrates that by involving Carys, along with the other young mums, in productive working relationships, they can be enabled to join in the co-design and co-production of services. Given that Carys is a qualified nursery nurse and three others have gained qualifications in early childhood education, their active participation in the educational programme design for the crèche should be sought. But there are other services that could be co-designed and co-produced, like the new-build multi-agency hub, which is potentially a good site to locate the crèche. It is also a place to bring the primary school staff into contact with staff in the health and welfare services on this site (see Jones's chapter 3). These sorts of co-design and co-production will prove useful on this housing estate, especially when it comes to helping set the trajectory for children and young people. My counsel to civil servants is to engage the local school-community, acknowledge that local resident families have much to give, build some trusting relationships so there is a joint effort in identifying their assets and strengths as well as their needs. Then invite children, young people and adults to be active change agents and a part of the co-design and co-production of local solutions.

Coming together

To bring an assets-based approach to school-community development to fruition and make it work, there needs to be some humility on the part

of the professionals working on this estate and beyond when it comes
to recognising the need for systemic and structural change. This could
well start with re-configuring the template for a school development
plan to give more credence to 'Working with the community'. From the
perspective of community development, the local pre-school and primary
schools are themselves an asset to the Trem y Mynydd housing estate
as places of learning and community, and as physical buildings where
people can come together; but these social institutions are generally
closed-off places where parents and others can be excluded. This is not
an invitation to set the school up as a business franchise open to outside
users, however. This is the gist of Wales's Education Minister Jeremy
Miles's call for community-focused schools.[11] Exclusion means yet
another missed opportunity for all concerned on two counts: assets such
as resident families and those working in community groups, third-sector
and voluntary organisations, could support pre-school and school staff
in a variety of ways, not least in helping with support for children and
young people. They also bring understanding of local history and culture,
including the ways of this particular school-community, and therefore
have the knowledge of how best to work with and educate their children
and young people. In sharing the benefits of relationship-building with
the wider school-community, they can often ease the job of schooling in
this place where there are great challenges confronting teaching staff (see
Evans's chapter 2, Maclean and Daws's chapter 7, French and Howard's
chapter 8).

One of the benefits of coming together as the data task group for the
Children First needs assessment, and then subsequently in the Bangor
PLUS project series of seminars, is that community development workers
managed to have conversations with the local primary school Head,
other multi-agency workers, local residents and critical friends like their
elected representatives and academic partners. This was so fruitful in
terms of meaningful and substantial engagement and should happen
more frequently. There are decisions to be made about how to improve
the lot of children, young people and adults on Trem y Mynydd, but
these need to be underpinned by common values and principles as well as
shared understandings about what is required. For instance, a colleague
and I committed to apply for funding to pay for additional support to
help address some of the challenges faced by the school. We could see
merit in the appointment of a family support officer who could support

children and their families troubled by any number of challenges that were getting in the way of schooling and education; we were prepared to propose drawing on funding from our own community activity programme to furnish this extra resource because we could see the benefits that this kind of support could bring to both resident families and the school.

This opportunity to work together on such a project would also build relationships for potential further collaborations on school-community development. It is a very exciting prospect for community development workers given that schools are notoriously difficult to access and are normally closed to outside agencies, which precludes any cross-fertilisation of ideas and multi-disciplinary perspectives. For example, I envisaged working with Carys and the young mums on an anti-violence programme that could be utilised in a number of fora on Trem y Mynydd. However, as the months passed by it became apparent that the school Head simply did not have the time to meet with us to discuss what needed to go into an application for funding. This was ironic because a family support officer would assist the school in response to incessant welfare demands and, by all reports, the school Secretary and the school Head are constantly in crisis management mode (see Evans's chapter 2 and Jones's chapter 5). They clearly need a designated staff member with time devoted to supporting resident families, getting to know them and building trust. All parties are then better able to tailor the right support.

This was a truly frustrating situation, especially given that it is a systemic problem despite the school development plan guidance on 'Working with the community', not to forget the orientation in the *Curriculum for Wales* classroom activities and learning experiences in the wider community and the call for community-focused schools. The way the education system is structured allows no space for any such collaboration to happen as it is seemingly not prioritised, valued nor measured. Despite all the promises of the school reaching out to its community, teaching staff are under so much policy and time pressures to meet existing policy obligations that anything outside that remit cannot happen. Yet these suggested collaborations between frontline workers, including school staff and multi-agency workers as well as resident families, have the potential to not only alleviate some of the challenges faced by schools in economically deprived areas, but to also co-design and co-produce support in all sorts of ways.

The cause and effect of poverty are displayed in so many ways on Trem y Mynydd, especially in the prevalence of family and social problems that have long-term consequences for children and young people, as well as adults. The case story on violence, noted above, drives home the point and heralds a warning, but so too a case story on self-harm. Sadly, this came to a climax on Boxing Day last year when a young man, who had showed such promise and shared his dreams of becoming an accomplished musician, took his own life. One way to process the grief is to come together as a school-community and consider ways to offer alternative visions of the future to resident families, which would be a great tribute to honour the memory of this young man. Were the pre-school and primary school, parents/carers, multi-agencies and community groups to come together, there would be an opportunity to pool resources and streamline services and also explore ways of working in that is locally responsive and contextually sensitive. This means identifying assets, building on existing strengths and talents, and working together to identify local solutions to different challenges and problems. This co-design and co-production towards school-community development needs to be a regular facet of the school's educative work on the Trem y Mynydd housing estate, but staff need to reach out, foster and embrace partnership ways of working. As it stands, most resident families remain supportive of the school's work but more can be done by the school-community and critical friends to offset the lived experiences of poverty effects, especially where they provoke student disengagement, alienation and absenteeism that hampers their life chances.

A local solution to childminding

Before Covid-19 struck, the group of young mums discussed earlier approached a community development worker in the drop-in centre after they had been talking to a community nurse about the lack of accessible childcare for 0–2 years. Bearing in mind that there was only one registered childminder on the housing estate, the nearest nursery was a bus journey away, which was inaccessible not only in terms of monetary costs for formalised childcare but because of the logistics and costs of public transport, working hours and the nursery's opening hours. The *Children First* needs assessment noted that residents' car ownership is low so public transport is the only option for several families, and working hours are often non-negotiable in places like the local hospital, which means shift work. Hence regular nursery opening hours – for example, 8am–6pm on weekdays only – would not suffice, even if it was practical to get there and back via the nursery twice a day on public transport. Confronted with this conundrum the young mums invariably rely on each other and family members for childcare, but this is chaotic in terms of provision and meeting families' needs. The mums' proposal was a classic example of motivated and capable local residents, confident enough to come forward with an idea that they wanted to achieve.

Their vision was for tailored local childcare provision in a 0–2 crèche that would operate to suit local working patterns and be staffed by qualified local residents who had knowledge of families, babies and toddlers. This was communicated in their bid for the Welsh Government's Foundational Economy Challenge Fund, and it came as something of a surprise that this was not successful. No doubt there were numerous competitive bids but, given that these are matters discussed in the Senedd, I was struck by the lack of foresight in not funding this bid.[12] The concept of a foundational economy has been much discussed in academic and policy circles, notably the Centre for Socio-Cultural Change, which publicised the idea in their manifesto and which provides a useful definition: 'What we will call the foundational economy is that part of the economy that creates and distributes goods and services consumed by all (regardless of income and status) because they support everyday life.'[13]

The young mums' proposal was a visionary local solution, inspired by the Sure Start model rolled out across the UK by the Blair/Brown Labour government (1997–2010). Sure Start was an area-based, and disadvantaged-focused, initiative aiming to give children the best possible start in life. This was to be through the improvement of childcare, early childhood education, health and family support, and with an emphasis on outreach and community development. Its funding was then axed in 2010 by the Cameron-Clegg Conservative-Liberal Democrat Coalition government when it came to power and rolled out its austerity programme, cutting back on public services. This was clearly a policy choice to not tackle poverty in the UK, but rather to promote the idea that poverty is personal, as if it is an individual's choice and not systemic nor structural. This is another instance of the problems created by UK governments foisting their neo-liberal policy frameworks on Wales, which then relies on Welsh Government to rise to the challenge. Again this was a frustrating situation because its Foundational Economy Challenge Fund was seemingly insufficient and not big enough to respond positively to the number of bids that needed to be supplied with necessary resources, albeit given the criteria for a successful bid.

The local council is alert to residents' need for good quality childcare: in part due to the findings of the *Children First* needs assessment and because of a post-Covid-19 collaboration between a senior policy officer and the community development worker who had lead the funding bid for the crèche. At the time of writing, they are working together to advance the plans for the mooted new multi-agency hub, jointly funded by Invest Local and Gwynedd Council, although further matched funding is being sought. The hub project is part of an assets-based approach to school-community development, but progress on the demolition of the old youth hall and the new-build is subject to long and lengthy processes of negotiation, not least because of the council's bureaucratic structures and ways of working, which includes its internal politics over available contributory funding: if a community decision is made that the hub is not the place for a crèche, then consideration must be given to an alternative site on the estate.

Years later the young mums' proposal for a crèche, enhanced by a vision for 0–2 education, remains the preferred local solution and it is a responsive local solution to myriad problems, not least meeting a self-identified need for good quality childcare on the estate. These women are mostly in insecure, low-paid and zero-hour contracted work, who already provide chaotic informal childcare for each other as well as relying on friends/family to help them escape a spiral of intergenerational poverty marked by unemployment. Their circumstances are a stark reminder that poverty and its effects are policy choices that put barriers in the way of them working their way out of poverty and alleviating family stresses. Their proposal was also educative to the extent that resident families would be party to their children's sure start, on track to a successful pre-school and primary schooling experience on this estate, and their request for training to gain the qualifications to run it informs the basis for an allied Not-NEET project.

Conclusion

To recap, there is no provision for a dedicated crèche for 0–2-year-olds
on this housing estate, whether run by Gwynedd Council or by the
private market, though there are council-run children's support services:
Flying Start-funded childcare for 2–3-year-olds; the Childcare Offer for
Wales reiterated by Gwynedd Council for 3–4-year-olds; and Gwynedd
Council-funded childcare for 4–5-year-olds. The young mums' proposal
for an on-site crèche is a local solution to the problem of not having
accessible and suitable childcare for babies and toddlers, given that
the closest provision is more than two miles away in one of the city's
privatised childcare settings. These are neither affordable nor easily
accessible for those families that can ill-afford the time and bus fare to
take their babies and toddlers twice daily there and back. The mums'
vision is to build capacity in their own school-community and provide
childcare marked by local knowledge of babies' and toddlers' needs and
family circumstances. These young mums want childcare available 24/7
to fit with flexible working hours, particularly with patterns of shift work:
they want to remove barriers to accessing employment, education and
training, and family services.

Their proposal to the Welsh Government's Foundational Economy
Challenge Fund should stand as a feasibility study. Their allied
Not-NEET project – 'Starting out for the future: 0–2 years on-site
crèche' (see appendix 5) – is to facilitate an on-site crèche run by qualified
parents with others in training. In turn, this is intended to build their
capacity to learn about and gain expertise in childcare, education and
schooling, especially as it coordinates with the local school and Gwynedd
Council in line with UNICEF's work in the UK to create safe and
inspiring places to learn.[14] Their ideas for tailored 'on-the-job' training
would expedite the facility's immediate opening and shape the nursery's
ethos, and clear, mapped career trajectories. The recruitment of new
parents, year-on-year, will help build childcare careers and community
transformation towards gainful employment, education and training.

At the time of writing we are in the process of writing a brief
for a second feasibility study for the multi-agencies hub/community
centre, which includes an options appraisal and business case for the
best solution going forward. There are two different sites and various
alternatives in terms of what is included within the hub/centre, including

the possibility of a crèche. Much work needs to be done before a decision is made regarding the most fitting option, including where the crèche facility would be best placed. There is some Invest Local and Gwynedd Council funding earmarked for the hub/centre but we need to apply for matched funding. This project began as a partnership project with Gwynedd Council to provide a community space with accessible services at the request of the residents; however, it has stalled due to Covid-19 and lockdowns and their effect – and continued impact – on the delivery of services.

I would advise ongoing efforts to maintain the young mums' group and its momentum, but it has experienced many setbacks during the last couple of years, given their bid to the Foundational Economy Challenge Fund was not successful and then Covid-19 lockdowns. This came with myriad challenges, not least for those trying to juggle chaotic childcare arrangements while maintaining their family employment status as key workers. Thankfully, more recently, there are positive signs that these young women remain keen on the idea of 0–2 years' provision given quite a few came together to organise an ad hoc baby playgroup as an interim step and want to resurrect the bid for an on-site crèche. In supporting them, my work experience suggests it is important not to promise anything too prematurely because disappointment has happened far too often before and because further setbacks sow the seeds of distrust, which then reflect badly on what social democracy should mean in Wales. This requires us all to focus on ways to realise citizen participation and how that can become better informed through school-community development. This brings me back full circle to building trust in the school-community. We must be intent on identifying its assets, then drawing on its understanding and knowledge, but also recognising, accepting, welcoming and trusting its local solutions. We must also be intent on working in a co-productive way with resident families from the outset, particularly in the co-design of projects and in the application for funding and resources.

This all readily lends itself to learning from our Not-NEET project, 'Starting out for the future: 0–2 years on-site crèche', where the young mums declared their need for resources to develop an on-site crèche as an asset with social value. These mothers wanted childcare and a family friendly centre, which would allow for an access-point for family services and for community-driven solutions to family problems. They wanted to facilitate early intervention where needs are high and build a seamless approach to multi-service access for whole-family needs. We – community development workers employed on the estate – have yet to respond appropriately, with a (financially viable) sustainable childcare provision solution before their enthusiasm for parent engagement in early childhood education, pre-schooling and schooling is lost. But, like all the other local solutions and allied Not-NEET projects included in this book, it requires the political will to make it happen. This means policies that herald fundamental changes in structures and systems, a cultural shift away from 'we know what's best', and the intelligence to acknowledge what is at issue and realise a partnership to affect some change.

Notes

1   For further critical discussion of the problematic nature of need, see Ife (2009).
2   For an extensive discussion of co-production in relation to community development, see Banks et al. (2019).
3   As noted by the Child Poverty Action Group (2017), the Joseph Rowntree Foundation acknowledges that there is no universal agreement defining human needs nor their relation to resources, and goes on to discuss the intricacies of the ways to conceive needs given particular sets of circumstances that includes modernity. The upshot was agreement with what CPAG co-founder Townsend (n.d.) called 'the ordinary patterns, customs and activities' of society that cost more than just the rent, food and utility bills. This prefaced further discussion about minimum standards (of living) that are to be expected at certain times, for example, in war time or given more contemporary calls for austerity (see pp. 18–19).
4   Here I should acknowledge the input from Lori Beckett, one of the academic partners working to help conceptualise the Bangor PLUS project: she could see the potential benefits of enhancing the application for funding a crèche with a vision for education for 0–2-year-olds. This has since been vindicated in Carys's case story about her aspirations for her children.
5   Again I should acknowledge the input from Lori Beckett and Graham French, the academic partners on the Bangor PLUS project: they could see the worth of conjoining community development and school development guided by common shared values and principles.
6   'Nurture Development' is a Community Renewal Centre and one of eleven partners of the ABCD Institute, as noted on the homepage of this website: *https://www.nurturedevelopment.org/who-we-are/* (accessed 21 April 2023).

7   '1-in-4 children living in poverty set to worsen during cost of living crisis'.
     Loughborough University: *https://www.lboro.ac.uk/news-events/news/2022/july/
     1-in-4-children-living-in-poverty-cost-of-living/* (accessed 21 April 2023).

8   OB3 is a research institute that provides services to government among
     others, as noted on their website: *ob3research.co.uk* (accessed 21 April 2023).

9   Co-production is defined by the Co-production Network for Wales on their
     website: *https://copronet.wales/home/coproduction/* (accessed 21 April 2023).

10   See *https://www.legislation.gov.uk/wsi/2014/2677/contents/made* (accessed 21
     April 2023).

11   See press release dated 21 March 2022 from Wales's Minister for Education
     and Welsh Language Jeremy Miles: *https://media.service.gov.wales/news/gbp-
     25m-investment-in-community-focused-schools-to-tackle-the-impact-of-poverty*
     (accessed 20 April 2023).

12   A *Manifesto for the Foundational Economy*, Working Paper 131, Centre for
     Research on Socio-Cultural Change: *https://foundationaleconomycom.files.
     wordpress.com/2017/01/wp131.pdf* (accessed 21 April 2023).

13   Various interpretations of the Foundational Economy are explored by
     the Institute of Welsh Affairs on their website: *https://www.iwa.wales/
     agenda/2019/02/what-is-the-foundational-economy/* (accessed 21 April 2023).

14   See *https://www.unicef.org/* and note the name change from UNICEF (the
     United Nations International Children's Emergency Fund) to the United
     Nations Children's Fund. Its aims are to reach the most disadvantaged
     children and adolescents, and to protect the rights of every child.

This shows the 4th Lord Penrhyn (middle/seated), Hugh Napier Douglas-Pennant (1894–1949), who sold parcels of land to Bangor City Council, some for social housing following enticements from the UK Government in Westminster to local councils to mitigate housing shortages in the interwar years.

7

LYRICISM AND HIP HOP TO COUNTER MISEDUCATION IN A SCHOOL-COMMUNITY IN POVERTY

Owen Maclean with Martin Daws (Letters Grow *project*)

Introduction

This chapter is written following numerous conversations and e-mail briefings from a resident creative artist on Trem y Mynydd housing estate, to use its pseudonym, who attended the local primary school and a local high school, but who has unhappy memories of those experiences. In his own words, I was targeted, teased and bullied, likely because of my dyslexia and learning difficulties that prompted my allocation into a Special Education Unit in primary school. We carried red folders, easily identified and called names in the playground. I was also punished for my English grammar, spelling and handwriting, which contributed to my being an angry teen going into high school, though I count myself lucky on two counts. It was boxing club that taught me self-defence and encouraged me to stand up against the bullies, and once I threw that first punch I garnered respect from my peers. Then, when I was old enough, I went to youth clubs where I met a number of youth workers including Martin Daws, who is also a poet. He taught me to rap and rhyme and encouraged me to stay on at school to do my GCSEs, which was some challenge! We connected again years later and it is sweet that he is now making a contribution to this chapter, following conversations via zoom meetings.

After I finished school, I worked in a few apprenticeships in the building industry, but these were not for me and I dropped out. I was wayward, though mine is a redemption story because my lot started to improve as I started to hone my music and song-writing skills, then teamed up with a few mates to start up a record label. I could also see a need on Trem y Mynydd for some sort of youth club-type sessions, given that so many of the children and young people were disenchanted with school and getting into trouble, no doubt experiencing what I have since come to recognise as miseducation.[1] The youth clubs had long gone and I was inspired to honour the memory and replicate the work of one of the youth workers, the late Paul Hockaday. The first iteration of my *Letters Grow* project on rap and rhyme was funded with a grant of £2,000 by our local drop-in centre called Mynydd Ni and I came to run an after-school music club. Then I enrolled in a Music Technology course at Coleg Menai, where I ran into Martin Daws and met one of his colleagues Martin Hoylan, who encouraged me to do 18 months of online mentorship training with Community Music Wales. These courses both provided me with so many opportunities to learn my craft and run community-based programmes.

Once again luck was on my side because I fell upon my music career path, which contrasted so markedly to the path I started out on as an angry teen that then carried into my twenties. Looking back I blame the teachers who did not see my worth and the education system for not then accommodating my learning needs and interests. This bottled-up frustration and negative emotion was then channelled into my work organising raves and shows, acting as a DJ, making and editing videos. I can only applaud the work of the *Children First* needs assessment (see chapter 1 in this volume), which registered local residents' concerns about education and skills, jobs and income under the heading 'Barriers and Threats' to health and well-being. This goes some way to describe my design of the *Letters Grow* project, which starts with the recognition that every child on this housing estate has potential. Working with Daws helped me hone my approach to teaching and learning music, lyricism and hip hop (rap), oral traditions and writing styles. This is spelled out in our publication, *The Letters Grow Handbook*, which guides my work with the children and young people who are ever ready to write verses on what they miss at school. This can be tied to the lived experiences of poverty and its effects like student disengagement, alienation and absenteeism.

Funding from Community Music Wales enabled me to run online sessions during the first Covid-19 lockdown, and I also worked with

Daws to apply for more funding. We were eventually successful and given £1,000 from Comic Relief, £2,000 from Mynydd Ni, £3,000 from Mantell Gwynedd and £10,000 from the National Lottery. This money enabled us to order a print-run of 400 of *The Letters Grow Handbook*, purchase equipment like Go Pro cameras, microphones and lighting, and pay for staffing costs. This ensures that I can focus and provide a consistent level of professional support for the project, which has teaching intent. Its many forms of creative activities encourage children and young people to find their voices and tell their stories in rap and rhyme and engage in creative expression. This is my local solution to meeting young people's needs, and I cherish the opportunity to work with the Bangor PLUS team and plug into our Not-NEET project, 'Acting on the future: student expression in the performing arts' (see appendix 6). I am keen to see opportunities for young people from Trem y Mynydd to train as youth workers but also working artists who are digitally competent and able to have supporting roles running gigs and events.

In this chapter, I recall some of my personal experiences in primary school and high school, and share my thoughts on children's unmet needs and the challenges that they present. I also report on my work here on the Trem y Mynydd housing estate, and how I came to meet and work with my co-author. I then discuss my concerns regarding miseducation, a handy term to describe the damage done inside the school system. This requires correction and community music works well in remedying this, and here I showcase the youth clubs held after school – but there is government conflict. I go on to describe our joint work, the responsive *Letters Grow* project, which is designed to meet the language and literacy needs of children and young people given the perpetuation of miseducation. It is constructed as a form of educative work akin to the tradition of the Celtic bards in the past but is also set very much in the present Wales. I then describe my local solution to miseducation in more detail and how it allies to the Not-NEET project that has the potential to connect with reshaping the wider 14–16 qualification offer in Wales. These analyses lead to my chapter conclusions, particularly my suggestion for a facilitation fund to be lodged with the Trem y Mynydd Co-operative, which would then take responsibility for allocating grants to the Not-NEET projects funded with public investment to secure the children's future.

The crayon kids

Such a derogatory term was bandied about in the playground to describe those of us in the Special Education Unit and it is lodged in my memory of the experiences of schooling on Trem y Mynydd, though I hasten to add that I am extremely proud to be part of this community. This is all the more so because my family are long-term residents who are well regarded; which is not surprising given that my maternal family history goes back to the 'early settlers' who relocated from Bangor. I can remember my Taid (grandfather) talking about working on the docks – Port Penrhyn – where so many of the men were employed and where they often went fishing, which probably helped to feed their families, especially with work so scarce after the Penrhyn Quarry closed down. The verse below registers my concerns about class-based inequalities, and my unhappiness from my parents' separation and seeing my mum battling hardship being a sole parent responsible for two children:

> No wonder we're living in a tragedy / 100 grand plus perks with their salary / So much hunger and pain / And they laugh man how can it be / Cutting free dinners / while giving up millions / To do up the Palace for the Lords and her majesty

Free dinners refers to free school meals, available to parents in receipt of benefits, a godsend to my mum and Nain (grandmother) who were trying to feed a family with hungry children and young people. I am sorry to say that this caused me some shame, because I was mocked, which added to my feelings of being discriminated against, and the stigma and my loathing of the discipline meted out in primary school for what now amounts to different ways of learning. I especially resented those primary schoolteachers who praised children with tidy handwriting, and I begrudged the music teacher in high school who made it known that she had no time for those of us from our housing estate. I remember lesson after lesson a group of us were ordered to stand away from the class playing their instruments. We were forbidden to make any noise, even tapping to the rhythm and using our desktops as percussion, acutely aware that our parents could not afford an instrument or any extracurricular music tuition. I did not realise I had any talents in music, and though I showed some aptitude for rhyming words in youth club it was years before I came to creative expression.

Martin Daws is a trained youth worker who was given a statutory contract in the youth club that operated out of the old youth hall between 6 and 9 p.m. two to four days per week in school term and during summer holiday programmes. This was under the auspices of Gwynedd Council, and different to the youth clubs funded by the Blair-Brown Labour governments' Communities First programme that operated in the new-build across the road. Children and young people attended both, likely oblivious to any differences, though Daws's concerns were mostly with creative expression and also its cultural form. At first this received a mixed reaction, especially from the boys and young men who were more interested in football and gym, but they came around to engaging with storytelling and talking. They stood by, observing at first; then came to participating while some got into the music and the way of rhyming and rapping. Slowly word spread and the youth club was attracting anything up to sixty-five children and young people, which meant that there needed to be a minimum of three staff members, but also adult volunteers supervising and safe-guarding. Daws stayed for eight years before he left the youth club – but he left his mark.

I met Daws on one of his return visits when I was 12 years old and already enthralled with rhyming, which was something he encouraged. I will always be grateful to him for coming into my life, for wisely using his time with us to give us a sense of purpose and a positive outlook on life, and showing us that a youth worker could also be a creative artist. I am delighted that Daws now calls himself the proud grandfather of our work on lyricism and hip hop on Trem y Mynydd. He planted a seed, it took root and then became the inspiration for my own teaching programme, originally called 'Let us Grow' but renamed by Andy Mario to become the *Letters Grow* project. Daws sees it generationally, having done youth work and mentoring with my age cohort when I was young and now seeing me develop my work with children and young people. It is a mark of respect that I invite him along to work on occasions. It has been a very fruitful eighteen-year relationship to date, which he says is rare because this sort of creative work is usually only ever piecemeal. I can only agree: it takes dedicated time encouraging youngsters' cultural expression and fostering health and well-being – its key role – is best done in continuous, ongoing sessions.

Coming back to my own story, I am the first to acknowledge that going through school I could read but I could not write, and I was not very good at conversation. If the teachers bothered me, I would challenge their authority and came across as abrupt. I had bottled up so much trauma, including my hurt being called 'a little shit' by an art teacher who barred me from class. In the following few years, my outlet was partying and playing the fool, including getting up to mischief whilst fuelled by alcohol. The police were coming to our home almost weekly as I was getting into more and more trouble, and so my mum encouraged me to stay home. In doing so, I was safe, not exposed to temptation and being part of the gang, and more likely to lose myself listening to music and writing expressive verses. Being bullied was at the heart of the bad behaviour, and it is gut wrenching to learn that all these years later it is still an issue for children and teenagers, as this essay-type verse from my little cousin shows:

> I want that all the bad kids in school to change and be good.
> I want that the bullies to stop being bullies.
> I want that all the bad people stop.
> I think the school should be a nice place with no bullies.

A community music programme

I am pleased to report that, despite my years as a wayward youth, I could see another way forward. I came to a fork in the road in my early twenties when I opted to use rap and rhyming to express how I felt. I realised that I needed to unburden myself and really clear my mind, which in effect was an emotional journey and a great way to start opening up about myself, my situation and the circumstances of my life. At long last I realised that I had some talent for rave music and song-writing, but I also yearned to perform. The opportunity came in a workshop run by Community Music Wales, where I recorded a demo CD and sent it to DJs, which led to a stage performance showcasing my verses. I then threw myself into research on African traditional music, and here I will share some critical reflections on my learning journey: the shame is that it was not a consequence of my schooling experiences but rather it was in spite of my miseducation: 'without the fear of what others thought, I started really expressing what and how I was feeling and out of a really dark time in my life came the spark that I needed all along'.[2]

The idea of miseducation is best captured in my verse written specifically for this chapter, but here I would ask the reader to look past the (strategic) lack of punctuation and spelling mistakes to the messages conveyed. My teaching intent is to remind those teachers who ignored my (creative) needs and (music) interests to look past regimented policy demands and provide some learning opportunities for students' (artistic) expression:

> Miss educated miss judged and miss led /
> Listen to everything that miss said /
> Misinterpreted missing the important stuff / a broken system repeatedly failing us /
> Raised voices and Pointed fingers in the face / your writting is a mess and your spellings a disgrace /
> Not many teachers understood / that it was hard to face the day /
> First lesson missed and lack of attendance / punishment is coming now another detention /
> Still Tied to so called current curriculum / all for currency / so wrongly taught in history /
> Not told about the Welsh knot / And how We had to break from the states of Emergency /
> Repremands for those who don't Represent / The Reputation / Kids Dodging school so they called it Miss Education!

The Welsh knot has various spellings, usually 'Welsh Not', and a WN chiselled into a slab of wood hung around a child's neck in school houses in the nineteenth century (see figure 12). This was a deterrence against speaking the language,[3] and it remains in living memory but only to the extent that some older residents remember their parents' and grandparents' stories of this sort of punishment and humiliation. In my verse I use the Welsh knot as a metaphor mostly to draw attention to the ongoing omissions of Welsh histories in children's learning, which can have the effect of suppressing knowledge of the Welsh language, culture and nation-building. This happens again and again when children and young people are turned away from schooling and then when the youth clubs shut down. This happened with the demise of Communities First project when its funding of youth workers was axed in 2010 by the Cameron-Clegg Conservative-Liberal Democrat Coalition government (see Thirsk's chapter 6). Its austerity programme impacted on Wales's local and national governments via cuts to funding of youth clubs, which then denies opportunities to learn and which – in my opinion – amounts to neglect.

This comes back to my teaching intent as it is stated in *The Letters Grow Handbook*: 'to enrich the collective oral traditions of our communities'. In my first venture in an after-school music club, I took in some pieces of digital equipment that I had bought with birthday money and savings earned through working various jobs; I saw it as an investment given that my dream was to start up a small business. During the session with the children and young people, we did some activities that amounted to a rhyming game that was then followed by some other tasks where the rhymes were bridged into verses. Another one of my friends, who had helped set up the equipment, gave demonstrations on music production: in those early sessions these were mainly beats to accompany the verses, which were later meshed into hip hop. The children and young people soon got into the swing of oral tradition, and responded positively.

After a couple of years continuing to hone my own of practice writing rap and being on the microphone at raves, mostly taking the role of MC, I wanted to learn to make more sounds better suited to my vocal expressions to mesh into rap. I enrolled on a music technology course in Coleg Menai Bangor and, looking back, I enjoyed it so much; no doubt because I thrived. I still struggled with writing, spelling, grammar and punctuation, but I was not criticised nor punished. My tutors were understanding and in tune with additional needs regarding learning and written expression. They brought good humour to their assessment feedback, and though they noted that my assignments featured very little or no punctuation, I was made to feel at ease and I learned a lot. They saw my potential, and pushed me to work on my strengths rather than pointing out my weaknesses. They noted the positive influence I had on the class, especially were I would encourage 'a community of learning'. I have great respect for them and I will always be grateful to them, especially for the joy their reports on my progress gave to my Mum.

The *Letters Grow* project

During my time at Coleg Menai, I met Martin Hoyland who sourced a budget to put me through a paid online mentoring programme provided by Community Music Wales. It taught me much about approaches and methods in various sorts of creative expression, and I went on to assist Martin Daws out in the field before Covid-19 hit. Though we were confined during lockdown, we moved to online working with youth services, charities and organisations across North Wales, right down to Merthyr Tydfil. Daws and I both see ourselves as freelance creative artists and social actors who are keen to help young people build a positive personal identity and connection to their community. Cultural expression is a great resource that helps us survive poverty because it shows us that we need to help one another through the challenges and share resources. As Daws says in the song 'Deyika's Dream', 'No one should have too much need / no one should need too much.'[4]

This spoke to all of us especially during the Covid-19 lockdowns, when the resident volunteers supported by elected representatives for Trem y Mynydd on Gwynedd Council and Mynydd Ni workers were on site to jointly develop contingency plans. Everyone came together to ensure families' basic needs were met at the same time that many local residents stepped up as key workers, though they remain the working poor. Daws maintains that as cultural artists we can help build the community, lend them support and give them strength, and this is culturally potent. In teaching my peers and me, he drew on his experiences of being a white working-class rapper and poet in London, and encouraged us to see that everyone has a story and everyone should be given the opportunity to share it. I came to see this as a powerful teaching strategy to improve Welsh and English language and literacy, which in turn helps to counter the lived experiences of poverty and socio-economic inequalities. By fostering self-belief and a sense of achievement and self-worth, this translates into better learning outcomes, which can lead to student engagement in schooling, educational qualifications, employment, and better life circumstances. In turn this speaks to inclusivity, given that we work with cohorts of children and young people who live in socially and economically disadvantaged school-communities, but we also alert them to different oral traditions and encourage a respect for difference and diversity. It has been a joy to relate hip hop to the cultural practices of the Welsh bards, and showcase the commonalities.

Their skill was/is phenomenal and my humble ambition is to record some folk stories in the form of raps, which is very much a poetry of the people. This is a much admired tradition across Wales, and we have only to think of the National Eisteddfod that alternates between north and south Wales every year.[5] I was in awe of the 2017 centenary celebrations of the Chair – so beautifully carved – being awarded to Hedd Wyn, which was the bardic name meaning 'blessed peace' used by Ellis Humphrey Evans, a shepherd who had been killed during the First World War. His prestigious prize, forever known as the Black Chair, now resides in his family home on the farm at Yr Ysgwrn near Trawsfynydd in Gwynedd. It was about this time that the idea of a handbook came to me as I wanted to pass on what I had learnt on lyricism and hip hop – which had taken me five years! The intention was to share my knowledge and empower the next generation, which is to follow in the footsteps of the quarrymen and port workers who raised funds for the University College of North Wales in the late nineteenth century and who hung the banner 'knowledge is power' on the portico at the official opening (see figure 6).

Another instance of my teaching intent is targeted at bullying, which remains an issue for so many children and young people. One session titled 'Tornado talk' in *The Letters Grow Handbook* is devoted to rapping in double time, identified as tongue twisters to demonstrate how large words should be selected to fit more syllables into the rhythm. This catchy title provides a golden opportunity to encourage talking about our collective experiences of trauma, intimidation, hurt, fear, and the like, but also forms of resistance. For example:

> I'm a saviour/changed behaviour/faked the faker/
> pen to paper/try be greater/than a stinking little hater/
> call the waiter/great escaper/instigator/
> instigate then see you later.

This verse is used as a teaching tool to encourage the session participants to try to construct their own verse using these words: saviour, behaviour, faker, paper, instigator, hater, waiter and escaper. The instruction is to use the larger words as key words with the double syllable and fill in the gaps with smaller self-chosen words. A teenage girl created a thoughtful rap on bullying and performed it outside the entrance to her high school. I filmed it and put it online, but because of the background signage the school Head demanded that it was taken down lest the school's reputation was damaged.

This scenario was enough to provoke this teenage girl's disenchantment – if not disgust – with high school, and calls into question the wherewithal of the school Head and teaching staff to appreciate schooling experiences for children and young people, never mind solicit the support available. This dovetails with the findings of the *Children First* needs assessment on Trem y Mynydd (see Lewis's chapter 1) given its children's and young people's problems with schooling: there are low attendance rates, their concerns are not identified and there is not enough support to stop young people from leaving school. Then there are barriers to them re-engaging with schooling because of a lack of confidence, additional learning needs and a lack of basic levels of communication. This is where our work in the *Letters Grow* project becomes apparent; another dream is to have a copy of our handbook in every school across Gwynedd and further afield. I am confident that it would help teaching staff trying to meet children's and young people's unmet needs (see Evans's chapter 2), as this teenage boy is asking for in the following verse:

What's up with school/they're treating us like fools/
So we're breaking all the rules/their methods aren't cool.

Acting on the future

This is where Wales's history, language and culture is crucial but, it is apparent that the majority of the children and young people who come to my sessions are not well versed on these sorts of matters – no pun intended! They are also shy, not always open to talking and telling their stories, and sometimes struggle with reading and writing English, as well as Welsh. Another instance of my teaching intent is to develop an interest in Welsh language and literacy, which will help young people develop their sense of self and their community but also find their place in the wider world. Here is one of my bilingual verses:

Let me teach you how to learn the language/
Dan ni'n mynd i ddysgu sut i siarad yr iaith/

We have hello how are you goes like/
hello sut mae / and tara rwan means to now say goodbye/

So Mooving forward now Dan ni'n symyd ymlaen/

Try to nor worry if your falling behind/
Paid â poeni pan ti'n disgyn yn ôl/
Cause most things take time/

Y rhan fwyaf o bethau'n cymryd amser/
So enjoy your life/
Mae bywyd i'w fwynhau/
looking to the blue sky/
Yn edrych ar yr awyr las/
And wondering why/
Meddwl pam/
There's too many lies/
Gormod o glwyddau/
Going on right in front of our eyes/
Mynd ymlaen o flaen llygaid ni/

We will stand like the dragon/
Dan ni'n sefyll fel y ddraig/

Welsh so there's music in our blood/
Cymry mae cerddoriaeth yn ein gwaed/

This is the sort of work that Daws encourages, it makes us stronger individually but also collectively, and this strength stays with you and because it's not in material form it cannot be taken away. This was evident in my 'pop-up' family festival that I organised last spring with a few of the local residents, staged one Friday early evening on the football field. It was to promote community well-being and we recruited some of the young people to help set it up, which provided them with work experience as it were: erecting the main tent, lighting, sound system, TV screens, ensuring e-supply, then filming and editing. The digital graphics were supplied by Dan Parry, a graphic designer and dear friend, who added much to showcase our after-school rap group's performances to parents and visitors, including community development officers and academic partners. It was a great gig and much appreciated by those in attendance, especially some of the parents who set up stalls to raise money for the old folks' home on Trem y Mynydd. It all brought to life Daws's lyrics for the refrain to the song 'Deyika's Dream': 'Good people got to take control / good people of planet got so much soul.'

This is also the sort of work I offer to run in after-school sessions at the local primary schools and high schools. In going back to Ysgol Trem y Mynydd, I wanted to showcase my form of educative work to the school Head and teaching staff, not that any of my old teachers are there now. The school Head, who has now left because of long Covid (see chapter 2), approved two programmes: an hour once a week for years 3 and 4 on Mondays and years 5 and 6 on Tuesdays, running over six weeks. It was extracurricular tuition in lyricism, hip hop, song writing and music video; the children performed their own work and loved it. This was then shared in the school-community and was very well received. While I had done this of my own volition it was a shame that the school Head could not access any funding to institute the programme on a more permanent basis a more permanent basis. My academic partners tell me that this project would sit well with *Curriculum for Wales* that came into force in September 2022. The school Head was worried about bedding it in because they were all preoccupied with welfare demands (see Evans's chapter 2). We need to join the dots because while the new curriculum has provision for outreach into the school-community, my work is endeavouring to reach into the school. I would very much like an opportunity to co-design and co-produce our allied Not-NEET project – titled 'Acting on the future: student expression in the performing arts' (see appendix 6) – which is in line with Beckett's argument in her response to Ysgol Trem y Mynydd's new curriculum online survey:

> Curriculum implementation must be undertaken by teachers who have nuanced understandings of the causes and effects of poverty that impact on pupils' and parents/carers/grandparents' learning opportunities, and who thereby hone their commitments to teaching the poor, their families and children.

Teaching needs to be research-informed to be intellectually robust because it takes inordinate skill to develop classroom pedagogies to engage if not re-engage those who are historically marginalised and excluded from schooling.[6]

In formalising my local solution in the *Letters Grow* project, it became apparent that I needed to set up a small business: I am sorely in need of help to manage my workload while I concentrate on my creative expression and educative work. This was suggested by one of the community development officers who has insight into my current ad hoc management arrangements and busy timetable. I would benefit from an administrative assistant to orchestrate funding applications, my diary full of meetings and bookings of gigs and events, correspondence, promotional work, finance and accountancy, our online presence, events management and other office work. Again we need to join the dots because there are so many teenagers and adults on this housing estate looking for work and who do work experience at various gigs of mine. This is one step away from becoming a PA, finance manager, accountant, events manager and dedicated events support staff, including technicians, video editors and graphic designers – not to forget youth workers! This could dovetail with reshaping the wider 14–16 qualification offer in Wales to mentor and support children and young people staying on in school, and gaining the training and qualifications as I did all those years ago following in Daws's footsteps.

The logistics

A facilitation fund would prove enormously helpful to sustain our project as a social enterprise: setting up a small business as a co-operative and/ or with shareholders' investment would take me away from my work as a creative artist for at least three months. I am currently operating out of the Mynydd Ni drop-in centre, so at least I am working with community development officers as colleagues and I can use their facilities, especially office space to see clients. Better still, extra funding could well be used to set up a multi-media studio as a creative space in the Youth Hall. My rationale for such funding is to secure continuity and longevity of my *Letters Grow* project as a local solution and to synchronise the education, employment and training opportunities provided by our allied Not-NEET project. I am happy to share my idea for a facilitation fund and have it managed by the Trem y Mynydd Co-operative, which is Pete Whitby's idea (see Fernley et al.'s chapter 4) that would operate in accordance with the legalities in line with advice from another community development worker (see Thirsk's chapter 6). A co-operative board could manage the finances and accountancy, which is in everyone's best interests. Otherwise it all remains ad hoc and children and young people's unmet needs remain unfulfilled, including the need for youth workers and mentors who can help to fill the void created by miseducation, and engage young people, and divert attention away from wayward activities.

I appreciate the need for a feasibility study, which was effectively reflected in my proposal for £1,800 continuation funding from Mynydd Ni to secure continuation of my hip hop programme for children and teenagers who were out of school during the summer holidays. It was tabulated to take into account the timetable: 1 x 6-week block of the 'hip hop stop' to continue through the summer, which required three tutors for 10 to 20 participants, though the number of participants always varies; and a 1 x 6-week block of the 18+ music and media lab, which required two tutors for 8 to 15 participants, though this also varies. The costing included fees for staff facilitation and delivery, materials and catering (which was akin to free school meals, bearing in mind that we had hungry children and teenagers). The justification was based on our past success, the children had shown amazing improvement in their creative expression, and there is ongoing need for consistency in the provision of tuition. Also, there is always a need for summer holiday activities to consolidate productive output and to provide a networking hub for musicians, along with experienced and budding creative artists on the estate.

As ever, my teaching intent is to help build capacity and confidence, and to provide advice not only on participants' creative journey but also on education, employment and training opportunities. These sorts of block sessions, like the after-school sessions in schools and youth club-type sessions, is all part of the *Letters Grow* project, which benefits from forward planning and success with funding applications. For example, we received £10,000 in a block grant jointly funded by Gwynedd Council's Haf o Hwyl (summer of fun) programme, Community Music Wales and Pontio Arts and Innovation Centre, located in the grounds of Bangor University. This was to help scale-up the inaugural 'pop-up' family festival that ran last spring on Trem y Mynydd, and to do this I worked cooperatively and collaboratively in alliance with creative artists in other nearby local communities. In the build-up to our second family festival, I invited the Llanberis circus troupe to join us in weekly mini-activity sessions and take the opportunity to learn the ropes – if I can use that metaphor here. The plan was for family festivals to run in other local communities before an extravaganza event showcasing performances from across the region to be held at Venue Cymru Theatre and Conference Centre in Llandudno.

To go full circle back to the beginning of this chapter, my aim has been to share my story about my sad and sorry schooling experiences as a prelude to put my local solution to countering poor kids' miseducation with my responsive *Letters Grow* project. This has the potential to become a cross-curriculum project on language and literacy in English and Welsh given the *Curriculum for Wales*. It also has the capacity to provide multiple education, training and employment opportunities via our allied Not-NEET project, 'Acting on the future: student expression in the performing arts', which dovetails with the wider 14–16 qualification offer in Wales. As well, this could be developed into a small business pending investment but, equally, it can operate as a social enterprise subject to a facilitation fund managed by the Trem y Mynydd Co-operative. Meantime, we are working with piecemeal funding, notably on local expansion that will stand us in good stead for would-be national development with creative artists. This should begin in those school-communities that participated in the 2018–19 *Children First* needs assessment (see the introduction and chapter 1).

To reiterate Daws's argument, as cultural artists we can help build community strength by encouraging interaction and positive energy, which is all culturally potent. We don't have all the answers but we have the expressive tools to empower people and make them stronger and healthier. The last word belongs to two parents of children and teenagers who attend our *Letters Grow* sessions on lyricism and hip hop:

> Martin and Owen have inspired me and my son to do something we never thought possible. It helps my son, who has anger issues, bring out what is really wrong through making the lyrics.

Letters Grow has immensely helped my daughter deal with a lot of her emotions. I would dread to think what state she would have been [in] if she couldn't have expressed these feelings. She finds talking to people about feelings hard. She can feel as low as to want to self-harm sometimes. But thanks to the work of Owen and Martin she has gained confidence in herself and done exactly what the group's name suggests: let her grow!

Notes

1 My thanks to academic partners for introducing me to these ideas and to Reay (2017).
2 These form part of my mini-biography in *The Letters Grow Handbook*.
3 See *https://www.library.wales/discover/digital-gallery/printed-material/the-blue-books-of-1847* (accessed 30 October 2022).
4 This song was penned for the late Deyika Nzeribe, Green Party candidate nominated to stand against Andy Burnham for the mayoral election of Manchester: see *https://www.theguardian.com/politics/2017/mar/02/deyika-nzeribe-obituary* (accessed 30 October 2022).
5 I only recently learned that my Nain's brother, my great-uncle Tom Huws, won the Crown for his poem 'Cadwynau' at the National Eisteddfod in 1959 in Caernarfon: see *https://eisteddfod.cymru/archif/enillwyr-yr-eisteddfod/enillwyr-y-goron* (accessed 30 October 2022).
6 Unfortunately, the online survey site is no longer available to access.

I am not impressed with the argument about distance from the town and various works. The present generation's advocates appear to think that a mile or two walk is harmful to them. There are any amount of men in Bangor to-day between the age of 60 and 70 who thought nothing of walking four to six miles to their work.

(3 Can we afford it? One feels after reading Mr E. H. Jones' speech that the Council and the town should think very carefully before embarking on a policy which may, however desirable, land the town in the same mess as the country was in in 1931. After making all calculations an allowance of at least 20 per cent. should be made.

It is true we should sacrifice for future generations but we are not asked to bankrupt ourselves. Idealism is excellent as long as it is practicable. I disagree with the suggestion of calling in some expert to advise us. The town is fortunate in all its officials and they are quite capable of advising on all points. It is the duty of the Council to formulate a policy and for the officials to carry it out.

Finally, I would say that what is required is dispassionate consideration on this important question. Our Councillors are no doubt doing their best, but if too much heat is introduced the citizens may be entertained but not enlightened.

I hope, Mr Editor, you will favour us with more of your leaders and waken the town up on this vital matter.—Yours, etc.,

DORIC.

Bangor,
December 9th, 1935.

This extract of a letter to the editor of the North Wales Chronicle, dated 13 December 1935, provides some insight into the public debates about Bangor City Council's plans for social housing that amounted to hundreds of new houses being built. Note the reference to future generations.

8

OUTDOOR LEARNING: ADDRESSING STUDENT ALIENATION AND DISENGAGEMENT BY BUILDING SOCIAL CAPITAL

Graham French (Bangor University) with Claudia Howard (Wild Elements)

Introduction

This chapter is written by an academic working in teacher education with a particular focus on outdoor learning and working as an academic partner on the Trem y Mynydd housing estate, to use its pseudonym. My contribution, as a member of the Bangor PLUS team working in support of the local primary school, Ysgol Trem y Mynydd, is to tender advice on addressing some of its many challenges and alert staff to some useful knowledge bases and practices including pedagogical approaches that are research informed.[1] My professional conversations with the school Head and allied multi-agency workers stemmed from concerns about a handful of primary-aged children (3–11 years old), who are troubled and who have been excluded from this school and others, and hence struggle to access educational provision of any sort. In response, I sought advice from a colleague, Claudia Howard, at Wild Elements, and we are agreed that personal and social development fostered through outdoor learning is key in addressing student disengagement, notably for those who have been excluded, which should help other families who find themselves in this situation.[2]

In my work as an academic partner, I have learned much about the lived experiences of child poverty and its effects on this school-community. This is tempered by a critical understanding of the policy pressures facing schools that have a bearing on the ways they deal with welfare demands. Without the requisite funding and resources, sometimes they have no choice but to exclude children who cannot be accommodated. This is mostly because a focus of education policy on measurable cognitive outcomes has come at the cost of the value of the contribution schooling can make in building children's social skills. By their nature these are less tangible or objectively measured, yet ironically it is a deficit in these social skills that manifest as poor behaviour and attendance, which in turn leads to school exclusion. I see it as a moral imperative to consider our work with teachers and multi-agency workers, children, young people and their families in ways to help address these issues that are more in tune with the child's unmet needs.

In order to act on the moral imperative, we needed a deeper understanding of the intersection of child poverty and the policies that drive Wales's education system, and how this can lead to students' disengagement and alienation. These problems are manifested as either a physical lack of attendance and/or inappropriate, anti-social or even violent behaviour. This is likely at the root of the case story about Cadi, introduced previously (see chapter 5), who is co-parenting a boy aged seven. Following his multiple school exclusions, she came back to the school Head of Ysgol Trem y Mynydd to request a reconsideration. She wanted her son, Rhys, to be on a phased return, and suggested some arrangements put in place with Wild Elements staff to provide him with outdoor learning experiences. This was a local solution to address behaviour problems, which is the inspiration for the work discussed in this chapter. Having gained an educational record from being excluded with the attendant risk of being identified as challenging, the school Head brokered arrangements for Rhys with the local authority, which was acceptable to his parents. Teaching staff, along with the school's family support officer and other multi-agency workers, needed to negotiate what would be involved in taking him back. This is one of the strongest arguments to explore innovative pedagogies with teaching staff assigned to work with these children.

This local solution to working with children on the edge of exclusion or who have already been excluded from school is to help them manage their emotional and behavioural responses to challenging situations, such as being confined in a classroom. It is crucial to engage with parents like Cadi, who was willing to consider learning outside the traditional classroom setting. Outdoor learning is an innovative pedagogical approach, especially given its focus on teaching social skills to build social capital alongside material from the *Curriculum for Wales*. Social capital can be thought of as the ability to bond within a social group for effective support, and bridge between different social groups, such as those encountered at school.[3] To this end my colleague Claudia Howard from Wild Elements has joined me in putting together a locally responsive programme to engaging children in STEM subjects: science, technology, engineering and maths education. We also co-designed our allied Not-NEET project proposal to engage those young people who either are, or are at risk of becoming, not in education, employment or training (NEET).

The intention of this chapter is to show what it means to be more responsive to children and young people's unmet needs through an educative outdoor learning programme that builds their social capital. We explore the meaning of social capital and why it is an important consideration in any child's education, even more so in the challenging environment of Trem y Mynydd where the causes and effects of child poverty collide with educational policy pressures in the school-community. There is also an argument that whilst the practical unmet needs in the schooling of a small group of children and young people are being met by alternative provision in an outdoor learning intervention provided by Wild Elements, there is also the capacity to have a more fundamental impact. Wild Elements is equipped to provide larger-scale, school-community wide outdoor learning programmes but this would require funding support, say from the facilitation fund to be managed by the Trem y Mynydd Cooperative with a board to be comprised of local residents and frontline workers, and governed in line with cooperative models.[4] This would guarantee a stronger connection between the children, resident families and those teenagers who are already NEETs or at risk of being so, which ties into the work of teaching staff and multi-agency officers working together supporting this school-community.

Outdoor learning: pedagogy, practice, partnership and potential

It is timely to set out our respective roles and what they mean in the context of the work with Ysgol Trem y Mynydd. As an academic in Bangor University my work is in initial teacher education, specifically in the field of outdoor learning. As an academic partner I provide practical advice and guidance on learning design, whilst not being directly involved in delivering programmes to children. This partnership allows me to bring academic experience and expertise to both influence programme design, but this mutually beneficial process because the outdoor learning programmes rolled out in school-communities can be shared and incorporated into the initial teacher education programmes. This is in keeping with the findings in a commissioned report I co-authored for Welsh Government that concluded that the health and well-being benefits of outdoor learning are such that greater resources need to be directed to support its development, and that in turn this should be reflected in initial teacher education.[5] One way these recommendations can be met at a local level and replicated more widely is illustrated in the partnership between the school, Wild Elements and the university described in this chapter.

In working for Wild Elements, Howard already co-ordinates and delivers programmes of outdoor learning to groups at Ysgol Trem y Mynydd. As a not-for-profit social enterprise organisation, Wild Elements has grown from small beginnings to offer a range of school- and community-focused projects and services, adhering to Wild Elements' ethic. I share this approach of complementing – not competing – and fostering partnership, working in line with the forest school ethos of self-driven learning, personal decision-making, empowerment, creativity and imagination. These values underpin all our shared endeavours. Ultimately, its mission involves building more resilient and informed communities with increased social value through their work in outdoor learning. The work of Wild Elements includes small group or individual intervention projects to re-engage children and young people who have found themselves outside formal education; programmes to foster a stronger engagement with learning of STEM subjects and connect with nature; social enterprise work in the hospitality industry at a local level; and supporting members of the community to green their more urban surrounding, including aspects of self-sufficiency and increasing home-grown vegetable and fruit production for local people (see Silvester and Joslin's chapter 3).

There has long been a partnership between Wild Elements staff and Bangor University, which began as a result of Welsh Government funding awarded to support outdoor learning in 2015. Some of the staff at Wild Elements are alumni of programmes at Bangor University which, given shared values, was instrumental to our Trem y Mynydd partnership. As the Bangor PLUS project developed and gathered momentum, our partnership was renewed as each of us gained greater awareness of the work of the other. Howard shared the established work of Wild Elements with Ysgol Trem y Mynydd, which brought into focus the rationale for delivering education outdoors. This showed that an alternative pedagogy appeared to engage some of those children facing challenges at school, and motivated the wider school population in their enthusiasm for STEM subject learning. At the same time, staff from Wild Elements were working with some of the children excluded from school, through Mynydd Ni, and feedback from parents and the school Head in both contexts – through questionnaires and conversations – was very positive. It was a logical next step to consider evaluating the effectiveness of the programmes to gain more reliable evidence of the transferability of an outdoor learning programme from in-school learning to out-of-school learning.

We found that the experiential nature of outdoor learning allowed children to construct knowledge and skills at their own pace, develop social skills and engaged those who found classroom-based sessions challenging. Importantly, we found that it was seen by school staff and the children not so much as enrichment but as entitlement. There is a difference between a short-term extracurricular programme that is only available for the few and an entitlement for every child in Wales to have the opportunity to experience outdoor learning, which sits well with children's right to education.[6] It was not a break from learning, or a specialist approach to be used for those with additional learning needs, challenging behaviour or as a reward; instead, it was seen as an effective educational tool that should be a part of every child's school experience. Outdoor learning was also seen to be aligned with the four purposes of the *Curriculum for Wales* 2022.[7] Howard and I concluded that collaboration between Wild Elements, academic partners and schools can ensure that a wide range of children gain the opportunity to learn outdoors. Wales is well placed to more widely adopt this approach with Natural Resources Wales and the Outdoor Learning Network groups which work to support school staff in developing their own pedagogy, as opposed to a financially demanding short-term outdoor education enrichment residential which is a more traditional approach to outdoor learning.

These evaluation findings, verified in a review of literature, informed our conviction that outdoor learning should be an entitlement that has a particular benefit to those children who have experienced school exclusion.[8] And whilst its benefits as a pedagogy are often conflated with *what* is taught (and hence the outcomes achieved), it is in understanding a pedagogical approach that social capital gains can be best explained. Here we draw on another study that outlined a pedagogical approach to learning outside, and in doing so set out some 'design principles'.[9] These include the experiential nature of learning outdoors, the element of managed risk and the personal and social learning focus of the learning activities. In other words, being outside whatever the weather, experiencing what it is that is being learned, getting wet when solving a leaky pipe challenge, for instance, and focusing on how the problem is solved, and not on the actual outcome. There may be some physical risk involved too as the task and outdoor environment are less controllable than a classroom.

Developing social capital: building trust within and beyond the community

Before proceeding, we should explain a little more what we mean by the phrase 'social capital'. There are two ways this can be understood, and we draw on other studies by colleagues who explored building social capital through outdoor education.[10] It is important to acknowledge that the concept of capital is more than, or distinct to, actual physical money.[11] The prefix 'social' adds a specific meaning, such as having the social skills to develop relationships within a peer group for support, and also to develop relationships outside that peer group to be able to form new relationships in different contexts; for instance, at school, with family, at work. These relationships require the ability to communicate thoughts and feelings and listen to others and process their reactions and respond, building appropriate trust. This helps us to think about those difficult-to-quantify outcomes that can be achieved through outdoor learning to help children who have experienced school exclusion.

These sorts of social skills are not easily measured by the tests rolled out in schools, where teachers are under policy pressures to demonstrate cognitive development such as literacy and numeracy skills, so the social learning that takes place in school is significantly undervalued. For the teaching staff and the children who are challenging them, teaching and learning about social skills is incredibly important. Of course, this already happens in schools in all sorts of ways, but some children do not pick up on these messages.[12] They likely need many more learning experiences, such as how to relate to others, appreciating how one's own actions and reactions influence other relationships, and opportunities to develop appropriate trust. This is precisely what we do in outdoor learning settings, but a person with less social capital will find levels of trust difficult to develop and judge appropriateness.

The terms bonding and bridging have been used to describe the two aspects of social capital that children who grow up in poverty found challenging. The idea of bonding is a life skill that allows children and teenagers to form trust within their peer group and thus develop the support networks to help them cope with the challenges of everyday life. This also allows them to develop a degree of resilience in challenging situations, like being confined in a classroom. Not having this type of trust results in difficulties in dealing with situations like teachers' reprimands for inappropriate behaviour, and results in feeling a lack of support when small challenges combine. This can find expression in acting out, which shows a lower emotional resilience, and which could lead to mental and emotional health problems. The idea of bridging and the trust developed in this context allows children and teenagers to believe that others outside their immediate social circle can be trusted, like a teacher or support worker, who are there for the young person's benefit. This allows them to function better in places like the classroom and carries over into other social spaces. A lack of this type of trust may hinder a young person from getting on in life.

A cautious approach to developing social capital is necessary. We tend to use the word 'appropriate' as a prefix to trust, and in both bridging and bonding, there needs to be an added aspect of judging whether either form of trust is appropriate, beneficial or perhaps even morally acceptable. For example, inappropriate bonding can lead to gang culture, anti-social behaviour towards the wider school-community or some forms of criminality, if there are any physical assaults or damage to property. Inappropriate bridging can be seen, for example, when adults come into the lives of children and young people offering material rewards for seemingly harmless behaviours. This can be in building up to child sexual assault or in county-lines operations and the movement of illegal drugs, which was the focus of one of the resident artist's video production projects on the Trem y Mynydd housing estate, funded by North Wales Police. According to Stoddart (2004), outdoor learning is effective when working with youth-at-risk at countering this issue in bridging and building appropriate trust beyond a peer group.

Outdoor learning is a good way to develop some deep knowledge and critical understanding of social skills that will surely help the children of Ysgol Trem y Mynydd when facing taxing social challenges (see Maclean and Daw's chapter 7). If they have low social capital, they will likely find themselves in difficult relationships with other children, teaching staff and other multi-agency workers, which can lead to a disengagement with schooling per se or even formal exclusion from school. This can have an impact on their quality of life, their prospects and physical and mental health and well-being. Outdoor learning has the potential to increase social capital so in speaking as an academic partner supporting outdoor learning programmes, or as a social-justice-minded not-for-profit organisation working in direct delivery with children, or training staff in outdoor learning pedagogy, we advocate for a wider scale adoption of outdoor learning as an entitlement, beyond enrichment for the select few.

An alternative to develop the affective

Our co-designed local solution is to position outdoor learning as a viable alternative to classroom-based teaching. It is important to re-state how this might deter children's disengagement and alienation and re-settle them in schools. The most obvious form of disengagement is manifested as non-attendance, sporadic or irregular attendance, or challenging behaviour when in attendance. However, many children who do not react overtly in disengagement still face challenges in taking a full part in school life and learning. The *Curriculum for Wales*[13] makes explicit the social aspect of learning where children should develop skills to speak and listen with each other, to value other views and opinions, and to make and nurture friendships. These skills are acknowledged as important yet have a somewhat slippery nature in that they cannot be measured in a conventional sense – using tests, forms or grades. Indications of disengagement can be seen in the cognitive behaviour of children (i.e. how they relate to learning activities), but signs of alienation can be observed earlier in the social behaviours of children (how they relate to their peers and staff).

This can all come to influence children's cognitive and psychomotor outcomes; for example, letter formation, reading skills or factual recall. It may be that this is a direct result of the poverty experienced by those children, for instance, a lack of books to read as books are expensive, or less parental engagement from parents/carers who are working more than one job to pay for food and meet rising energy costs. Or it could be a result of simply finding the structured world of a primary school challenging. Whilst Wild Elements has been effective in working with some of the most disengaged and alienated young people, we advocate a more sustainable and inclusive outdoor learning experience. There needs to be a move towards providing an equitable development of social capital for every child. This means more outdoor learning opportunities, but not as a subject to be taught with content to cover, even within personal and social learning. Outdoor learning is such an effective pedagogy that all children should be entitled to experience it as part of their day-to-day education, rather than it being for only those who are seen to have additional needs, who need re-engaging in schooling or who can financially afford a perceived specialist approach.

Returning to the example of Cadi, who pointed out that there is some reluctance about schooling for Rhys, not least because he clearly does not warm to any school, although he has responded well to working with her partner Aled and staff from Wild Elements. He enjoyed going on a woodland walk with one of the community development workers, a colleague seconded from Wild Elements, an academic partner and accompanied by his parents and he engaged in conversations about his schooling options. He responded well to a fruit-picking activity, which framed learning about where food comes from, what could be eaten safely and what could be saved for cooking. Cadi wanted people to know that, although seemingly troubled, which led to his exclusion from school, Rhys is a good boy. The outdoor learning activity on the walk connected with him and taught him about food in the wild, and how to listen to someone explaining a task that would benefit the group. This illustrates a transferable social skill relating to others – earlier described as bridging – appreciating how one's own actions and reactions influence the ways others relate to us. This also provided an opportunity to develop appropriate trust with someone outside the peer group.

These tangible outdoor learning activities deliver authentic learning experiences with explicit outcomes and consequences. For example, lighting a fire and boiling water for a cup of hot chocolate is learning about how fires use fuel, oxygen and heat, and how a fire with lots of fuel but no oxygen is less effective at boiling water than a fire with less fuel but more air flow. At the same time, the cooperation required to carry out tasks like this in planning, designing and then building the fire prior to lighting it simultaneously develops the social capital that will allow the transfer of these skills to different contexts that may be less tangible. This may be in common classroom tasks such as creating short verses and putting them to music, in simply sharing classroom equipment or in relating to their teacher when they are asked to do something. An understanding of an effective way to work with someone whether they are a peer or teacher and the results of working together are beneficial, can be transferred from an outdoor learning scenario to the classroom.

Wild Elements has been occupied with a sustainable local approach to developing social capital through outdoor learning, working with Ysgol Trem y Mynydd to deliver STEM learning sessions, utilising an outdoor learning approach to teaching and learning. This work, allied to our Not-NEET project, 'Rooting for the future: Wild Elements outdoor learning' (appendix 7), provides potential career paths for those who want to deliver outdoor learning sessions themselves. They can gain experience and qualifications in leading and teaching sessions in a variety of ways: either through the outdoor learning programme at Ysgol Trem y Mynydd, or through the outdoor learning after-school club which allows children to gain their John Muir Award.[14] The school-based outdoor learning sessions have been piloted to evaluate their effectiveness in engaging children. A previous Wild Elements programme at Ysgol Trem y Mynydd developed a forest school site that is appropriate and accessible for the children and which is being further utilised. The school-based sessions and after-school club provided opportunities for teenagers to give back to the community, through mentoring or leading sessions, recognised for their Welsh Baccalaureate community challenge as part of the 14–16 curriculum offer.[15]

An entitlement to develop social capital

The small-scale nature of the development work, as in the fruit picking with Rhys, although pertinent to working with a few of the most troubled youngsters, has provided useful anecdotal evidence of why, in the children's eyes, outdoor learning is more effective than a classroom-based approach to learning. This in turn demonstrates the challenges children with less social capital find in mainstream primary school. We have described these problems as difficulties in bonding and bridging and set out the need for social capital to develop relationships within and without a direct peer group. Children find the outdoors more engaging than classroom-based learning because it offers authentic individual experiences which they can see, feel, touch and smell, and can develop how they deal with other individuals. They enjoy being active in their learning, both physically and mentally, and find the direct consequences governed by circumstance, as opposed to an adult in authority, a more realistic extrinsic motivation. There is a perception imposed by the nature of four walls that proves more than just a powerful metaphor that an enclosed body can also be an enclosed mind.

The range of outdoor learning providers in Wales is diverse, and this in turn contributes much to the transferability of a programme with similar aims to the Wild Elements work. Many schools across Wales engage with providers of outdoor learning, but it is uncommon to do this on a medium-/long-term basis. Intervention projects are extremely valuable, but often only work with low numbers and are frequently seen as only suitable for small groups or those who have behavioural or other problems, and therefore fall under the heading of enrichment. We have argued that social capital growth is so important for children and young people that outdoor learning needs to move beyond enrichment for those that can afford it. It should be understood as something so fundamental to effective education that it becomes an entitlement for every child in Wales. Our Not-NEET project outlines how outdoor learning work in school and in an after-school club provides opportunities for teenagers to be trained in leadership and teaching roles. We have given indicative costs of a feasibility study and how this type of work could be replicated in other *Children First* areas that seek innovative approaches to engage or re-engage children with schooling or to support those who have been excluded and are in need of alternatives.

The focus of this chapter has been building an argument for our co-designed local solution to disengagement from schooling and alienation form education. We posit outdoor learning as a workable approach to teaching and social learning that can deliver cognitive and social capital gains for children and young people in Wales and beyond. In an education system that struggles to articulate the value of social learning despite a tacit acknowledgement, we have presented an alternative to classroom-based pedagogy with evidence as to its impact. We have illustrated children's positive engagement through programmes of outdoor learning-based activities where they can develop social capital. This is crucially important to the education of all children and young people in Wales. The Wild Elements programmes are an example of working with those who have less social capital and fewer opportunities to build it because of the challenging situation they find themselves in. Outdoor learning as a pedagogy sits well with a number of curriculum projects and can deliver a positive impact on health and well-being. The task here remains to articulate the logistics of rolling out our Not-NEET project in the school community of Ysgol Trem y Mynydd that can be expanded.

Our pilot programme/feasibility study for social capital development work ran over a 30-week period delivering 30 days of outdoor learning-based STEM activities, facilitated by Wild Elements and supported by school staff. It was aimed at the older primary schoolchildren (ages 8–11) and allowed two classes of children per day of activity. The focus was the regular *Curriculum for Wales*, and the sessions used outdoor learning to provide authentic learning experiences. These were designed to build social capital and engage the children as they learned the required skills and knowledge in science, technology, engineering and maths. School-staff evaluations in questionnaire form demonstrated a positive effect on the children and in particular their engagement with the STEM material and their social interactions. Feedback from the Wild Elements staff delivering the sessions highlighted how much the children enjoyed the different approach to their usual classroom sessions. The outdoor learning after-school club provided opportunities for the teenagers to train in the leadership of outdoor learning sessions and helped children build social capital outside curriculum time and engaged with nature.

We have come full circle from what was stated at the start of this chapter, about what social capital is, why it is important and how outdoor learning can be used to develop it. Rhys began to develop his bridging social capital in the short outdoor learning activity of fruit picking, and the feedback from school staff on the pilot programme also illustrated how the children engaged with outdoor learning as an alternative approach to teaching and learning curriculum subjects, developing their bonding social capital at the same time. Our Not-NEET project, 'Rooting for the future: Wild Elements outdoor learning', provides opportunities for teenagers to gain skills, recognition and potentially a career in outdoor learning, and children and young people to develop their social capital as they connect with nature. A programme of outdoor learning offers an alternative model to traditional intervention-type provision, because it focuses on the equitable use of outdoor learning for more children, for its social capital and cognitive value, rather than being exclusive to those who can afford it.

Notes

1   There are other opportunities outside the scope of this chapter to facilitate professional learning development work with school staff, mentoring and supporting them to become research active; and to gain recognition and/or qualifications.

2   Wild Elements is a not-for-profit community interest company providing outdoor learning programmes, training, environmental projects, and nature connection experiences for schools, communities, public bodies, and youth organisations across North Wales.

3   The work of Putnam (2000) *Bowling alone* is considered one of the most influential books on social capital and it concluded that a decline in social capital is reflected in increased political and civic disengagement, fewer informal social ties, and lower tolerance and trust.

4   The facilitation fund was so named by one of the residents, Owen Maclean (see chapter 7), and the co-operative was suggested by Pete Whitby, another resident contributing a local solution (see chapter 5), while Gwen Thirsk provided advice on the legalities: see *www.cwmpas.coop* (accessed 1 December 2021).

5   The report authored by French et al. (2021) can be accessed here: *https://hwb. gov.wales/professional-development/the-national-strategy-for-educational-research -and-enquiry-nsere/research-studies-on-the-impact-of-the-covid-19-pandemic-on -the-welsh-education-system/research-study-6/* (accessed 1 December 2021).

6   In July 2022 an opportuntity to begin the process that would lead to presenting a private member's bill to the Senedd, The Outdoor Education (Wales) Bill. It sought to provide an outdoor education residential experience for every child in Wales and the requisite funding needed to provide this for every child.

7   The *Curriculum for Wales* 2022 is based on four purposes and should produce ambitious, capable learners, ready to learn throughout their lives; enterprising, creative contributors, ready to play a full part in life and work; ethical, informed citizens of Wales and the world; healthy, confident individuals, ready to lead fulfilling lives as valued members of society. Outdoor learning connects directly with these by adopting an enquiring nature, teaching problem-solving in an ethical manner (and in relation to the natural environment) and developing physical and mental health and well-being in connecting with nature.

8   Outdoor learning has been demonstrated as an effective pedagogy in improving engagement (for example, in Wales: French et al., 2022; in Scotland: Mannion, Mattu and Wilson, 2015; and Christie, Higgins and McLaughlin, 2015; in Denmark: Mygind, 2007, 2009).

9   Williams and Wainwright (2015, 2019) proposed and justified a specific pedagogical model for outdoor and adventurous activities which has transferable components to a broader outdoor learning approach.

10   Beames and Atencio (2008) – this study focused on how outdoor learning can develop social capital and drew on Putnam's (2000) work and the work of Stoddart (2004), working with youth at risk in Cumbria specifically using an outdoor learning programme in this context.

11   This follows the work of French sociologist Pierre Bourdieu.

12   For an extended discussion, see Lingard (2013).

13   Personal and social development is distributed throughout the Areas of Learning and Experience within some of the progression steps; however it is consistently and explicitly referred to in the Health and Well-being Area of Learning and Experience statements of What Matters.

14   One aim could be achieving the John Muir Award, a free award scheme that has different levels of achievement and values connecting with nature.

15   The Welsh Baccalaureate is a qualification all students aged 14–16 in Wales have to follow and compliments other school work, comprising qualifications in literacy and numeracy, supporting qualifications such as GCSEs or Agored Cymru vocational qualifications and a specific skills certificate which itself requires an individual project; an enterprise and employability challenge; a global citizenship challenge; a community challenge.

PUBLIC WORKS, ROADS AND TRANSPORT CONGRESS (1937).

WEDNESDAY, 17th NOVEMBER, at 3.0 p.m.

Practical Aspects of Housing Design

BY

B. PRICE DAVIES,

F.S.I., F.R.I.B.A., F.R.San.I., M.Inst.M & Cty.E., M.T.P.I.

City Engineer, Bangor, N. Wales.

(NOTE.—This Paper was submitted for the Open Competition arranged by the Congress Council and was awarded the First Prize of a Gold Medal and One Hundred Guineas).

Notes which are added since the submission of the paper in December, 1936, are shown in italics.

I.

INTRODUCTORY.

The Congress year of 1937 is of historical importance. It is the Centenary of Queen Victoria's ascension to the throne of our beloved country and it is the Coronation Year of her great-grandson, King George the Sixth. A hundred years lies between ; on the one hand we are inclined to look backward a hundred years while on the other hand we are inclined to look forward. We will do both in sequence.

Shall we venture to state that the past hundred years is a wonderful period of progress in public administration, and that in consonance with the title of this paper, we will search the situation of a century ago in connection with housing.

9

COLLABORATIVE SCHOOL IMPROVEMENT: DEVELOPING RESEARCH-INFORMED SUPPORT FOR SOCIAL JUSTICE

Richard Watkins (GwE, gwasanaeth gwella ysgolion rhanbarthol Gogledd Cymru)

Introduction

I am writing this chapter in my capacity as the research and evaluation lead for GwE, North Wales regional school improvement service (GwE, gwasanaeth gwella ysgolion rhanbarthol Gogledd Cymru). I also write in my capacity as Honorary Senior Research Fellow, Bangor University, to focus on our Bangor PLUS team's school-community development work in relation to the regional school improvement strategy. As a school improvement officer, my concern is with the systematic use of evidence-informed approaches in North Wales to support schools and also help reduce inequalities in educational outcomes, and I am guided by Thomson, Lingard and Wrigley's (2012) unifying trope, that is, *ideas for practice* at systemic, policy, school and pedagogic levels.

Over recent years, education policy in Wales has been used proactively to address the impact of socio-economic inequalities and improve outcomes for disadvantaged learners. During this period both local authority school improvement services and initial teacher education (ITE) providers in Wales have undergone significant reform to improve the quality of their provision. In North Wales a collaborative model has emerged from these reforms, where the regional consortium works closely with both ITE and research staff in its partner higher education institutions (HEI) to better coordinate the training of associate teachers, and also to support schools to use effective interventions and strategies to support struggling learners and improve teachers' professional enquiry skills.

This is how I came to work with the Bangor PLUS team, and I consider myself an academic partner even though I work from a distance in GwE. It is a testament to our partnership that I have been asked for my response and advice on how the Bangor PLUS project and its seven co-designed local solutions and Not-NEET proposals described here stand with GwE. My initial thoughts are such that the team has developed a model way of working and its output can be used to support collaborative school improvement initiatives. This is in keeping with GwE's work with Welsh Government, Bangor University and other HEI partners to support schools to mitigate the impact of disadvantage through the use of more evidence-informed teaching strategies.

There are caveats of course. First, we all need to consider the use of additional, targeted deprivation funding for schools. Though it is a promising approach (Gorard, Siddiqui and See, 2019), there is still a challenge to support schools to use this funding effectively by providing access to more evidence-informed approaches. From 2014 onwards, GwE and Bangor University recognised the potential for a more structured collaborative framework to enable schools to access information and training to enable them to make more informed choices about how best to deploy supplementary catch-up provision more generally (Tyler et al., 2019).

This strategic working has enabled larger projects to be constructed that involved multiple schools working together on projects that not only provided schools with high quality training, but also generated important implementation research findings for the wider education system. The projects spanned important aspects of school provision, such as the creation of positive school culture and improving learner behaviour, and improving basic literacy and numeracy skills for struggling learners. Many projects involved teachers working with researchers responding to national policy initiatives or from requests from schools and/or clusters of schools to evaluate provision.

Second, since 2011 there have been coordinated efforts by governments across the UK to use additional, targeted funding for schools to improve educational outcomes for disadvantaged pupils (Welsh Government, 2015). In 2012 Wales introduced the Pupil Deprivation

Grant as a method of providing additional funding to schools to improve outcomes for pupils eligible for free school meals (eFSM). There have been few reliable evaluations of the impact of targeted deprivation funding in the UK, although a recent study by Gorard, Siddiqui and See (2021) indicated that the attainment of disadvantaged learners has improved in more disadvantaged areas of England since the introduction of Pupil Premium funding.

Early evaluations of the impact of the funding of the Pupil Deprivation Grant in Wales have proved inconclusive, with concerns raised about the capacity – and willingness – of schools to access and apply external research evidence for more promising approaches (Welsh Government, 2017b). Research shows that schools face many challenges in engaging with more evidence-informed approaches, with little evidence currently available to suggest how educators might use evidence to improve learner outcomes (Gorard, See and Siddiqui, 2020).

Third, since 2014 there has been a clear divergence in the style and tone of education policy-making in Wales compared to England. This divide is characterised by Welsh Government's ongoing desire to cultivate a more empowered teaching workforce fostered within a more collaborative, self-improving education system compared to the more 'anaemic, top-down, test-driven, reductive accountability approaches that now pervade many schooling systems across the globe' (Thomson, Lingard and Wrigley, 2012: 3). Two key policies set the framework for this 'profession-controlled … richer, more intelligent forms of educational accountability' in Wales: *Qualified for Life* and *Education in Wales: Our National Mission* (Welsh Government, 2014, 2017a).

Together, these landmark policy documents set Wales on course to improve both the quality and training available to teaching staff, and also the quality and relevance of the school curriculum for pupils aged 3 to 16 years through the realisation of the new school curriculum, *Curriculum for Wales* (Donaldson, 2015). By utilising enhanced levels of teacher agency and professional trust delegated to schools by Welsh Government, school leaders and teachers are now empowered to provide more relevant and engaging learning experiences sensitive to local contexts. This increased autonomy also extends to schools' ability to utilise supplementary funding to help disadvantaged learners catch up, and a number of regional evidence-into-action projects have been set up in North Wales to provide schools with practical support and guidance for promising teaching approaches.

Against this policy backdrop, the Bangor PLUS team have identified a number of innovative ideas to help disadvantaged communities to mitigate the impact of child poverty on schooling, but they are likely to be seen as alternative ideas, albeit ones that show some promise. It is important to point out that the team's work is research-informed and is considered an 'ethnography that makes a difference' and draws on the funds of knowledge approach.[1] Accordingly, the work of the Trem y Mynydd school-community, to use its pseudonym, in co-designing local solutions span important goals of the Well-being of Future Generations (Wales) Act 2015: such as improved well-being, economic prosperity, the local environment and, importantly, the impact of schooling on children's life chances. Their allied Not-NEET projects, as the term implies, have direct implications for education and schooling.

For example, the proposed 'Rooting for the future: Wild Elements outdoor learning', 'Acting on the future: student expression in the performing arts', and 'Rigging the future: Welsh slate boats and World Heritage', provide teachers in Ysgol Trem y Mynydd with excellent opportunities. Among these are the chances to develop co-designed local curriculum solutions in line with the ethos and requirements of *Curriculum for Wales*, and through the numerous opportunities these Not-NEET projects provide, they have the potential to foster the four purposes and six Areas of Learning and Experiences that frame the school curriculum in Wales. This would enable teachers to use their ability to construct an engaging and relevant curriculum sensitive to the needs of the community by drawing on the rich history of Penrhyn Port and Penrhyn Quarry.

This adds something positive to Wales's progressive schools' policy framework that has also encouraged the generation of more practice-based research evidence. In particular, those researchers working in The Collaborative Institute for Education Research, Evidence and Impact (CIEREI) at Bangor University have identified the need to review and improve the use of additional deprivation funding in schools, and to ensure that this is utilised on more promising approaches. We also argue that some of the savings from this disinvestment might be reinvested into some of the co-designed solutions specific to this school-community, as they are described in this book.

In this chapter, I provide an overview of my role with GwE, Welsh Government and HEI partners, including CIEREI and Bangor University, and I describe our work over recent years to improve school uptake and the implementation of more evidence-based strategies and programmes to help struggling pupils catch up. I then describe how some of the key education policies have set Wales on a distinctive path towards the creation of a more collaborative, research-informed education system. I begin with my response to the Bangor PLUS team from my perspective as a critical friend on their work as a model way of working. These analyses lead to my advice in two parts: on the utility of the team's seven co-designed local solutions and Not-NEET projects, which is a way of emphasising context-specific school-improvement to help inform 'school-community development'; and on the ways these closely align with the principles of recent Welsh education policy, and how GwE's collaborative research outputs could help schools use deprivation funding to these ends.

School improvement and the culture of collaboration

The main focus of our collaborative research and evaluation work in North Wales over recent years has been the promotion of evidence-based approaches to improve school provision. This is a relatively new and exciting initiative in education in Wales, and requires a more collaborative approach to be taken by schools, school improvement professionals and higher education researchers to provide schools with access to a greater range of evidence-based ideas and strategies. The policy context has enabled the development of more collaborative working in Wales, and particularly between GwE school improvement professionals and Bangor University researchers through the creation of CIEREI (Watkins et al., 2018). My background in the natural sciences and experience working in industry continues to guide my philosophy for the importance of placing evidence at the heart of decision-making, and we now have a receptive education policy backdrop in Wales to make this a reality.

Welsh Government's response to the disappointing results in the Programme for International Assessment (PISA) published in 2010 resulted in a fundamental change in the nature and style of school improvement services in Wales. From the previous model of often disparate and poorly coordinated services provided by each of the twenty-two local authorities, Welsh Government led the formation of four regional consortia in 2012 tasked with providing a more coordinated and effective approach to school improvement (Welsh Government, 2012). These new regional consortia had responsibility for the provision of all key aspects of school improvement services, including teaching, leadership and performance accountability and, importantly, how schools utilised their Pupil Deprivation Grant funding to help disadvantaged learners catch up (Welsh Government, 2015).

Initially, the consortia focused on the implementation of a national school categorisation (or banding) system alongside a new national testing framework to monitor pupil outcomes. Together, these initiatives formed a core of Welsh Government's response to a new PISA-driven improvement and accountability culture in Welsh education (Welsh Government, 2016). The OECD (2014) improving schools report recommended the adoption of a more collaborative approach to school improvement and accountability in Wales that was aligned more closely with system-wide capacity to deliver the necessary improvement goals. This OECD review led to the landmark Welsh Government *Qualified for Life* report, which outlined a five-year improvement plan for Wales and paved the way for a fundamental overhaul of the curriculum in Welsh schools through the Donaldson *Successful Futures* (2015) report.

A central role of the work of GwE's supporting improvement advisers is to guide and signpost schools on their progress towards their implementation of *Curriculum for Wales* alongside other key national policy initiatives, including the need to foster an increasing sense of professional curiosity and autonomy. Much of the focus of GwE's leadership, teaching and curriculum provision has been to provide teachers with the necessary knowledge to ensure that they have a sound understanding of not only the key concepts and ideas in teaching but, importantly, a greater understanding of when and why those strategies should be used to maximise learner outcomes. Schools in Wales now retain a considerable degree of autonomy on how they utilise the two main supplementary grants provided to schools: the Education Improvement Grant and the Professional Learning Grant.

Schools such as Ysgol Trem y Mynydd are encouraged to audit staff skills and align training provision according to need. In addition, Ysgol Trem y Mynydd has been working with partner schools in its cluster to develop a common understanding of curriculum reform, professional learning and also the additional learning needs reforms in Wales.

School leaders and teachers have also worked with GwE and schools in their cluster and beyond to access advice and support to create more evidence-informed education systems to improve outcomes for learners and improve value for money.

The reform agenda set out in *Qualified for Life* and the vision for the new *Curriculum for Wales* set out by Professor Graham Donaldson in the *Successful Futures* report required an overhaul in the nature and quality of initial teacher education (ITE) in Wales. The Welsh Government-commissioned report by Professor John Furlong (2015) highlighted the need to radically overhaul both the structure and quality of ITE provision in Wales to better prepare university staff and trainee teachers for 'situated learning', where trainee teachers are exposed to theoretical, practical and empirical professional knowledge as a product of close partnership working between universities, schools and regional consortia.

Furlong's recommendations have led to a more robust accreditation and monitoring process of ITE programmes against Welsh Government criteria and ensured that more specific consideration of how the programmes will raise the quality of provision and attract the best quality candidates into teaching. They have also led to an increase in the number of partner schools that now share responsibility for the collaborative provision for the new ITE programmes: for example, the CaBan partnership in North Wales includes Bangor University, Chester University, GwE and schools across the region. Universities and schools have also invested heavily in this reformed ITE provision that now supports student teachers to make sense of teaching knowledge and experiences using a range of academic reflection and school-based practicum. ITE provision in Wales is now fundamentally different from some of the favoured ITE models in England that are mainly based on direct school experience alone.

All these important policy changes in the nature of the school curriculum, ITE provision, professional learning and the promotion of evidence-into-action ideas has characterised a uniquely Welsh education policy. Welsh Government has moved systematically to create a new school improvement framework that balances challenge and support whilst systematically fostering greater trust in teachers' professional judgements. Enhancing teacher agency is at the heart of recent reforms and has been marked by the careful transfer of intellectual responsibilities to schools. Or, as Priestley (2015) describes, teacher agency is, 'an emergent phenomenon, something that happens through an always unique interplay of individual capacity and the social and material conditions by means of which people act'.

In Wales, the careful reform of school improvement services into more coordinated regional consortia provided the foundation to coordinate professional learning and communicate new ideas and approaches to large numbers of schools. One of the benefits of this newly emerging culture of collaboration was the ability to harness and transfer knowledge from research findings to help schools identify and use more promising teaching approaches. It followed that GwE and Bangor University researchers came to work together to provide a variety of evidence-into-action projects to help schools provide effective, supplementary support for struggling learners.

This enables me to gain some perspective on the Bangor PLUS team's work, but first, it is helpful to explore the history of education reform in Wales since devolution in 1999 as it has attempted to address inequalities in educational outcomes through a series of landmark policies. It is also helpful to consider the impact of these policies on teachers, school leaders and key stakeholders in Wales.

Tackling disadvantage through education reform in Wales

Devolution empowered political leaders in Cardiff to steer Welsh education policy away from the ideas pursued in England; this has given them the opportunity to craft landmark policies such as *The Learning Country* (Cynulliad Cenedlaethol Cymru, 2001), *Qualified for Life, Education in Wales: Our National Mission* and Wales's landmark *Curriculum for Wales* (Welsh Government, 2014, 2017a). Evans (2021) has documented this policy evolution and framed it within three key phases: first, devolution and a licence to innovate (1999–2010); second, PISA and the age of accountability (2010–15); and third, *Curriculum for Wales* and a culture of collaboration (2015–present).

Importantly, the introduction of the Pupil Deprivation Grant in Wales in 2012 (now called the Pupil Development Grant) coincided with the second phase of national policy development, namely a move to a period of increased accountability characterised by the use of more high-stakes performance measures and school comparisons.

During this time, schools in Wales were mainly focused on operating within a compliance culture with a high-stakes inspection system and limited teacher autonomy. With the onset of the third phase of Welsh policy development (the culture of collaboration) from 2015, a new phase of curriculum and professional autonomy began that has since been underpinned by the National Strategy for Educational Research and Enquiry (NSERE) and is continuing to encourage a more evidence-informed approach in all sections of Welsh education policy and planning.[2]

When the OECD published its *Improving schools in Wales* report in 2014, it signalled the start of a policy shift away from the performance-driven, accountability culture that had characterised the preceding years, to a period focused on renewed collaboration and engagement with the teaching profession. This move away from some of the previous neo-liberal initiatives that had characterised education policy in Wales (e.g. National School Categorisation system and National Reading and Numeracy Tests for pupils from 7–14 years) was locked into policy through the publication of Welsh Government's *Qualified for Life* (2014) five-year policy framework (Evans, 2021).

Qualified for Life set out a vision for a more skilled education workforce that would be able to improve outcomes for disadvantaged learners through the realisation of four strategic objectives: to improve the quality of the teaching workforce; the range and relevance of the curriculum; the nature of the qualifications young people achieve; and, education leaders working within a more supportive, self-improving system. These foundational policy initiatives, including the landmark new *Curriculum for Wales*, required schools to work more collaboratively with each other in the goal of improving the quality of teaching and school provision. When aligned with the nascent *Curriculum for Wales*, schools in Wales were now empowered – and expected – to both develop innovative curriculum responses to meet the needs of local stakeholders and also take ownership for the evaluation and monitoring of their provision.

Following the foundations laid down by *Qualified for Life*, in 2017 Welsh Government continued its reforming education policies with the publication of *Education in Wales: Our National Mission* (2017). Central to *Our National Mission* was the continued development of the *Curriculum for Wales* and its associated improvements in both professional learning and also initial teacher education. One of the four enabling objectives of *Our National Mission* was to develop 'Strong and inclusive schools committed to excellence, equity and well-being' to 'expand the Pupil Development Grant so that schools can improve on the life chances of our most deprived younger learners through earlier intervention, which will support the ambition to improve the first thousand days of our most vulnerable children'.

This renewed focus on the provision of the Pupil Development Grant was aligned with additional support and guidance from the regional consortia in Wales to help schools support more vulnerable pupils to catch up through the sharing of knowledge and ideas about what works and why. Although *Our National Mission* was a consolidation of the progressive policy-making of previous years, it also provided a renewed impetus for school improvement officers to engage with academic partners to improve the uptake and use of evidence in schools.

Before coming back to the Bangor PLUS model way of working, we have already seen that collaboration between schools and their stakeholders is closely aligned with Welsh Government education policy initiatives. One of the underlying themes of *Qualified for Life* and reiterated in *Our National Mission* is the desire to develop more local solutions for communities and the schools that serve them in an effort to mitigate some of the barriers and challenges for school leaders (see chapter 2).

It follows that the Bangor PLUS team involving school leaders, Gwynedd Council officers and other agencies working together to devise local solutions is a feature of schools' enactment of the nascent *Curriculum for Wales*. Ysgol Trem y Mynydd is required to engage with its stakeholders and school communities to build a locally relevant and engaging curriculum for its learners that builds on the foundational Areas of Learning and Experience laid out in *Curriculum for Wales*.

I have already noted the Bangor PLUS team's work is research-informed, and so they embed a funds of knowledge approach in their allied Not-NEET projects, which can be extended to include a range of GwE school improvement projects. For example, over recent years Ysgol Trem y Mynydd has been involved in a range of evidence-into-action projects, including the use of a phonics-based reading programme and the introduction of evidence-informed behaviour strategies to help build a positive school climate.

This is only a step away from a serious consideration of the co-designed local solutions identified by the Bangor PLUS team, who are well placed to provide support for the development of a more engaging and relevant school curriculum for Ysgol Trem y Mynydd. This corresponds well with how Welsh Government education policy has evolved to foster a more collaborative, self-improving system through the provision of enhanced professional learning and the more systematic use of research and enquiry findings. One of the main aims of these reforms was to improve both the quality learning experiences through a more locally responsive and relevant curriculum as well as enabling schools to provide effective supplementary provision for learners, especially those from more disadvantaged communities.

The Bangor PLUS project and Wales's education policy

In providing advice to the Bangor PLUS team, I was mindful of the research and evaluation findings generated in North Wales over recent years that have identified the need to support schools to use their deprivation funding more effectively. This might lead to a process of disinvestment in less promising approaches and the opportunity to reinvest in more innovative local solutions.

Foremost was the need to consider ideas and initiatives that would point to meaningful contexts for learning as schools in Wales are tasked with creating a more engaging and relevant curriculum to improve pupil experiences. As Donaldson described in *Successful Futures* (2015: 10):

> A further significant challenge is that disadvantage in its many forms too often has a pernicious effect on the educational achievement and personal well-being of children and young people. It is essential that the curriculum is designed in ways that will engage the interest of all children and young people and enable them to achieve. A curriculum that promotes high expectations for all can help schools to defeat the circumstances that condemn so many to educational underachievement.

This progressive education policy context in Wales now allows schools the chance to fulfil this vision for a new curriculum that engages all learners, and schools such as Ysgol Trem y Mynydd are able to work collaboratively to co-design local solutions and take that next step to co-produce the allied Not-NEET projects. This might sound daunting but the Bangor PLUS team have pre-empted concerns about any likely extra demands on school Heads and teaching staff to engage in school-based curriculum design and to develop resources.

Area-based local curriculum committees have been proposed, who can oversee these tasks, and this is a common proposal across all their projects, as noted in the appendices. It remains to be seen if there is widespread support and funding for their initiatives on Trem y Mynydd but the Bangor PLUS team have aimed to expand to the other four *Children First* needs assessment areas. As I said above, this all shows promise because the local solutions allied to their Not-NEET projects are designed to be cross-curriculum projects, and flag partnerships with specialists including education representatives from Undeb Cenedlaethol Athrawon Cymru (UCAC), NASUWT Cymru, NEU Cymru, ASCL Cymru, Gwynedd Council, GwE and Bangor University and local agencies who are invited to contribute to the design of the learning programmes.

From my perspective in GwE, enabling schools to work across school-communities with key stakeholders will help address some of the impact of disadvantage on education outcomes, but educational solutions alone are unlikely to be sufficient mitigation for entrenched disadvantage. We already know that a combination of educational and economic measures as part of a funds of knowledge approach involving a range of key stakeholders is likely to be a more promising undertaking. Hence one of the central aims of *Curriculum for Wales* is to set learning within four purposes to help students in Wales become: 'ambitious capable learners'; 'enterprising creative contributors'; 'ethical informed citizens'; and 'healthy confident individuals'.

Seen through the lens of *Curriculum for Wales*, the Bangor PLUS team's Not-NEET projects offer children a wide range of valuable experiences in the six Areas of Learning and Experiences within the context of the four core purposes of education. They will help schools meet the challenges that come with using this framework to construct a more detailed, local curriculum for their learners. They will also help children practise some of the four integral skills: planning and organising, creativity and innovation, critical thinking and problem-solving, and personal effectiveness.

The allied Not-NEET project 'Cultivating the estate: establishing community food gardens' draws on children's lived experiences with both Wales's call for feeding hungry children and the cost-of-living crisis concerning food poverty, and it offers them empowering learning experiences in horticulture that point to work in the food industry, starting with the Hive Café.

The 'Powering the estate: a home-grown energy supply' project also relies on children's lived experiences with both Wales's nation-wide energy crisis and the cost-of-living crisis concerning fuel poverty, and it also offers them engaging and relevant learning experiences in STEM subjects with a view to career paths in the energy production and supply industries.

The enhanced 0–2 years education vision in 'Starting out for the future: 0–2 years on-site crèche' links to pre-school and beyond, and provides a vital gateway into formal schooling through collaborative links to Ysgol Trem y Mynydd and, importantly, the ability to identify children and young people who are at risk of poor outcomes through effective, evidence-informed early intervention.[3]

The 'Co-ordinating the future: building the new multi-agency hub' project is a welcome addition to the local plans for the new-build eco-friendly multi-agency site with recreation facilities already lodged in a development application with Gwynedd Council. It guarantees that curriculum learning opportunities are not lost by tagging a required element of paid work experience, education and training in the requisite contracts for demolition and building, landscaping and recreation facilities, among other areas of expertise.

'Acting on the future: student expression in the performing arts' initiative provides direct and relevant curriculum learning opportunities to promote the expressive arts, which is one of the six Areas of Learning and Experience in the *Curriculum for Wales*.

The 'Rooting for the future: Wild Elements outdoor learning' project provides myriad suggestions for teaching and learning with its pedagogical approach to wide-ranging learning opportunities, and it has implications for Ysgol Trem y Mynydd's response to its welfare demands, and makes the important argument about outdoor learning being an entitlement for everyone.

The 'Rigging the future: Welsh slate boats and World Heritage' project develops even more comprehensive learning experiences through maritime heritage conservation that engages local Welsh history and also family histories. It provides children with a deeper understanding of the part played by the Penrhyn slate quarry as one of the largest and most productive slate quarries in the world; and how the wealth created by its owners, the Pennant and Douglas Pennant families, was sustained through the use of slave labour in sugar-growing estates in Jamaica. In undertaking this work, schools will be enacting the very essence of teacher agency and fulfilling the aims of *Curriculum for Wales*.

Taken together, these seven Not-NEET projects provide children with rich and rewarding learning experiences that include one of the five cross-cutting themes described in *Curriculum for Wales*, including learning about local, national and international contexts. There are clearly many other Areas of Learning Experiences that can be explored in ambitious themes such as these, and one of the challenges for teachers and school leaders is to identify and be very clear about the main learning outcomes that they wish to focus on.

In closing this chapter, I am reminded about how a collaborative approach to school improvement in North Wales has enabled the transfer of research knowledge to benefit learners in disadvantaged communities served by schools like Ysgol Trem y Mynydd. Partnership working between schools, GwE and Bangor University enabled the uptake of evidence-informed approaches in schools whilst simultaneously creating important research outputs focused on the implementation of such promising propositions. These CIEREI projects in North Wales have been planned within a systematic evidence-gathering framework to help move teaching from *evidence-informed* to *evidence-based* practice (Owen, Watkins and Hughes, 2022).

The Bangor PLUS team have provided all of us with an excellent example of how collaborative working and using the funds of knowledge approach can operate effectively in the context of school improvement. I would certainly like to see education policymakers work more closely with this team to consider how to support schools to use funding more efficiently on these promising projects, and especially in schools serving more disadvantaged communities. The Bangor PLUS co-designed local solutions sit neatly within Wales's progressive education policies that have enabled knowledge building between universities, school communities and key stakeholders. We can now build on this foundation through the judicious use of deprivation funding on evidence-based approaches that can be an effective tool in the twin task of addressing child poverty, education and social inequalities.

Notes

1   See Mills and Morton (2013), specifically chapter 13; and Zipin, Sellar and Hattam (2012).
2   See *https://www.gov.wales/national-strategy-educational-research-and-enquiry-nsere-vision-document* (accessed 21 April 2023).
3   See *https://www.eif.org.uk/* (accessed 21 April 2023).

This shows Port Penrhyn with sail boats ready for loading dressed slates at the quay built in 1821. These were likely part of a fleet owned by the Penrhyn family and though others had shares in shipping, in 1897 the 2nd Lord Penrhyn purchased a fleet of steamers from the Anglesey Shipping Co.

10

SCHOOL HEADS: ENACTING SCHOOL-COMMUNITY DEVELOPMENT IN RESPONSE TO CHILD POVERTY

Eithne Hughes (Association of School and College Leaders)

Introduction

This chapter is written by a former secondary school headteacher with twenty-seven years' experience at senior leadership and eleven years as head. I am currently the director for the Association of School and College Leaders Cymru, which is part of a UK trade union representing over 22,000 school and college leaders. I was awarded the OBE for services to education in Wales education in 2016 and was given an honorary professorship from Bangor University for my work in developing Initial Teacher Educational programmes. During my career I have worked with a range of policy-makers and those responsible for implementation, and with Welsh Government.

My work both as a practitioner and as a trade union official gives me a unique insight into the significant, stubbornly persistent challenges faced by schools trying desperately to swim up-stream against the effects of child poverty. We talk of equity and equality. We talk of excellence and recovery. We talk of policy and strategy. Unless any of this breaks the shackles of suppressing talent and potential, they are just words.

Having heard about the school-community-based Bangor PLUS project at a presentation given by Visiting Professor Beckett at Bangor University, I am delighted to add to the debate in exploring a variety of possible avenues to support these school-communities. We do need, however, to be clear that there are no quick fixes. The ensuing problems coming from the causes and effects of poverty are knotty and wicked.

Schools are facing a period of reform overload. Essentially the majority of policies relating to schools that can be changed either is in the process of doing so or has recently been shifted. It is not that reform is not important: it needs to happen to improve the lot of young people but the timing, the volume, the rationale and the energy left in an already exhausted workforce needs to be seriously considered.

To name but a few policy directives that require a seismic shift in implementation terms, we have the very positive *Curriculum for Wales*, which demands a complete rethink of curriculum design and assessment; a labyrinthine additional learning needs bill which is worthy but heavily bureaucratic; Initial Teacher Education reforms taught in collaboration between schools and higher education institutions; a tertiary bill; a ten-year Welsh language plan; schools as learning organisations; announcements about all schools being community schools; changes to the organisation of the school year; self-evaluation and accountability; and on it goes.

All of this comes on top of a vital pandemic recovery agenda as school and college leaders try to re-establish learner routines, encourage attendance and re-engagement, and support the most vulnerable who have become more so in our most disadvantaged communities. The pandemic has shone a bone-white light on this unequal and inequitable society. Yet again, in and among this blizzard of reforms, schools are expected to solve these system failures.

For too long, policy on the area of child and community poverty has had little traction since it is conceived at a distance and generally by those who are already advantaged. The intentions are good, however. No nation wants its children to live in poverty; this is exemplified in the universal offer of free school meals for all primary-aged students.

Demands on school Heads

Things on the whole are not working as they should be. Wales has the highest child poverty rate in the UK and the widest attainment gap at GCSE when compared to England.[1]

The work of schools such as Ysgol Trem y Mynydd, to use its pseudonym, is to be commended for actioning a research-informed school-community response to child poverty against the backdrop of the pandemic and the sheer volume of reforms in the education system in Wales. It is time to rebuild a national mission through policy and practice, which gives life and breath to the worthy principles of the Well-being and Future Generations (Wales) Act 2015 and the *Children First* needs (and assets) assessment from 2018.

I would argue that school competition, previous heavy-handed accountability, exams that can appear irrelevant to individuals and a diminution of support services for schools renders leaders and classroom teachers weary and feeling frustrated from trying to solve the effects of poverty on the children they serve – and, indeed, they cannot do this alone. All of this is compounded by a cost-of-living crisis driving families into further poverty.[2]

I have seen first-hand as a former school Head the child who is dark-eyed, hungry and tired. Hungry children cannot learn. Families living in poverty need easily accessible, coherent and effective wraparound support as do the schools who serve those communities.

The Bangor PLUS project is an acknowledgement in action that evidence-based local solutions, allied to so-called Not-NEET projects in this case, leap over the public policies that this Ysgol Trem y Mynydd school-community has apparently found to be of little practical value. And there are many such communities across Wales desperately trying to deal with food and housing poverty in this deepening economic crisis who understand that education may just provide a future for their young people. Further support, however, for these communities that reaches beyond the here and now to upskilling the whole community as learners is also needed. There is much to be done.

Schools are extraordinarily busy dealing with the urgent day-to-day issues from trying to deal with the fallout of the pandemic, a rise in behavioural difficulties, low learner attendance, stretched budgets and a bloated portfolio of reforms. Time, resources and the ability to do much other than react are all in short supply. Schools absolutely cannot do this by themselves.

The logistics of rolling out the Bangor PLUS project into school-communities, if only in those other four areas selected for the 2018 *Children First* needs assessment, will require a robust, fully costed, evidence-informed and persuasive rationale to be presented to policy-makers and those who hold the purse strings. There will be the inevitable issues to be debated around not adding to the complexity of funding mechanisms for schools or indeed schools having to work with yet another middle-tier body in order to serve the most vulnerable.

The inter-relatedness of the services offered by local government, social services, the private sector and the interface with Welsh Government will need to be carefully mapped out. Further to this, any such expansion would need to be based on strong foundations, be sustainable and underpinned by a demonstrable collective will to succeed. It would clearly need project management at local level, tight budgetary controls and evaluated success criteria. Will this alone, solve the complex problems of the causes and effects of poverty? There will inevitably be more to do.

The creativity of thinking in arriving at co-designed local solutions allied to Not-NEET projects for local school-communities demonstrate what can be done where there is collaboration, strong evidence and a collective will to succeed. Linking into the *Curriculum for Wales*, which is a contextualised curriculum for a locality, is too good an opportunity to be missed.

The challenges faced by leaders and their schools serving high areas of deprivation are multifarious. The hard-to-reach parents frequently remain so and the pandemic has served up the knotty and complex issue of very low learner attendance, particularly for those on free school meals. Anecdotally, behavioural problems have increased as schools try to reset boundaries blurred by school non-attendance during and after the pandemic struck. Challenges around the mental health of youngsters in poverty continue with little to no specialist support for schools and unhelpful, lengthy waiting times to access educational psychologists and CAMHS.

School leaders work desperately hard to connect with communities in order to engage disadvantaged learners in schooling, despite depleted specialist out-reach support as a result of year-on-year chronic under-funding. Some schools have tried to address these issues through opening their own pupil support centres which offer a place of refuge for vulnerable learners with trained staff who know and understand family circumstances. Schools will, where resources allow, employ pastoral support workers who make direct contact with families to discuss academic progress, attendance and any behavioural and emotional needs. School uniform exchange services are set up and parents in some schools are assisted with form-filling to claim benefits.

Where learners are entitled to free school meals every effort is made to avoid stigmatising or identifying these young people through biometric systems. That free school meals for primary-aged students were rolled out from September 2022 was a much welcomed policy initiative. We would hope that the same provision will extend to secondary-aged learners. Again, where funding allows, some schools have employed their own school counsellors and support staff.

The idea of school-community development

In discussing the idea of school-community development, I would make it clear that this is not the same as community schools or community-focused schools which have had multiple iterations over the years.[3] This is about a contextually appropriate, relevant and fully funded set of partnerships between schools and their communities, which provides specialist long-term support driven by the needs of children.

Schools do not exist in isolation from either their communities or indeed those who create policy and then hold schools to account, either at a local level or by the inspectorate, local authority scrutiny panels, the regional consortia or Welsh Government. The pressures to serve so many masters with so little funding and resource constrains schools and, from what I have seen, the multi-agencies working alongside them. We do not need the blunt instruments of narrow accountability but, like their counterparts, schools need agency and capital to do what they know to be effective for their most vulnerable learners and families. The recent widening of accountability measures in Wales recognises that the delicate eco-system of a school cannot be judged solely by exam results, however important they are. This too is to be welcomed.

Parental engagement is sometimes difficult. A parent who has had a bad experience at their own school may be reluctant to engage with their child's school. Parents may feel that they simply cannot help their child with their schooling and feel inadequate as a consequence. There is a strong argument to develop learning communities to upskill adults in the basics of literacy and numeracy. Parents will want to help their child succeed in school but if they do not have the wherewithal, this can only serve to alienate parents from children and then from their school. Parents know the urgency of dealing with the daily causes and effects of poverty on a day-to-day basis. They also know the importance of education in the medium to short term.

What is vital is that someone in the school setting and in the wider support services knows and understands families who are in financial difficulty and opens up a dialogue with them. This requires substantial funding which allows for the recruitment of school-employed pastoral support mentors, family liaison officers and wraparound specialist support personnel. None of this is new. Slashed funding has resulted in a damaging depletion of such support for those who are most vulnerable. It is now time to repair, reform and rebuild.

Community engagement takes time, resource and specialist support in outreach services. Schools need to be freed up to deliver on high-quality teaching which is highly skilled in delivering for each and every learner, not regardless of her/his background but by being cognisant and responsive to it. There is a challenge.

Clearly the significant problems that confront these school-communities have been exacerbated by the effects of the global pandemic and now the economic crisis which will affect these families the hardest. The Bevan Foundation (2022) estimates that those families with an income below £20,000, which accounts for one in five families, 'sometimes or often cannot afford to buy the basics'.[4] The report goes on to describe children going hungry, an increase in mental health problems, and families being unaware of some of the support offered by Welsh and UK governments. Post-pandemic, attendance rates for statutory-aged students are already woefully low. The cost of fuel sees some children unable to afford to get to school. The material deprivation suffered in the teeth of deepening child poverty cannot be overstated.

Schools in the middle of all of this are not immune. At a time where more resource is needed to support the recovery as we emerge from Covid-19, school budgets are struggling to meet increasing costs. The persistent underfunding through austerity policies has seen the wraparound services of welfare support being cut back. While none of this is a deliberate attempt to make things worse on behalf of young people, the effect is felt keenly.

Schools, despite the challenges outlined continue to work very hard for the communities that they serve and many do so very successfully. However, they are working in very difficult circumstances without always having the specialist out-reach support staff or the capacity to resource staff internally. The competing pressures on public funds is a reality and to be acknowledged. The economist Sibieta in his report on school funding in Wales, states that: 'The latest empirical evidence shows that higher spending on schools can improve learner outcomes, particularly amongst disadvantaged learners.'[5] The Bangor PLUS team recognises that learners need to have the buying power of qualifications to fulfil their ambitions, realise their dreams and shake off the limiting effects of poverty. We have a unique opportunity in Wales to shape a set of engaging and relevant qualifications based on the *Curriculum for Wales*, which should allow all learners to show what they know and can do. The qualification system needs to be designed to meet the ambitions of this new curriculum rather than having the effect of reducing its aspirations and limiting the life chances of young people in Wales.

We have to argue for equity to get to excellence in the system as a whole with every moving part contributing. Schools will and do play a part but are not the only actor on the stage. There of course needs to be an emphasis on research-informed policies and strategies for working with academics at home in Wales, just as there are in the international arena. Wales is not alone in tackling the effects of child poverty and this current administration will be keen to look for best practice across the globe.

Conclusion

The Bangor PLUS team's model could provide a way of working, alongside other explorations of 'what works'. Partnerships with local businesses and the higher education institution alongside further education demonstrates the connections needed to support the whole school-community and its young people. This, if it to be expanded, requires funding and an alignment between local and national policy. It further may require that schools collaborate closely in support of one another to share good practice and conduct close-to-practice research on the efficacy of innovative practice.

Engaging the community is vital in support of young people's attainment and sense of self-worth. This is not about a narrow definition of community schools per se, but about engagement with the community and a laser-sharp focus on inclusivity, equity, relationships and high-quality teaching that works for every child. This engagement

454

needs to come from schools, welfare support services, local businesses, the police and health services in an integrated, coherent, funded and planned-for strategy. The Bangor Plus model shows a potential way forward.

There is, however, much to be done.

Notes

1 See *https://endchildpoverty.org.uk/wp-content/uploads/2022/07/Local-child-poverty-indicators-report-2022_FINAL.pdf*; *https://epi.org.uk/publications-and-research/inequalities-in-gcse-results-across-england-and-wales/* (accessed 21 April 2023).
2 See *https://www.bevanfoundation.org/resources/a-snapshot-of-poverty-in-summer-2022/ (/* (accessed 21 April 2023).
3 See *https://www.gov.wales/sites/default/files/publications/2018-03/27-community-focused-schools.pdf*; *https://gov.wales/25m-investment-community-focused-schools-tackle-impact-poverty* (accessed 21 April 2023).
4 See *https://www.bevanfoundation.org/resources/a-snapshot-of-poverty-in-summer-2022/* (accessed 21 April 2023).
5 Luke Sibieta (2020). 'Review of school spending in Wales', Cardiff: Welsh Government. Available at: *https://gov.wales/sites/default/files/publications/2020-10/review-of-school-spending-in-wales.pdf* (accessed 21 April

The Slate Landscape of Northwest Wales
World Heritage Site Nomination

Welsh
Slate...
Roofing
the World

Llechi Cymru
Wales Slate

This front cover of a booklet prepared by Llechi Cymru provides details of the key areas of the slate landscape located in Gwynedd and the vision to protect, conserve and enhance its Outstanding Universal Value. Inside it notes the heritage industry contributes £180m to the local economy.

11

THE CONSEQUENCES OF CHILD POVERTY AND INEQUALITIES FOR FUTURE GENERATIONS

Sue Whatman (Griffith University)

Introduction

This invited chapter is written by an Australian teacher education academic located in Australia and well known to the Bangor PLUS team. I came to Wales to attend the 2019 British Educational Research Association (BERA) conference in Manchester, which was before Covid-19. I took that opportunity to visit academic partners and two of the community development officers on site on the Trem y Mynydd housing estate, to use its pseudonym. The intention was to talk through mutual concerns about child poverty and schooling in the two different devolved systems of education, and the hope was to find common ground to share with other city-based teams in Australia and the United Kingdom keen to join forces in a multi-cities ethnography. The academic partners were already acquainted through BERA and Australian Association for Research in Education (AARE) conferences, special interest networks and publications, sharing an interest in the Brisbane team's focus on how schools with students living in poverty approach learning engagement[1] and well-being (Whatman, Thompson and Main, 2019).

The Brisbane team's projects took particular care to investigate where support for well-being can be found in not only national, state and school policies and state curricula but also within school communities. The project developed in response to the disturbing trend of de-professionalisation of teachers, also noted in the United Kingdom (Beckett, 2016; Nuttall and Beckett, 2020), where the possibility for them to formulate their own, tailored responses to meet the needs of students living in poverty is unfeasible. This is due to the central regulation of teachers' work[2] and proliferation of external well-being providers in the school marketplace.[3]

The effects of child poverty on schooling and teachers' work are not unique to any one nation or school-community, given our common histories of neo-liberalism, globalisation, de-industrialisation and austerity, and now compounded by Covid-19. In comparing notes and literature with academics and teacher partners in Brisbane and Bangor, it is possible to name patterns consistent with what Finnish educator Pasi Sahlberg called the Global Educational Reform Movement, or GERM.[4] The GERM, developed from the ideas of Andy Hargreaves and colleagues,[5] has fundamentally shifted teachers' work away from contextually supporting students in learning to generically surveilling and reporting not only student performance, but also school and teacher performance. These measures have had similar impacts upon teachers' work around the world, with the micro-surveillance of teachers and accountability regimes now common practice in schools across Australia and the United Kingdom but also other nations like the USA and Sweden (Ozga and Lingard, 2007).

Understanding child poverty as exacerbated by these neo-liberal policy symmetries across the world, especially given the GERM, assists us in viewing the impact on teachers' work in new ways. It encourages us to reframe the intense pressures on teachers not as something they are doing wrong and to shift the focus away from the oxymoronic label of 'failing schools' (Beckett, 2016) that mindlessly blames teachers, students and their parents for what transpires. Instead, a critical view of the GERM spotlights the failures of government to properly invest in all children's futures, providing teachers with a collective voice to demand better for their students.

In this chapter, I provide an overview of what child poverty means in school-communities and concomitantly in teacher education to drive home the point that it is not peculiar to any one school in its community either in Australia or elsewhere: it has wider structural origins nationally, transnationally and globally. I then explain my role as an Australian academic in teacher education, my commitments to equity and social justice, my interest in the Bangor PLUS team's project in Wales and the multi-cities ethnographies, including our projects in Australia. I then concentrate on my university-school partnership work in several school-communities, which illuminates the teachers' and school leaders' work occurring here, showcasing our responsive and educative work in the interests of student well-being. This leads to a discussion about the inspirational story of Wales and the Well-being of Future Generations (Wales) Act 2015, designed by Jane Davidson, the then minister for environment, sustainability and housing, and the ways the Bangor PLUS project is seeking to place local solutions and 'school-community development' at the heart of regenerative and sustainable practices.

These analyses lead to my chapter conclusions, which include a set of recommendations for governments, universities, teachers and researchers to be creative with local solutions addressing child poverty in school-communities. It counters the pessimism surrounding teaching today that we are too far along the GERM pathway to reclaim teacher professionalism and research-informed partnerships. Our shared stories from the multi-cities ethnographies via our international collaboration, including the Bangor PLUS team's work here with Ysgol Trem y Mynydd, all demonstrate how a local school-community can build a research-active support network of practitioners working with academic partners to develop responsive/educative work. With support from future research partners with academics, these become the local solutions and 'school-community development' at the heart of the 2015 Well-being legislation, in order to reclaim regenerative and sustainable schooling practices.

Child poverty in school-communities

A helpful starting point is to have a definition of child poverty and an explanation of what it means within school-communities. Poverty is often described from an asset-based view, where poverty is aligned with a lack of material resources or income (Farver, 2014). This is consistent with definitions used by corporations such as the World Bank (World Bank, 2022), who state that poverty is living on less than 1.55 GBP (US$1.90) per day, and charities like World Vision, who state that poverty is a lack of access to services and essential goods. UNICEF noted that children are more likely to be living in poverty than adults and are more vulnerable to its effects. Welsh Government estimates that 31 per cent of children are living in relative income poverty, after housing costs.[6]

These statistics are real but conceal much of the story of poverty. They reinforce an individual-in-view, deficit-based understanding of poverty and, therefore, direct attention away from a complex interplay of social identity, or class, geopolitics and cultural identity, and the machinations of capitalism. Families do not choose to live in poverty (as in a lack of material resources) but rather are positioned there as the result of a racist, classist system (Smyth and Wrigley, 2013). For example, Wales has lower pay for people in every sector than the rest of the United Kingdom, so impoverishment of households via deliberate lower wages is systemic. For low-income families, the availability of childcare, particularly outside normal working hours, is paramount in enabling parents to work in insecure, casual and hospitality industries. Two-fifths of local authorities in Wales do not have enough childcare of this type and much of it is unaffordable.[7] The 'culture of poverty' view propagated by conservative political narratives (that is, poverty must be the fault and/or choice of the individual) damages, demeans and pathologises individuals and communities impacted by poverty, all the while serving the neo-liberal conservative economic agenda to keep them there (Smyth, 2012).

It is important that teachers understand that prolific views about poverty are socially and politically constructed, and are reinforced by educational policy directives that tacitly maintain the status quo of lower paid workers. Teachers have a moral and ethical imperative to reject this view of self-made poverty in their professional work (Smyth, 2012); to do this, they must be critical consumers of their own employers' policies. Let us take the Australian example of 'Every child succeeding State School Strategy 2022–2026' (Queensland Government, 2022). The four pillars or measures for student improvement are achievement, engagement, well-being and transition. The mantra of every child succeeding is every child attending, meaning that the key measure of a successful student is attendance. Students not attending, and by extension, their families who 'fail' to send their children to school, are pathologised as not valuing school. State schools have policies for community engagement, as though outreach to families and communities is something that schools already do well. And yet, education departments and many schools render what students actually need as outside their remit. School breakfasts and lunches are not provided by Queensland state schools: they are sometimes provided by partnered charities. Free public transport to and schools is dependent upon your locality and, even then, low-income families tend not to live in suburbs or towns well serviced by public transport.

An article in *The Conversation* offers not only a perspective on the role of schools in tackling child poverty but the relationship between poverty, race, class and learning achievement. 'I just go to school with no food' (Redmond, 2022) brings to light the reality that one in six Australian children are living in poverty. These averages range from one in four for children with English as another language, or indigenous identity, to one in eight for children who are white, English-speaking background. Learning achievement averages are similarly tied to cultural background and socio-economic status.[8] The authors described student poverty as not having cars, computers, food every day, money for excursions and/or material things that help students fit in with daily schooling. Most teachers can identify who these children are but not necessarily what their role is in ameliorating the effects of poverty in the educational system. The issues raised in the article was shared as an impromptu professional learning opportunity over the Australian Council for Health and Physical Education (ACHPER, 2022) Facebook group in early 2022 to raise critical awareness in the health and physical education (HPE) teaching community: that raising student academic performance means tackling structural inequality, and that the effects of living with poverty cannot be professionally ignored.

Clearly, teachers cannot do everything. It is important to focus on what schools and teachers can do to understand child poverty and take appropriate action and this is where academic partners come in. This book outlines chapter by chapter ways in which schools and academic partners have collaborated to generate research-informed initiatives and evidence of how teachers and schools can make a genuine difference to the schooling of children living in poverty. We collectively show that teachers are not meant to tackle structural inequality alone. The next section returns to the two Brisbane school-university research collaborations to unpack ways in which research-active teachers can make a genuine and lasting difference to the schooling experienced by children affected by poverty and under-served by education.

The Brisbane research collaborations

I am an academic in health and physical education at Griffith University, in Brisbane, Australia and have worked in teacher-education for more than thirty years. I have been particularly interested in health inequalities in my research and practice initially through my PhD study into health education for Torres Strait Islander girls and my professional role as an advocate for Aboriginal and Torres Strait Islander students at university between 1993 and 2010.[9] My commitment to equity and social justice was forged through this advocacy, regularly requiring me to stand up to the racism in the academy endured by indigenous students. My research work and knowledge around health and well-being, particularly with children living with poverty was borne out of collaboration with the Independent Aboriginal and Islander (Murri) school,[10] the Titans Learning Centre (TLC)[11] and our current study with the Multicities Ethnographies collaboration on shaping positive engagement and well-being in the primary years,[12] with the research evolving to be more collaborative, research-informed support for schools on learning engagement and student well-being.

The shaping positive engagement project was just getting off the ground when we heard about Lori's work with the BERA Poverty and Policy Advocacy Commission at the 2017 AARE conference in Canberra, Australia and we invited Lori to become an adjunct professor at Griffith University for a three-year appointment.[13] Pre-Covid, we worked together in Brisbane in the multi-cities ethnographies workshop, an international gathering of scholars working on poverty, racism, well-being and schooling. I also visited Bangor in 2019, on the back of another presentation to BERA in Manchester, whereby I had the privilege of meeting the Bangor PLUS team on the Trem y Mynydd housing estate. This work was cut short by Covid-19, with travel suspended in the third year of Lori's adjunct position.

Despite Covid-19, we continued our international collaboration with a virtual 2021 BERA symposium including Ian Thompson from the University of Oxford, Katina Zammit from Western Sydney University, Terry Wrigley who had been working with Manchester Metropolitan University (and sadly passed away a short time later), and Lori representing the team from Bangor (Whatman et al., 2021). The 2021 BERA symposium highlighted the strengths of analysing school-community relations through Basil Bernstein's (2000) model of pedagogic rights for students and families, and again focused upon real programmes and local solutions being offered in various countries. So, this is how it is that an Australian academic came to be writing this chapter for schools in Wales and to show the history of school-community and academic collaboration that has underscored our previous projects.

The Titans Learning Centre: building social and emotional resilience and academic potential

The teachers at the Titans Learning Centre (TLC) approached our university as they wanted to collect evidence showing that their programme was 'working'. We, as academic partners, wanted to understand what and how the teachers and players were teaching and what and how the learners were learning to draw out the relationships between resourcing and attention paid to particular things around student emotional well-being and better student academic outcomes. The TLC was a bespoke alternative primary schooling programme with a state-approved rationale to re-engage young learners (aged between 9 and 12 years, across grades three and four) identified by their regular classroom teachers as being 'at-risk of disengaging' from schooling.

Three days a week, students were collected by the team bus from their regular school at the start of the day to bring them together in a TLC classroom attached to another state primary school. The TLC teacher delivered a custom curriculum drawn from mathematics, English, the arts, technology, and health and physical education (HPE). Students completed the return journey to their regular school by bus in time for parental/guardian pick-up. Professional rugby league players also would teach the students certain parts of the curriculum and play handball with them during lunch breaks, which served a dual purpose as an emotion regulation session.

We paid close attention to the alternative curriculum, teaching and learning practices of the TLC. Modes of alternative schooling can be widely variable, but that it is typically not administered through state-sanctioned mainstream educational programmes, and rather 'the flexi, second-chance or last-chance schools ... those that develop innovative structures, environments, curricula and pedagogies to engage young people in learning' (McGregor et al., 2017: 4). We found that HPE served as an integrating curriculum for the other subjects and emphasised the social and emotional well-being and development of social skills in TLC students. What else made the TLC programme so unique amongst many alternative schooling programmes was its local community partnership with an Australian (national) rugby league or NRL club whereby players were actively engaged in classroom teaching and lunchtime physical activity, and its primary school setting.

Another critical finding was that many of the TLC participants were living with extended family, in state care or in one-parent households. These young learners' lives were shrouded with overarching structural factors that exacerbate social marginalisation, such as intergenerational unemployment, family and housing instabilities, making them more 'vulnerable to further social exclusion, with consequent weakening of their sense of social citizenship and community obligation: that is, a disposition to disaffection' (Sandford, Armour and Warmington, 2006: 253). The students learned in the TLC that the school would not change their home life circumstances today but, rather, ensure that their experiences of schooling could be consistently positive, affirming and equitable with demonstrable gains in their academic achievement – to enable students to take more control over their futures through the benefits of schooling. The TLC ensured that students were collected and returned to their regular school in normal hours and that they incurred no extra expenses to be part of the programme; and the follow-up data from their teachers once they returned to mainstream schooling was that they did re-engage with schooling and achieved better academic outcomes.

The research-active teachers collaborating in this project learned to collect and analyse longitudinal data from validated surveys, such as the Social Skills Information System (SSIS) (Gresham and Elliott, 1990) and the Productive Pedagogies Audit tool (Mills et al., 2009), to thematically analyse and discuss qualitative interview data and to create vodcasts on their exceptional teaching practices to share with other teachers. They emerged with a better understanding of how well-known and used theoretical concepts such as social and emotional learning (SEL)[14] and productive pedagogies gave them a shared language to talk about their practices with other professionals.

Shaping positive engagement in the primary years

The second project emerged out of what we learned from the TLC – that targeted well-being programmes in the middle years of mainstream schooling were less common than in secondary school and yet the ages of 9 to 12 are such a critical period of children's self-awareness and social comparison. The TLC was a bespoke, alternative schooling programme that was discontinued in 2017, due in part to a state government decision to devolve budgets from regional office. This decision, a hallmark of neo-liberalism, was ostensibly to give individual principals more choice about what programmes they would like to fund at the local level, but it fractured communal regional support for an effective programme. We then wondered what were schools who appeared to be doing well-being 'well' in the middle years were doing, and how they were doing it, particularly since regional support for well-being programmes was no longer forthcoming. We approached schools who had been partners with the TLC programme – schools that had recommended individual students in the past, and who appeared to be 'doing well-being well', to paraphrase Stephen Ball's phrase of 'doing policy well'.[15] As there was evidence of much sharing of the benefits of the TLC with partner schools (Main and Whatman, 2016), we had an educated guess that they might bring across to mainstream schooling similar curriculum innovations, teaching approaches, community partnerships and extra-curricular opportunities.

Two primary schools took us up on the offer to examine how they approach well-being. Beach School was previously a low socio-economic status (SES) postcode but was experiencing rapid gentrification and population change. Due to increasing enrolments in the local public primary school, the principal was able to capitalise on more funding opportunities from the state government and education department, council support for upgraded footpaths, pick-up and drop-off areas, playground and building upgrades. Beach School benefitted from increasing SES status, as wealthier and more highly educated families moved into the suburb and investment in its physical environment, a key element of a health-promoting school, was extensive. The school also allocated budget towards a chaplain and psychologist, part-time occupational physiotherapist, maintained partnerships with breakfast club charities and commercial outsourcers for social and emotional learning programmes across the year levels, but particularly in middle years.

Ocean School was in the next suburb over and was a founding primary school in the area. It was very old, had buildings with high maintenance costs and a decreasing student population, making it ineligible for the kinds of capital grants that Beach School was able to secure to improve its physical environment. In short, Ocean School was falling down around its teachers and students and keeping buildings safe and habitable preoccupied the leadership team. So, they invested in low-cost measures to change routines in the school day to promote well-being, such as changing up the playgrounds that the early and middle years students typically used. Another significant trial was to spend ten minutes at the start of the school day to enable students to begin with a variety of mindfulness and relaxation programmes with their regular teacher before the formal start to the curriculum. Ocean School also invested in a fee-for-service, annual national survey of student well-being, gauged through age-appropriate self-report questionnaires for students, parents/carers and teachers. The leadership team mapped the academic performance of the students against their annual well-being scores and behaviour data, such as school attendance and the number of 'blue slips' – behaviour referrals – that students accrued.

We found that both schools took the approach that every teacher was a well-being teacher and that it was part of their professional role to implement specific learning experiences and devote time to responding to children's well-being needs every day. Both projects demonstrated that research-active teachers with academic partners and supportive leadership staff took control of their school-based responses and professional responsiveness to student well-being needs. The academic partners negotiated ethical clearance with the education department and university ethics committees to be able to share the learning in the form of conference presentations, workshops for staff professional learning and publications. More importantly, these partnerships created an internal research culture in the schools over which the teachers involved took ownership.

Learning from Wales: Well-being of Future Generations (Wales) Act 2015

I now turn to the background behind the Well-being of Future Generations (Wales) Act 2015 into the narrative. Like Queensland, where states have responsibility for the education of their residents, Wales now has devolved responsibility for education for Welsh children and have seized the chance to charter a new policy environment that is responsive to the needs of future generations and the planet. The well-being and sustainability focus underpinning the Act is quite extraordinary and deserves the praise of the United Nations shared in Jane Davidson's (2020) book.

In particular, the three policy triggers that lead to the creation of the Well-being of Future Generations (Wales) Act have caught my attention and provide a type of blueprint to how other devolved jurisdictions might work towards policy environments that tackle structural inequality. Davidson recounts her time as a minister in the Welsh Government and documents the creation of three sustainability development policies – 'Learning to live differently' (1999–2003), 'Starting to live differently' (2003–7) and 'One Wales, one planet' (2007–11) – as the foundation of the well-being Act. As Wales responded to each policy, Davidson came to realise that compartmentalised policy was not enough to guarantee lasting change to whole of government, and indeed, whole of society, well-being and sustainability practices. Hence, the Act emerged from these iterative sustainability policy cycles to become a whole of government responsibility. In Australia, we have a nation-wide policy for education, known as the Mpartnwe Declaration (Australian Government, 2020), in which well-being and sustainability are goals of Australian schooling, with key accountabilities distributed across federal and state governments. That said, Australia is a long way off from having a whole of government approach such as the 2015 Well-being of Future Generations (Wales) Act.

During my time in Wales, in 2019, I visited Trem y Mynydd housing estate with members of the Bangor PLUS team to see first-hand their efforts to unite multi-agency stakeholders, teachers, school leaders and service providers in their shared agenda to improve schooling and educational outcomes for children on the estate. The chronic underfunding of this public housing area was obvious at every turn, from the empty commercial buildings to the lack of public transport. Houses were well kept, yards were neat, the pride, perhaps relief, in having a place to live was also obvious. Trem y Mynydd school was new, the buildings indicating a significant investment in the physical environment in which students would learn. My visit inside the school was not possible that particular day but we discussed the strategies in place between the Bangor PLUS team in nearby council facilities.

What struck me as unusual and exciting about the Bangor PLUS team was the diversity of the team itself, which built on the *Children First* team that Lewis had brought together: local government officials, school leaders, not-for-profits organisations, academics, teachers and local council staff – everyone in fact who saw students affected by poverty as a stakeholder in their professional work and lives. Lori followed suit (see the introduction and chapter 1). Having such diversity on the Bangor PLUS team showed me and the other international partners in the multi-cities ethnographies project what ethical and sustainable collaboration can look like and how to sustain it. The Bangor PLUS team tackled the issue of child poverty one fragment at a time, with local initiatives in each member's professional remit. For example, Lori, as an adjunct university professor, mobilised additional university research support for the team through the university's infrastructure, bringing in additional academics and connections, particularly the library. The council staff and school leaders provided suitable venues for community meetings. Importantly, the group could share intel and data in ways that inspired and enriched everyone's daily work. Such collaborations are the gold standard for health-promoting schools, as defined by the World Health Organisation (WHO, n.d.) and are key to the sustainability of the work of Bangor PLUS on Trem y Mynydd and elsewhere.

Conclusion

On the basis of our project work in Australia and experiences of collaborating with knowledgeable and committed teachers, there are a number of ways forward in the interests of our future generations. First, all levels of government with devolved responsibilities for education and health should audit their operations with respect to the WHO health-promoting schools framework in which health promotion defines the education (curriculum, teaching and learning), environment (organisation, ethos and physical spaces) and partnerships (parents, communities and services) of those schools. It means that schools must work with their communities, just as the Bangor PLUS team in Trem y Mynydd has done, to develop local solutions for the health and well-being of students. The HPS framework has been in place for many years and countries like Australia have principles and audit tools available through their advocacy networks to support teachers and schools in this work (Australian Health Promoting Schools Network, 2022).

Secondly, universities, charged with the professional and moral education of future teachers, must resist GERM logics which overshadow external accreditation processes that now overburden preservice teacher coursework with literacy and numeracy training and practicum with data collection. University coursework should actively combat these market logics by regaining sociological, philosophical and disciplinary-focused coursework to graduate critical teachers knowledgeable and proficient in their fields of expertise. Universities and schools need to work together to support new teachers into the practices of teaching and this includes trusting the university sector to design the curriculum teachers need. Public institutions such as universities are not meant to be accountable to market logics – we are accountable to our future generations to create educational systems that promote equity, social justice and opportunity (Cochran-Smith et al., 2018).

Finally, I implore teachers, newly graduated or highly experienced, to trust themselves in their knowledge and their professionalism to develop local solutions for their students. The marketisation of education relies on teachers doubting their ability to design and deliver quality teaching and learning experiences across the breadth of the curriculum. Market logics would have the sector believe that an anonymous content creator designing attractive-looking websites is more qualified than a four-year, tertiary-educated teacher to design appropriate lessons and resources for their students. Hold fast in your professionalism!

These three points may seem overwhelming to individual teachers but the cases in this chapter and elsewhere in the book point to the veracity and effectiveness of research-active teachers and university partners, combining with multi-agency workers to support local school-communities underscored by poverty. Such collaborations help teachers and school leaders to develop a professional appreciation of how the GERM has shaped the everyday living and demands of and upon schooling but now with critical awareness of their role and remit to resist it. As the Bangor PLUS on Trem y Mynydd have done, unite and collaborate to reclaim an education system that cares about the well-being of this and future generations of students.

2023).

Notes

1   Whatman and Main (2018). This paper provides further detail of one of the Brisbane team's projects and specifically how partnership with a local football team was an integral feature of the programme.
2   Sellars and Lingard (2013). This paper explains the effects of hyper-surveillance of teachers and reductionism in school curricular offerings.
3   Williams and Macdonald (2015). This paper explains what is outsourcing, why it is flourishing and how it can have detrimental effects on the professional work of teachers, and quality of student learning.
4   Sahlberg (2011). This article gives an excellent explanation of the GERM and its origins.
5   Hargreaves et al. (2001). Sahlberg acknowledges this book as the catalyst for his development of the concept of GERM.
6   Wales Government (2021). Available at: *https://gov.wales/child-poverty-final-report-income-maximisation-action-plan-html* (accessed 14 April 2023).
7   Joseph Rowntree Foundation, *www.jrf.org.uk* (accessed 14 April 2023). This website contains up-to-date statistics concerning children and families living in poverty in Cymru, Wales.
8   Scanlon (2015). This book discusses the academic performance of students in disadvantaged schools, showing clear links between performance and socio-economic status. Scanlon debunks the myth of 'disinterested parents' in their children's attendance and achievement.
9   Whatman (2008). This book recounts my PhD fieldwork into community participation in health education decision-making for Torres Strait Islander girls in a remote part of Australia. It is also accessible in a journal article here: Whatman and Singh (2015).
10 The Aboriginal and Islander Independent Community School (the Murri School) is an independent, non-state government school, run by an indigenous community board for indigenous students and their families. You can read more about it here: *http://murrischool.qld.edu.au/* (accessed 14 April 2023).
11 Main and Whatman (2016). This is another paper from one of the Brisbane projects. It focuses on the audit of the classroom pedagogies in use and how social and emotional well-being is supported by these teacher-led pedagogies.
12 Whatman et al. (2021). This conference paper was the most recent

opportunity for the Multicities Ethnographies teams from Australia and the United Kingdom to present their work.

13 We invited Lori to become an adjunct of EDJEE, a research collaborative within the Griffith Institute of Educational Research. You can read more about it here: *https://blogs.griffith.edu.au/gierinsights/edjee-research/* (accessed 14 April 2023).

14 Collaborative for Academic, Social and Emotional Learning (CASEL), *https://casel.org/fundamentals-of-sel/what-is-the-casel-framework/* (accessed 14 April 2023).

15 Ball (2015). This paper provides an excellent review of Ball's research legacy around educational policy, following the publishing in 1993 of his influential book.

This photo of a Welsh Not artefact held in Bangor Museum was hung around a child's neck for speaking Welsh in nineteenth-century schools, a consequence of anti-Welsh bias notably in the 1847 Reports of the Commissioners of Inquiry into the State of Education in Wales, later known as the Blue Books.

12

TOWARDS A CRITICAL UNDERSTANDING OF WALES'S PRESENT FOR FUTURE GENERATIONS

Lori Beckett, Graham French, Carl Hughes (Bangor University) and Gwen Thirsk (Swyddog Buddsoddi Lleol)

Introduction

This co-authored concluding chapter recounts the Bangor PLUS team effort to date to respond to the brutal lived experiences of child poverty on the Trem y Mynydd estate and undertake an 'ethnography that makes a difference'.[1] This is being done with and for the residents who typify the strength, determination and grit of this local school-community to put things right for their children and young people. The majority represented here are on universal credit, ranked as the working poor or unemployed,[2] having suffered income and wealth inequalities recognised as the greatest social threat of our time.[3] They are adamant that they do not want their children to experience the same fate. Without exception, they wish they could have their time at school all over again and that their understanding could have been different; now they want their children to continue with their schooling and do well enough to find a path into employment, education and training. These residents' ideas about making life better for future generations while struggling to provide for their families plug into the central thesis of this book: emergency social actions are required simultaneous to make a difference to the lives and life chances of their children and young people. This requires a major shift in Welsh Government policy thinking, especially in schooling and education, which would be a strong counter to the suffering, stigma, discrimination and demonisation that so many families and children from the Trem y Mynydd housing estate feel, as recounted in previous chapters.

Before proceeding it is important to revisit the history of Trem y Mynydd, which has come into view with the images that appear across this book, a result of the team's archival work on primary and secondary sources such as maps, photographs and other documentation. While we had to be mindful of ethical considerations and make them anonymous, it is hoped that the imagery will offer some contextualisation for the reader. The local history of this place, reaching back to the Penrhyn dynasty's slate quarries, not to forget their slave plantations in Jamaica, is the backstory to Wales as a nation-state fraught with inequalities. This is not to overlook counter measures. The details of Price Davies's (1937) account of Bangor City Council's public investment in social housing to be built on multiple sites, given the 1930 Housing Act, was significant given consultations with the working classes on their housing needs to inform the approach to the design of the homes on the estates. An item also found in Gwynedd Archives showed there had been heated debate about the working families' welfare in relation to the proposed sites among councillors and the public at large leading up to the 1936 vote on the purchase of Penrhyn's land for Trem y Mynydd, which was carried. This is particularly poignant, considering the point about future generations made nearly ninety years ago in a letter to the editor of a local newspaper (see figure 8). This account helps us to build a better understanding of the Trem y Mynydd housing estate and its history of disadvantage in the present to provide insights into the locality, the school-community and contemporary lived experiences of poverty, suffering and punishing hardship.

In turn this critical understanding of the local history of the Trem y Mynydd housing estate, which dovetails with labour history, is key to a critical understanding of the national story of Wales given it remains part of the UK marked by post-Brexit Conservatism. Another item found in Gwynedd Archives on the Penrhyn slate quarry dispute at the end of the nineteenth century provided details that are crucial to maintaining a focus on the inequalities that remain:[4] a transcript of 'The Interview with Lord Penrhyn' states that this was a full copy of the official report of a meeting between Mr E. S. Douglas-Pennant, MP and Mr E. A. Young (chief manager), on the employer's side, and an appointed deputation on behalf of the men. An interpreter and two further men were present, one for taking notes in Welsh and one in English, and it all took place at the Port Penrhyn Office on 18 March 1897, three years before the lockout. Edward Sholto Douglas-Pennant (1864–1927), a British Conservative politician, had stood in for his father, and he immediately took control and dominated the meeting, but the men identified by name – who must remain anonymous to protect the identity of the place – were clearly up to the task of negotiation. The twin point to be made here is that these men were no doubt self-educated and articulate, alert to the ways that wealth confers political power, and they too were forthright and not intimidated. The Penrhyn Quarry industrial dispute was central to the formation of the Welsh Labour Party to represent the working class. This gives voice to Raymond Williams's question, 'Who speaks for Wales?' We sought answers in the Trem y Mynydd school-community, where some of the working men's descendants live.

In building a critical understanding of Wales's present for future generations, we recount the raft of local solutions, mostly devised by local residents, whose ideas go some way to ensuring that their children do not end up in the official category of NEETs. These inspired their Not-NEET projects that are described throughout the book and are tabulated in the appendices. The first tranche recaps small enterprises like the community Hive Café, community crèche, Wild Elements outdoor learning programme and performing arts initiatives. The second tranche recaps larger public works, such as the mooted new-build community centre as a multi-agency hub, which calls for the inclusion of school staff in the developing plans, greening the estate for community food production and social eco-housing. The seventh local solution and its allied Not-NEET project, 'Rigging the future: Welsh slate and World Heritage', is aligned to this chapter and its argument about public investment. These identify Trem y Mynydd aligned with the slate landscape of northwest Wales, now inscribed as a UNESCO World Heritage Site, to draw on some of the supposed social and economic benefits but not only derived from tourism to Port Penrhyn. All seven local initiatives interconnect with the Bangor PLUS team's efforts to forge a notion of school-community development, which is asset-based and can be reasonably done locally to institute regenerative and sustainable practices at the heart of the 2015 Well-being legislation and the 2018 *Children First* initiative.

A point to be reiterated in this concluding chapter is that the Bangor PLUS team is trying to convey a sense that child poverty is not peculiar to the resident families in this school-community: the circumstances that see parents being unemployed or trapped as the working poor has both historical and wider systemic and structural origins. Another point to be reiterated in charting a way forward is that pressure must be kept up on Welsh Government to realise the implementation of its suite of progressive policies, not to add to schools' and multi-agencies' workloads, but to effect systemic and structural changes to ameliorate child poverty. Though such changes may well challenge the status quo, there is an immediacy to the social actions required to stem the suffering and alleviate the hardship of so many local families and children in poverty. This requires an extraordinary concerted effort, but the Bangor PLUS team has shown the way with its model way of working. The local solutions and allied Not-NEET projects almost superseded its original intention to work towards research-informed policy advocacy, but with little response to our early efforts, we then devised concrete proposals for innovative policies and practices. All seven local solutions and Not-NEET projects have implications for the *Curriculum for Wales*, rolled out from September 2022, and its revised 14–16 Qualifications Framework, but this all requires the political will in Cardiff and Caernarfon, and support from GwE and the ASCL as well as local colleges, Bangor University and Uchelgais Gogledd Cymru (Regional Skills Partnership).

In what follows, we recap our efforts to date strategising in the face of the current humanitarian disaster with an 'ethnography that makes a difference' to work with local residents in concert with school staff, multi-agency workers, elected representatives and critical friends. We describe the archival work that adds to the sequential images with caption-commentary in this edited book to provide more details on the history of this place, to shed light on class-based inequalities and counter measures like public investment. Building on this history of disadvantage in the present we focus on some labour histories, which are key to critical understandings of the national story of Wales, especially 'Who Speaks for Wales', where it stands for social democracy, equity and social justice. We point to the future with our seven place-based local solutions and Not-NEET projects, characterised by ideas on sustainable economic development to boost local employment, education and training, which opens up the debate about a foundational economy for Wales. This leads to our chapter conclusions, joining forces to develop a briefing for a business case and encourage Welsh Government to reconsider its raft of progressive policies for school-communities confronted by child poverty. This requires politicians, policy-makers and power brokers, along with teachers', children's and parent/carers' learning about what it takes to build school-communities that are socially just.

Give us another chance

This volume has been organised to sequentially present some of the challenges that come with living in poverty in an apparently affluent western European nation. All the chapters are focused on Welsh children growing up in poverty, which primarily is a result of the UK's consecutive Conservative governments' policy choices, and this school-community's responses. The findings of Lewis's *Children First* needs assessment on Trem y Mynydd was effectively confirmed in Alston's (2019) probe into *Extreme Poverty and Human Rights in the UK,* which drew attention to Wales:

> Wales faces the highest relative poverty rate in the United Kingdom, with almost one in four people living in relative income poverty. Like the rest of the United Kingdom, employment has not proven to be an automatic route out of poverty in Wales. In-work poverty has grown over the last decade, despite considerable improvement in the employment rate. Twenty-five percent of jobs pay below the minimum wage, and low-paid, part-time or insecure jobs are often disproportionately taken up by women, due to difficulties in balancing work and caring responsibilities.[5]

These lived experiences are not confined to this housing estate: Whatman's penultimate chapter in this volume pointed to Australia, which has fallen under the influence of neo-liberalism and the Global Education Reform Movement (GERM), and discusses how select Brisbane school-communities responded to very similar challenges.

Following the recent UK campaign to elect Prime Ministers Truss then Sunak, the Conservative Party was seemingly keen to defend their policy choices: Thatcher's de-industrialisation, Cameron's austerity, May and Johnson's Global Britain agenda apropos Brexit. This also included universal credit, a main focus in Alston's report and an initiative of Iain Duncan Smith who became Work and Pensions Secretary in the Cameron-Clegg Conservative-Liberal Democrat Coalition government of 2010–15.[6] The idea behind universal credit was to streamline the administration of the six main existing benefits – income-based jobseeker's allowance, income-related employment and support allowance, income support, working tax credit, child tax credit and housing benefit – and merge them into a single monthly payment. There is much to be said about consecutive UK Conservative governments' punitive sanctions on recipients of benefits and the shame and punishment visited on the poor, which may well provide right-wing conservatives political leverage at election time. These give rise to major ideological disparities with Welsh Labour given its devolved responsibilities[7] and inclination to provide support regarding benefits, health, social care, and social housing – lifelines to those in poverty whether unemployed or working poor.

The Bangor PLUS team studied Wales's response to Alston in its first series of seminars alongside the Well-being of Future Generations (Wales) Act 2015, *Education in Wales: Our National Mission* and Prosperity for All agenda (Welsh Government, 2017a, 2017c), all underpinned by a programme for government and government administration. These have been policy choices to celebrate, but they have been ineffectual in addressing child poverty. This is not surprising after Wales's Jones Labour government (2009–18) shifted away from its child poverty strategy and launched Prosperity for All in its stead. Though there have been multiple consultations and subsequent inquiries, such as the Child Poverty Progress Report 2019, resident families on the Trem y Mynydd housing estate continue to live in poverty. This is despite their protestations that nothing ever changes in the wake of local/national governments' anti-poverty policies and research inquiries. They continue to battle the causes and effects of poverty that deliver serious suffering, punishing hardship, the social emergencies that came with Covid-19, and now the humanitarian disaster that comes with the cost-of-living crisis. This is not to ignore systemic and structural impediments like school exclusion that border on human rights infringements. These are all fertile grounds for grievance and disorder, and extremist right-wing conservative populism taking hold.

The principles underpinning the 2018 *Children First* needs assessment and its findings galvanised this school-community to embark on an 'ethnography that makes a difference', but there remains much to be done to break the poverty cycle and its confluence with student disengagement, alienation and absenteeism. The early chapters in this volume provide some deep knowledge about the unmet needs in the Trem y Mynydd school-community, while the following chapters then recount the great efforts made to co-design and co-produce local solutions and their allied Not-NEET projects. These are all intended to put things right for the children and future generations and show where some of Wales's key social democratic ideas/ideals can begin to take root. It was disconcerting to see Education Minister Jeremy Miles in Wales's Drakeford Labour government (2018–present) turn to the GERM and its tired neo-liberal policy foci on high standards and aspirations to infuse the schooling system with notions about 'closing the gap' and 'raising attainment'. Seemingly Miles's intentions in tackling the impact of poverty are limited to test-based performance and accountability[8] reinforced in community-focused schools[9] with family engagement officers and community managers to liaising with outside agencies.

This dominant managerial approach seemingly disregards inequalities, understood here as the lived experiences of poverty, its causes and effects. This does not preclude the Bangor PLUS team working in support of the school's work in concert with the local school improvement consortium GwE, especially as it espouses Welsh Government's progressive policies. Yet there is something coy about Jeremy Miles being led by the GERM and especially England's successive Education Ministers' neo-liberal agendas underpinned by Thatcherism in Conservative, Coalition and New Labour governments. This creates policy tensions, which impacts on schools' work. The more progressive approach would be for Wales's Education Minister to engage research-informed policy advice, which means acknowledgement of academic critiques of sound bites like 'gap talk', 'raising attainment', community-schools, and school improvement for that matter. This is the preferred approach by the contributing authors in this volume, which is concerned with social justice in and through schooling and which lends itself to deep knowledge about the local context. Such an approach gives rise to contextualised school improvement if indeed this is to remain a central plank of Wales's schools' policy platform. It is a long way from the punitive sanctions that can come with 'closing the gap' and 'raising attainment' that can provoke children's and young people's disengagement, alienation and absenteeism. This only adds to resident families' grievances about the sanctions that come with universal credit.

Out of sight, out of mind

A fruitful study of the local history of Trem y Mynydd provided plentiful insights into the local context and this was greatly facilitated by archival work. We have pointed to the abundance of primary and secondary sources such as maps, photographs, and other documentation held in Bangor University Archives, Gwynedd Archives and Wales's National Museums including the Bangor Museum and National Slate Museum, as well as Wales's National Library and the so-called National Library in London. The images contained in this edited book are strategically intended to offer some contextualisation for the reader. They also showcase what could be done by teachers in Ysgol Trem y Mynydd given that they have responsibilities for the implementation of the *Curriculum for Wales*, effectively another one of Welsh Labour governments' social democratic ideas/ideals, rolled out in September 2022. An orientation to local history sits well with advice from Welsh Government[10] on designing their curriculum and developing their vision, which required consideration of a number of questions:

- what should we teach and why?
- how should we teach it?
- how will this support our learners to realise the four purposes?

In turn, these four purposes were said to be the starting point and aspiration for schools' curriculum design. The ultimate aim is to support learners to become:

- ambitious, capable learners, ready to learn throughout their lives
- enterprising, creative contributors, ready to play a full part in life and work
- ethical, informed citizens of Wales and the world

- healthy, confident individuals, ready to lead fulfilling lives as valued members of society.

This is precisely the focus for the Trem y Mynydd school-community, where school staff, multi-agency workers and academic partners joined forces with resident families and critical friends to push back against child poverty, especially its ongoing influence on schooling success. We took seriously Welsh Government's advice[11] that the school's curriculum should be an ongoing conversation for the whole school and beyond, engaging with parents/carers and the wider community, including business, academia and public services. This too is precisely what the Bangor PLUS team have done in regards the seven local solutions allied to their Not-NEET projects, and it was what was said in Beckett's response to Ysgol Trem y Mynydd's new curriculum survey online. In reply to a question about how the curriculum should be implemented, she said that it needs to be grounded in the present, contextually sensitive, well-designed and locally responsive to this school-community's lived experiences of inter-generational poverty. This way children come to know and understand their family circumstances and the worth of learning to improve their lives and life chances, mindful of the precarity of employment and income gaps, especially for key workers. Teaching needs to be research-informed to be intellectually robust because it takes inordinate skill to develop classroom pedagogies to engage, if not re-engage, those who are historically marginalised and excluded from schooling.

In response to a question about any one of the four purposes of the *Curriculum for Wales* being more important than another, Beckett said that they are inextricably intertwined and lend themselves to socially just outcomes from schooling. But in this era of public health concerns it is more important to be developing 'Healthy, confident individuals who are ready to lead fulfilling lives', though it is open to question whether these children will come to be seen 'as valued members of society' given the way things stand: they already experience the stigma of poverty more so now with health and welfare inequalities and social stratification exposed by Covid-19 and climate inaction. This is underpinned by social policies like competitive schooling with streaming, setting and sorting students to become the working poor, but this can be addressed in part through these four purposes of the new curriculum. These are crucial to self-consciously harness schooling and education to Wales's post-pandemic recovery and reconstruction,[12] and not just reigniting a competitive economy but investing in the foundational economy and improving the social conditions of children's lives, their worth and dignity: this collective responsibility lies with all stakeholders in local school-communities and should not be left to the individual.

In response to a question about classroom activities and possible experiences within the wider community and outside areas, Beckett replied that more frequent focal points for teaching and learning should follow public health's lead, including on climate action initiatives. This is not only in the present but also those rooted in history, such as Bangor City Council re-modelling unhealthy areas and building adequate social housing following the 1930 Housing Act on advice from the then Ministry of Health. Local history studies on Bangor's housing schemes for public improvement of living standards, and local history walks in Bangor city, Port Penrhyn, on the Penrhyn estate (now run by the National Trust), and also on their former farmland housing estate sold by the fourth Lord Penrhyn, would well inform teachers' design of classroom activities and learning experiences. This all lends itself to knowledge-building by children of resident families about their wider community, including the history of public debates about poverty going back to the Penrhyn Quarry disputes and the controversies on social housing played out in the newspapers of 1935–6, all in documentation held by Gwynedd Archives. Coming into the present, such new curriculum work will provide insights into the origins of social housing, which should dispel stigma, install pride and provide some perspective on hardship as described by the Child Poverty Action Group (2017): living in impoverished living conditions, going without essential goods and services, not least a good basic diet, adequate clothing and footwear, heating in winter, social activity and so on.

The political will and public investment are two main keys to this sort of work by teachers in collaboration with the Bangor PLUS team, especially in regards the seven local solutions allied to their Not-NEET projects that explicitly link to the *Curriculum for Wales* and the 14–16 Qualifications Framework. Yet again, it is crucial to delve into a fruitful study of the local history of Trem y Mynydd and recount Price Davies's (1937) details of Bangor City Council's public investment. He was quite matter-of-fact in his assertion that private businesses could not meet the need for new housing, which resonate today given the privatisation agenda of public services. Delving into the archives, Bangor city councillors' debates had some bearings on the location of these social housing estates with critics in turn publicising concerns about resident families being relocated away from the city and away from its amenities, then being 'out of sight, out of mind'. These concerns persist today where the eradication of child poverty on Trem y Mynydd remains out of sight, out of mind because it simply is not visible to the wider Bangor community. An opportunity is lost, given that Education Minister Jeremy Miles's policy focus relies more on wordplay: tackling the impact of poverty on young people's attainment reinforced by a mooted appointment of family engagement officers and community managers, rather than seriously tackling the causes and effects of child poverty and looking to systemic and structural change.

Who speaks for Wales?

These appointments are a far cry from the Family Support Officer proposed by community development workers to the school Head of Ysgol Trem y Mynydd, where school staff and other frontline workers have good insights into the locality, the school-community and resident families' lived experiences of poverty. Yet such insights are not necessarily the preserve of newly appointed family engagement officers and community managers, nor the wider Bangor city community, nor broader local/national electorates. In working with the community development workers during the Bangor PLUS project, we came to learn their opinions on 'closing the gap' as being more in keeping with the reality gaps that come from living off site, even in the city centres of Bangor and Caernarfon, or the wider north and south of Wales, especially Cardiff, not to forget the UK Government's base in London. To even broach 'raising attainment' on Trem y Mynydd is to ostensibly suggest that the school Head and teachers, along with the school-community, either need to do more or they have got it wrong. As this volume has shown, the odds are stacked against the appointment of a Family Support Officer in the school, who would be able to tackle inequalities as the relationship between student achievement, family and social backgrounds, which would mean acknowledging the interconnections between disadvantaged students' lives, learning and urban schooling experiences.

As the Bangor PLUS team has made clear in this book, Welsh Labour governments' social and educational policies' claims to a productive social reality, especially for families and children in poverty, are sorely tested in practice. This provoked us to do some further study of Wales's policy touchstones:

- Future Generations Commissioner for Wales's *Future Generations Report* (2020);
- Laura McAllister and Rowan Williams's work co-chairing the Independent Commission on the Constitutional Future of Wales;
- Institute for Public Policy Research's *Future Welfare State* (2020);
- Welsh Government's *The Co-operation Agreement* (2021) (effectively a cooperative alliance between Plaid Cymru and Labour).

This brought us back to Raymond Williams's question of 'Who speaks for Wales?', which prompted a re-consideration of resident families' designation.[13] The Bangor PLUS team have used the terms unemployed and the working poor, but this raised twin questions about their identification and representation. It is not obvious that they see themselves as the traditional working class, the new working class or the marginalised working class, though there is an interaction between the marginalised working class and poverty in Wales.[14] They are certainly capably served by their elected representatives on Gwynedd Council, and by their elected Plaid Cymru politicians in Wales's national parliament in Cardiff and the UK's parliament in Westminster. In ongoing conversations, it was apparent that there are shared concerns about current policy choices that give rise to child poverty, both directly and indirectly.

From the outset the Bangor PLUS team made its intention to engage knowingly in research-informed policy advocacy, but our first efforts are noteworthy only to the extent that our briefings were mostly politely and cordially received but nothing really came of them: it was disappointing to say the least given the time and effort that went into our invitation to the national manager of *Children First* to do an 'estate walk', our team presentation to Sally Holland and Alasdair Macdonald, Beckett's briefing to Wales's Child Poverty Strategy Review and our teams' attendance at the Llandudno forum. It was much the same with

Beckett's submission on post-Covid-19 recovery and reconstruction in Wales and her submission on Ysgol Trem y Mynydd's new curriculum, although in a face-to-face meeting the school Head responded positively. The caveat was that there needed to be top-down policy instructions before any actions can be taken at local level. This came as no surprise given Welsh Government's advice to schools on 'Developing a vision for curriculum design': 'It should be informed by the school's values and ethos, as well as by its location and surroundings. However, it should retain an approach that is consistent with the learning set out in national guidance.'[15] No doubt national guidance precludes teachers' educative responses to child poverty, despite the school's welfare role and its impact on staff and their own health and welfare, which is not to forget the stated intentions of the *Curriculum for Wales* to be oriented to its school-community.

We came to learn to target policy advocacy in the three tiers of government. Gwynedd Council in Caernarfon, in control of local government, has responsibility for the provision of social services and housing, with oversight of education and schooling and transport services. Its funding comes in the form of allocations from Wales's devolved national government in Cardiff, but while it has some revenue generating powers its own income comes from the UK Government in Westminster. This all has ripple effects, acutely felt on Trem y Mynydd, and it is not easy lobbying for local residents' unmet needs, even with local solutions allied to their Not-NEET projects, given the policy tensions between these three tiers. Thankfully there are positive signs in Cardiff given the Co-operation Agreement between Plaid Cymru and Welsh Labour, both centre-left parties, to realise social democratic ideas/ideals and to provide long-term political stability for the nation. However, the shadow of consecutive right-wing Conservative governments in London looms large and there are consequences for Wales as a result of Prime Minister Johnson's Brexit, his handling of Covid-19, the cost-of-living crisis and the war in Ukraine.[16] Wales may well have a social democratic vision for itself and indeed modern Britain if it were to remain part of the UK, but it is anchored politically to Westminster, and currently with the right-wing Sunak Conservative government.

This is most keenly felt in the funding and delivery of universal credit, which was a major focus in Alston's (2019) report but not yet a devolved responsibility to Welsh Government. In conversations with local elected Plaid Cymru politicians, we were advised that negotiations with Westminster are underway to relocate the administration of universal credit to Cardiff to ensure a more humane approach. We made the suggestion that should this happen, it would be advantageous to the school-community if Welsh Government were to embrace the idea of added monetary incentives to encourage resident families on Trem y Mynydd into education, employment and training. This would counter tendencies to 'blame the victim' or engage deficit readings, which can be a hallmark of emphasising high standards and aspirations, 'raising attainment' and the like. This volume has clearly shown that resident families have great aspirations for their children, and have devised local solutions and inspired their allied Not-NEET projects. Some recalibration of Welsh Government's education and social policies would surely make it better for resident families – children, young people and adults – and forge a new future society for Wales that is just, rational and humane with human rights at the fore.

Closing the reality gaps

Welsh Government faces huge challenges, captured in the 2020 call for submissions on Wales's post-Covid-19 recovery and reconstruction in the face of health risks; jobs at risk; public finances at risk; and vulnerable communities at risk. There was recognition that the recovery would impact all areas of Welsh people's lives and that it was profoundly important for public services, for the economy and society. There was also a declaration that applying the lens of the new post-Covid-19 realities to established policies needed to be fearless and radical. There may have been no response to Beckett's submission but the Bangor PLUS team has been fearless and radical in applying a new approach to our policy advocacy with a brief for a business case. This is on the strength of our responsive educative work in our local solutions allied to Not-NEET projects that run across a number of portfolios. None of this is to divert attention away from the necessary local/national responses to the social emergency unfolding on Trem y Mynydd, in other *Children First* areas in Wales, and beyond.[17] In the current set of circumstances, blighted by ineffectual policies, frontline workers have to lend emergency support and humanitarian disaster relief to local residents while the Bangor PLUS team looked to the future.

The epithet attributed to Jane Davidson (2020) in the front of this volume stands as a provocation, and so the idea of public investment has been reiterated throughout this volume. This draws on Welsh Government's foundational economy[18] and though education is not listed it is recognised by the Foundational Economy Collective (2018) in its book, where it is included as a providential service, part of the collectively consumed infrastructure of everyday life. They suggested, on a matter of principle, that citizens are asked what they want, and so we asked. They want assets-based school-community development with their locally devised solutions operationalised and their allied Not-NEET projects enacted. They want links made to the *Curriculum for Wales*[19] and Wales's 14–16 Qualifications Framework, and they want local curriculum committees established. They want responsibility for cross-curriculum projects coordinated across local school networks by nominated teams of teachers working with partners in local agencies. They want their small-scale enterprises and larger proposed public works reflected in the design of the teaching and learning programmes. They want a facilitation fund, so named by one of the resident artists, Owen MacLean (see Maclean and Daw's chapter 7). They want the Trem y Mynydd Co-Operative set up, as suggested by another resident, Pete Whitby (see Fernley, Whitby and Peisley's chapter 5). They took advice on the legalities,[20] initially from Trem y Mynydd community development worker, Gwen Thirsk (see Thirsk's chapter 6), who directed them to seek further advice on what is involved in registering as a company limited by guarantee but also with charitable status.

There are four local solutions allied to their Not-NEET projects, listed at the beginning of this chapter, that are considered small-scale social enterprises in need of investment and ongoing funding. They are tabulated in the appendices, and they benefit the school-community in different ways by working directly to support resident families and children. The community Hive Café provides a safe space, sense of community and meals with the offer of advice on shopping, cooking and nutrition. Likewise, the community crèche, once it is set up and operated as per the young mums' proposal to the Foundational Economy Challenge Fund, will support parents/carers to get engaged as key workers and shift workers but also institute an enhanced 0–2 education programme to advantage their very young children. The outdoor learning programme is designed to help children and young people connect with and enjoy the natural environment, improve their health and well-being, and build social capital. The performing arts initiatives all seek to re-engage children and young people at risk of alienation from school while teaching them new skill-sets including language and literacy. The investment and funding of these four projects will guarantee continuity and security for those who have already demonstrated their worth and impact.

The next three local solutions allied to their Not-NEET projects are considered to be larger-scale public works that address some of the most serious challenges facing this school-community. The mooted new multi-agency hub with capacity for responding to welfare demands disclosed in the local school makes frontline services more accessible and streamlined for users, and more efficient for Gwynedd Council. With frontline workers interconnected on the same site, education, health and welfare matters can be more readily addressed akin to a full service schools model. Establishing significantly sized community food gardens to supply the Hive Café and provide some food to resident families meets unmet needs in regards food insecurity, empowers local residents who get involved as volunteers, bestows health benefits in terms of nutrition and physical activities with gardening, and instils pride in the built environment. Promoting social eco-housing for energy efficiency and getting involved in producing renewable and sustainable electricity also meets unmet needs in regards fuel poverty, managing energy resources, producing and supplying more affordable energy. The investment and funding of these three projects will better protect Trem y Mynydd from cost-of-living crises and counter the immeasurable costs to resident families' health and well-being.

The seventh local solution and its allied Not-NEET project, 'Rigging the future: Welsh slate and World Heritage', also ties into the local history of the Trem y Mynydd housing estate and dovetails with labour history, but here a more contemporary national story of Wales comes into view. The point to be made here is that were resident families to miss out on some of the social and economic benefits to be derived from the slate landscape of northwest Wales UNESCO World Heritage designation and potential tourism to Port Penrhyn, they would be forever be condemned to be the marginalised working class. This can very easily happen but we have sought advice from the relevant team in Gwynedd Council in trying to access Heritage Lottery funding for our local project, which prompted the wordplay on this Not-NEET project.[21] In doing so, and maintaining a focus on inequalities, it is possible to redress the balance and deliver poetic justice given that so many families of the working men employed in Port Penrhyn and Penrhyn Quarry were relocated onto Trem y Mynydd from the waterfront at the time of 'early settlement'. This detail came to light from family history conversations, and also in a surveyor's report found in in the National Library Archives in London, which provided details of Bangor City Council's intentions regarding populating this particular social housing estate.

Conclusion

Given the grim realities of life on Trem y Mynydd, it is crucial to keep a more contemporary national story of Wales to the fore, and a way forward as we have shown throughout this book is a participatory approach to identifying needs and assets and then responding practically. On the one hand, this requires channelling research-informed evidence and policy recommendations from the grassroots into local/national governments, and not just to be cordially received but acted on: in our experience this means coordinated social actions by our elected representatives to Gwynedd Council as well as its power brokers and policy-makers, the national manager of *Children First*, Wales's Children's Commissioner, ministerial advisers, and politicians in Cardiff and Westminster. No doubt there are political pressures and political arithmetic, including re-appointments and re-elections, and constraints operating on local/ national governments to meet legislative obligations, but the local need is urgent. On the other hand, recognition of our jointly devised local solutions allied to Not-NEET projects is required, which means systemic and structural changes, particularly in the ways schools and other institutions operate with public investment and funding to deliver on the promise of Welsh Government's idea about 'Prosperity for All'.

Our briefing for a business case to address the problems of suffering and punishing hardship, social emergencies and humanitarian disaster, and to realise the promise of anti-poverty policies, is straightforward: 'better bang for the buck'! This was effectively the argument put on disinvestment and reinvestment by Lewis in chapter 1 and Watkins in chapter 9 this volume, which was to make more of the investments and public expenditure already ploughed into Trem y Mynydd. Such an economic imperative aligns with the moral and political imperatives for addressing welfare demands, but not just with emergency grants although these are crucial to buffer the fallout from the cost-of-living crisis, including children and young people disengaging from education. Disinvestment and reinvestment is in keeping with the Well-being and Future Generations (Wales) Act 2015, the 2018 *Children First* needs assessment and the principles of asset-based school-community development as we have outlined. More than that, it shows a realistic response to Alston's (2019) report on *Extreme Poverty and Human Rights in the UK* with its major focus on universal credit, which are fertile grounds for grievance and extremist right-wing conservative populism taking hold. To avert such catastrophe more streamlined funding is better spent on reconfigured frontline services in concert with locally devised solutions allied to their respective Not-NEET projects co-developed with the Bangor PLUS team.

In the case of building a replica timber slate boat (see figure 10) we also considered seeking a corporate sponsor, benefactor and/or shareholders, which harks back to maritime history when shipping expanded with the slate industry. Archival work[22] shows that there were only a few private companies with no one prominent person or stock company. Prior to steam ships, the early boats were built of wood and construction was facilitated by the investment of small sums by a large group of shareholders including quarrymen, who all received a small dividend. Apparently shares were sold by auction, an interesting idea that informs our efforts at fundraising, though we also investigated other more contemporary sources such as crowd-funding and matched funding from Welsh Government, Wales's National Slate Museum, Gwynedd Council and Heritage Lottery Funding.[23] This all pointed to a 'meeting of the minds' in terms of the practicability of thinking about wider systemic and structural origins of the resident families' lived experiences of poverty on Trem y Mynydd, as recounted in this book. This also means coordinated support from all quarters to help realise our vision for education and training, work experience and apprenticeships with a view to future employment.

Our approach challenges Welsh national/local governments to do things differently on two counts: move on from the GERM's tired neo-liberal policy foci on high standards and aspirations, tackling the impact of poverty on attainment and insisting on community schools with managers. Secondly, shift away from allocating budgets in any one election cycle to ministerial portfolios then relevant departments funding ineffectual policy initiatives and frontline workers, who mostly operate in silos. This all precludes joined-up thinking, which requires a new social democratic policy focus on requisite coordinated social actions at grassroots level. In our policy advocacy we emphasised assets-based school-community development to counter poverty causes and effects and to get stuck into what can be reasonably done to achieve the policy visions of the Well-being and Future Generations Act and the *Children First* needs assessment. Our driving force was what we could do locally to push back against child poverty but also to secure a stable Welsh social democracy for future generations, which is akin to the approach taken by Europe's Committee of the Regions.[24] The local/regional area assumes responsibility to identify its own social, economic and environmental needs and opportunities, and the resources required to fund an integrated approach to education, employment and training. These are the sorts of public debates that informed academic partners' teaching and research activities,[25] but this work has required an extraordinary concerted local effort to date.

To carry it still further, to expand if only into the other four *Children First* areas, we invited chapters that are responsive and advisory from GwE (see Watkins's chapter 9) and from school Heads, specifically the Association of School and College Leaders in Wales (see Hughes's chapter 10), but also from international academic partner (see Whatman's chapter 11). Hughes reminded us of the complexity of current policy demands on school Heads and the desperate need for matched funding and resources, but she acknowledged the creativity in our local solutions allied to their Not-NEET projects and firmly indicated that we needed 'a robust, fully costed, evidence-informed and persuasive rationale' for expansion. We tried to secure £5,000 funding from Bangor University to commission a business case, given the briefing to support our modest request for opportunities in employment, education and training, at the same time as we set out to consolidate partnership ways of working with other major institutions, including local government, convinced in the key principles devised by Welsh Government:

A *Children First* approach brings together organisations to improve outcomes for children and young people around a 'place'. A long-term strategic focus is developed with communities for that place, to reduce the inequalities faced compared with children in more socially advantaged places.

Garnering a positive response is not easy because it is all in the face of post-Covid-19 austerity cuts. For example, Bangor University is going through yet another restructure while Gwynedd Council is rumoured to be facing £42m budget cuts, and those responsible for education are confronted by professional concerns with school inspections, student alienation, disengagement and absenteeism following Covid-19 lockdowns, as well as teachers' strikes, among myriad other issues like the costs of the school day. We fight on, trying to bring the Bangor PLUS team together with politicians, policy-makers and power brokers as well as civil servants in the hope of joining the dots, acting on local solutions and providing learning opportunities through our co-designed Not-NEET projects. In doing so, we are drawing on our social democratic social imaginary, co-constructing a different vision of the future, and throwing out a lifeline of hope to resident families, including children and young people. In this concerted effort, we are conjoining the local and the national in Wales in order to provoke systemic and structural change, push back against child poverty and confront the challenges for schooling future generations.

Notes

1   This is the title of chapter 7 in Mills and Morton (2013).
2   For an indication of their income, see *https://www.gov.uk/universal-credit* (accessed 1 April 2022).
3   As discussed in the opening sentence to Dorling's (2014) book, and is raised by journalist John Harris in a feature article titled 'This is a social emergency. Why is no one acting like it?' (*The Guardian Journal*, 8 August 2022) and again by Aditya Chakrabortty in his article, 'In this Welsh town the UK's humanitarian crisis has begun', *The Guardian Journal*, 20 August 2022.
4   This is a teachers' pack (n.d.) with a bilingual title, *Llechi Slate* and subtitled *The Slate Industry of North Wales. The Quarrymen's Union*. It contains numerous items, some ready for reproduction for classroom use, all listed in

the booklet titled *Introduction. The Development of Unionism*. It includes the interview transcript cited.

5 See *https://www.ohchr.org/documents/issues/poverty/eom_gb_16nov2018.pdf, p. 21.* For the full report, please see *https://documents-dds-ny.un.org/doc/UNDOC/GEN/G19/112/13/PDF/G1911213.pdf?OpenElement* (accessed 1 April 2022).

6 See *https://en.wikipedia.org/wiki/Universal_Credit#:~:text=The%20Universal%20Credit%20mechanism%20was,Party%20annual%20conference%20in%202010* (accessed 1 April 2022).

7 Coincidentally, devolution came under fire in the UK Conservative Party's public debates between Liz Truss and Rishi Sunak, the contenders to replace Prime Minister Boris Johnson.

8 This again was the substance of Wales's education minister Jeremy Miles's announcement to the Bevan Foundation on 16 June 2022, but the irony is not lost given global neo-liberal ideas touted in such a revered Welsh institution: see *https://media.service.gov.wales/news/radical-action-needed-to-create-a-truly-equitable-education-system-for-all* (accessed 1 April 2022).

9 See Welsh Government press release, 21 March 2022. Available at: *https://www.gov.wales/25m-investment-community-focused-schools-tackle-impact-poverty* (accessed 21 April 2023).

10 See *https://hwb.gov.wales/curriculum-for-wales/designing-your-curriculum/developing-a-vision-for-curriculum-design/#curriculum-design-and-the-four-purposes* (accessed 1 April 2022).

11 Ibid.

12 This is a reference to Beckett's submission to Wales's post-pandemic recovery and reconstruction online survey (no longer available to access), and yet again it was cordially received. A follow-up phone call was significant in that the nominated officer in Welsh Government could not answer questions on what would come of the survey results.

13 Daniel Williams's (2003) presentation of Raymond Wiliams's work has this for its title which presents selected writings of, and interviews with, Williams.

14 Adamson tracks the subtle but important change in the understanding of these terms in his chapter in Mannay's (2016) book.

15 See n. 11.

16 Truxal's chapter in the above work speaks of austerity and Brexit as the twin destroyers of social democracy and state provision, in this case specifally of legal aid.

17 See Harris, 'This is a social emergency. Why is no one acting like it?'.

18 See *https://gov.wales/healthier-wales-foundation-economy-programme* (accessed 1 April 2022).

19 As noted in Beckett's Editor's Introduction, this is akin to Moll (2019), which builds on Gonzalez et al. (2005). Also see Lingard (2013).

20 See *www.cwmpas.coop* (accessed 1 April 2022).

21 During the production of this book, Lori Beckett came to work with the Gwynedd Council team responsible for the World Heritage designation, who requested a list of possible heritage activities that could be easily implemented.

Lori indicated that these could double as taster sessions on Trem y Mynydd. They were favourably received, and Lori was then invited to a major workshop event to meet the partners involved with Gwynedd Council, which proved to be a golden opportunity for networking and soliciting support for our local solution building a replica timber slate boat allied to its Not-NEET project, which coincidentally put a spotlight on maritime heritage conservation.

22 This follows economic historian Jean Lindsay (1974).

23 The Bangor PLUS team is certainly inspired by the purchase and restoration of the Welsh bard Hedd Wyn's family home at Yr Ysgwrn near Trawsfynydd in Gwynedd (see chapter 7). This project, which included a new-build cultural centre with education facilities, bookshop and cafe, came about as a result of a partnership formed by the Snowdonia National Park Authority (SNPA), the Welsh Government and the Heritage Lottery Fund.

24 This was recounted in Roger Read's letter to the editor (*The Guardian*, 11 July 2022), then seemingly taken up in a main feature article on UK Labour's own 'levelling up agenda' by Lisa Nandy, shadow secretary of state for levelling up, housing and communities (*The Observer*, 24 July 2022).

25 See the budget for the two seminar series in appendix 1, and please note that at the time of writing we have sought funding for including a social geography mapping by Danny Dorling (Oxford), which takes direction from collaborative work done with colleagues in our BERA commission on poverty and policy advocacy.

APPENDICES

Appendix 1

Shaping the Future: budget for two seminar series

Preamble

The *Children First* needs assessment completed in 2018 in Bangor was followed by two series of six-monthly seminars: the first to initiate a place-based action study that became known as the Bangor Poverty and Learning in Urban Schools (PLUS) project; the second series to plug into the multi-cities ethnography taking shape across the UK and Australia. This work, recounted in this edited book, is ripe for expansion if only in the other four *Children First* areas across Wales, but it should begin with another needs assessment that is combined with an assets assessment, preferably done in 2023 at the end of a five-year cycle that included Covid-19 and a cost-of-living crisis. The logistics are such that there needs to be 'a robust, fully costed, evidence informed and persuasive rationale to be presented to policy-makers and those who hold the purse strings' (see Hughes's chapter 10). To this end, there remains much to be done, but we start here with a budget on costings to get started.

Number of partner organisation delegates	20
How frequently/will project run?	Two series of seminars: 2 x 6 x 2-hour seminars, 2-hour prep. for each with 1 staff on prep. and 1 staff in support at events = 72 staff hours on seminars Networking meetings: 2 hours per meeting, 20 meetings, 1 staff = 40 staff hours on meetings

Staffing costs (no. of hours x no. of staff x staff cost per hour)	40 = 72 staff hours @ £100 per hour (academic/facilitation staff) = £7,200
Resources (consumable materials, etc.)	Flyers, printed reading material for delegates, pens, paper, etc. £500
Capital expenditure (larger one-off items)	Books/e-books for project £1,000
Venue hire	12 sessions, 2 hours each plus set up time = 36-hour venue hire, e.g. cost £200 per session = £2,400
Travel costs	Guest speakers brought in £500 x 4
Subsistence (for groups or staff)	Lunch/tea/coffee, etc. 12 seminars, x 20 people at £ per head = £6.60 12 x 20 x £6.60 = £1,584
External support/quality assurance/awarding, etc.	Guest attendance (max. 4) £500 x 4
Miscellaneous costs (please detail)	£1,000
5% contingency fund (of total project cost)	£660
Total	**£14,844**

Appendix 2: the Not-NEET project tied to chapter 3

Co-ordinating the future: the Youth Hall as a multi-agency hub

Preamble

Mooted plans were underway on Trem y Mynydd to demolish the old youth hall and build an eco-friendly multi-agency site with recreation facilities and potential space for a crèche, which sits with consultations with local resident families. Covid-19 caused delays and consideration must now be given to new work practices like working remotely, on-site, or a hybrid mix, but this pause worked in our favour because this presented an opportunity for Mynydd Ni in receipt of Building Communities Trust (BCT) funding in concert with Gwynedd Council to not only consolidate investment on the estate but also consider poverty alleviation through major public works. These plans are in flux given austerity and funding cuts but the opportunity stands were the situation to change. This is an alternative to having external contractors on-site, doing the work and re-investing in their own profit-making businesses, and allows for negotiations on a Full Service Schools model for the provision of education, health and welfare services.

Locally devised solution

By providing opportunities for education, employment and training including paid work experience in the on-site building project, resident families, particularly children and young people, will learn about and build expertise in the associated professions of building design, town planning, the trades of demolition and construction industries, including green industries, landscaping and gardening, together with estate management and the service industries. These opportunities to actively participate in building an eco-friendly multi-agency site with recreation facilities and potentially a crèche will give the young people, and especially teenagers, the incentives to engage with mentors, see the worth of work and making a living, as well as ways to develop their own career path. This would contribute to building green industry on the estate.

Precedents

While this local solution is exemplary insofar as it provides incentives and opportunities in postcodes of concentrated poverty and unemployment, it sits well with the philosophy of the BCT's mission: to enable residents to build on the strengths and talents within their communities, and take action to make their areas even better places to live (see *http://www.bct.wales/about-us/*). Likewise, there are efforts underway to encourage apprenticeship initiatives in Gwynedd and across Wales to engage young people (see *https://careerswales.gov.wales/apprenticeships*).

Links to *Curriculum for Wales*

This Not-NEET project facilitates teaching and learning about major public works and a Full Service Schools model for the provision of education, health and welfare services. It aligns with several areas within the *Curriculum for Wales*: STEM subjects and other areas for learning, notably: health and well-being; humanities; languages, literacy and communication. There are several statements of 'What matters' to guide curriculum design that are directly relevant here: see *https://gov.wales/sites/default/files/publications/2021-11/curriculum-for-wales-statements-of-what-matters-code.pdf*. This Not-NEET project also supports the four purposes of the curriculum, specifically helping young people become: ambitious, capable learners who are ready to learn throughout their lives.

Logistics

The burden of work on school Heads and teaching staff for this project is eased by advice and output from a local curriculum committee, where Beckett and French join specialists and other partners in local agencies invited to contribute to the design of teaching and learning programmes: including but not confined to representatives from Betsi Cadwaladr University Health Board working with education representatives from Undeb Cenedlaethol Athrawon Cymru (UCAC), NASUWT Cymru, NEU Cymru, ASCL Cymru, Gwynedd Council, GwE, Coleg Menai and Bangor University, and other educational institutions.

14–16 qualifications on offer in Wales

This Not-NEET project provides differing skills for the different phases of the project. There will be opportunities to experience many trades connected to construction for which there are myriad vocational qualifications such as those offered by City and Guilds. There may also be connections with vocational GCSEs such as engineering and design work, along with practical skills in construction. These can progress to university-level work in terms of design/civil engineering. There are also links to the Welsh Baccalaureate Skills certificate in the areas of the enterprise and employability challenge and the community challenge.

Potential partners

- Uchelgais Gogledd Cymru (Regional Skills Partnership);
- Building Communities Trust and Invest Local Trust;
- Gwynedd Council;
- Bangor University;
- Coleg Menai courses;
- City and Guilds accreditation courses;

Facilitation Fund

Like the other Not-NEET projects, this one would benefit from a Facilitation Fund to be managed by the Trem y Mynydd Cooperative with a board to be comprised of local residents and frontline workers and governed in line with cooperative models.[1] This means:

- a start-up grant for a feasibility study £2,000 on a Full Service Schools model/hub;
- a pilot study £5,000 to set up curriculum committee and produce sample teaching materials;
- an evaluation £3,000 with advice on expansion into four areas that participated in the 2018 *Children First* needs assessment – for costs of the Bangor PLUS project as a whole;
- a full-scale 'Co-ordinating the future' project subject to a feasibility study report.

Allied businesses and industries

This enables us to reiterate an argument for the re-industrialisation of Bangor and Gwynedd:

- building design;
- town planning;
- the trades of demolition and construction industries;
- green industries;
- landscaping and gardening;
- estate management;
- recreation industries.

Note

1   The Facilitation Fund was so named by one of the residents, Owen MacLean (see chapter 7) and the co-operative was suggested by Pete Whitby, another resident contributing a local solution (see chapter 5), while community development worker Gwen Thirsk provided advice on the legalities: see *www.cwmpas.coop* (see chapter 6).

Appendix 3: the Not-NEET project tied to chapter 4
Cultivating the estate: establishing community food gardens

Preamble

Resident families on the Trem y Mynydd housing estate experienced food insecurity during the Covid-19 pandemic that required emergency food provision orchestrated by resident volunteers and supported by their elected representatives on Gwynedd Council, Mynydd Ni workers, Welsh Government, Gwynedd Council and the Betsi Cadwaladr University Health Board. The situation abated only to the extent that the emergency passed after lockdowns ended, but returned with the cost-of-living crisis felt across Wales and the UK. This requires concerted efforts to guarantee the right to food, to develop a food security strategy, and to deliver education/social policies that impact local communities.

Locally devised solution

The local solution at the time of the pandemic was to rally in support of resident families in distress who were experiencing punishing hardship, to provide emergency food crates and parcels on request. This local solution evolved with changing sets of circumstances and the community group's practical experience of responding to unmet needs. The Hive Café, having re-opened to the public in the church hall, moved from budget cooking and feeding hungry families to providing a communal space with food. The volunteers working on the community kitchen gardens to supply fresh seasonal produce for eating and the cafe, looked to start a social enterprise in market gardening on Trem y Mynydd. This would contribute to building green industry on the estate.

Precedents

There is a large-scale social enterprise producing and supplying food locally to Bwyd Da Bangor in line with plans developed by Paul Gordon, a colleague in Penrhyn House, to provide training opportunities for its recovery community. Gordon won Heritage

Lottery funding and in-kind support from Gwynedd Council in the form of asset-transfer to release a brownfield site on Trem y Mynydd for food production, and a condition of the funding was to coordinate with local networks of schools and educational institutions. This ties into our Not-NEET project that allies with the work of the Trem y Mynydd community garden group's work emulating *Incredible Edible*.

Links to *Curriculum for Wales*

This Not-NEET project facilitates teaching and learning about horticulture, agriculture, the economy of food production, food supply chains plus the practicalities of growing food in cross-curriculum food projects with potential for expansion locally, regionally and nationally. There are several statements of 'What matters' to guide curriculum design that are directly relevant here: see *https://gov.wales/sites/default/files/publications/2021-11/curriculum-for-wales-statements-of-what-matters-code.pdf*. This project also supports the four purposes of the curriculum, specifically helping young people become: enterprising, creative contributors who are ready to play a full part in life and work; ethical, informed citizens who are ready to be citizens of Wales and the world.

Logistics

The burden of work on school Heads and teaching staff for this Not-NEET project is eased by advice and output from a local curriculum committee where Mead Silvester and Beckett join specialists and other partners in local agencies invited to contribute to the design of teaching and learning programmes: including but not confined to horticulturalists, representatives from Betsi Cadwaladr University Health Board working with education representatives from Undeb Cenedlaethol Athrawon Cymru (UCAC), NASUWT Cymru, NEU Cymru, ASCL Cymru, Gwynedd Council, GwE, Coleg Menai and Bangor University, other educational institutions and Penrhyn House.

14–16 qualifications on offer in Wales

This allied Not-NEET project also draws on these collaborations to facilitate innovative and vocational qualifications to provide knowledge and skill sets regarding opportunities to learn about RHS qualifications in horticulture, HEI undergraduate and postgraduate science programmes in plant sciences, environmental studies, all geared to learning about and building expertise in growing food, self-sufficiency, health and well-being, and a sustainable and environmentally friendly local food industry along with home economics in relation to family maintenance, household budgeting, etc. There are also links to the Welsh Baccalaureate Skills certificate in the areas of the individual project, the enterprise and employability challenge, and the community challenge.

Potential partners

- Uchelgais Gogledd Cymru (Regional Skills Partnership);
- Penrhyn House;
- Wild Elements lectures and short courses;
- Coleg Menai courses on 'gardening the basics';
- Treborth Botanic Gardens 'get to know plants' courses;
- National Botanic Gardens courses on growing organic foods;
- National Trust (horticultural training);
- Royal Horticultural Society (horticultural training);
- Keep Wales Tidy.

Facilitation Fund

Like the other Not-NEET projects, this one would benefit from a Facilitation Fund to be managed by the Trem y Mynydd Cooperative with a board to be comprised of local residents and frontline workers and governed in line with cooperative models.[1] This means:

- a start-up grant for a feasibility study £2,000 to build up community food gardens;
- a pilot study £5,000 to set up curriculum committee and produce sample teaching materials;
- an evaluation £3,000 with advice on expansion into four areas that participated in the 2018 *Children First* needs assessment;
- a full-scale 'Cultivating the estate' project subject to a feasibility study report.

Allied businesses and industries

- horticulture;
- agriculture;
- DIY suppliers;
- market gardens.

Note

1   The Facilitation Fund was so named by one of the residents, Owen MacLean (see chapter 7) and the co-operative was suggested by Pete Whitby, another resident contributing a local solution (see chapter 5), while community development worker Gwen Thirsk provided advice on the legalities: see *www.cwmpas.coop* (see chapter 6).

Appendix 4: the Not-NEET project tied to chapter 5

Powering the estate: a home-grown energy supply

Preamble

Resident families on this housing estate have personal lived experiences with both Wales's nation-wide energy crisis and the cost-of-living crisis concerning fuel poverty. This is tied to the UK-wide climate crises, Brexit and a struggle not only with soaring energy bills, old and inefficient appliances and whitegoods, but also the unaffordability of heating aged, inefficient housing. Coupled with low incomes this results in judgement calls on 'eating or heating': feeding the family or staying warm, both greatly impacting on health and well-being.

Locally devised solution

The proposed local solution to the problems of fuel poverty and climate crises targets the energy market, specifically green energy, to encourage government policy choices away from inward investment from external companies more concerned with profit extraction providing no impact on the price of energy to provide renewable energy whilst generating assets. The solution is to re-tool the economy away from fossil fuels and develop local community-based energy sources to facilitate major public works and local ownership of energy production and supply. This is marked by the allied Not-NEET project, a place-based education, employment and training programme that contributes to the re-energising of Bangor and Gwynedd through the reconstruction of fuel and energy sources, their use and efficiency. This would contribute to building green industry on the estate.

Precedents

There are green energy/local community energy projects underway across Wales with the potential to coordinate nationally via the member-led organisation Community Energy Wales. Examples in Gwynedd include Ynni Ogwen in Bethesda, Ynni Padarn Peris in Llanberis and Ynni Anafon in Abergwyngregyn. Cyd Ynni, a local consortium of community energy groups, has trialled energy efficiency work and further afield there are numerous examples of people working together in their communities to address fuel poverty and the climate crises. The GwyrddNi movement in Gwynedd, funded by the National Lottery's Climate Action Fund, provides exemplary practice on putting the community in the lead of this type of work.

Links to *Curriculum for Wales*

This Not-NEET project facilitates teaching and learning about green industries through new technologies, eco-services, regeneration and recycling that extends to site visits, work experiences and more. These provide opportunities to learn about the challenges of renewable energy production, supply and efficiency in cross-curriculum energy projects with potential for expansion locally, regionally and nationally. There are several statements of 'What matters' to guide curriculum design that are directly relevant here: see *https:// gov.wales/sites/default/files/publications/2021-11/curriculum-for-wale s-statements-of-what-matters-code.pdf.* This project also supports the four purposes of the curriculum, specifically helping young people become: enterprising, creative contributors who are ready to play a full part in life and work; ethical, informed citizens who are ready to be citizens of Wales and the world.

Logistics

The burden of work on school Heads and teaching staff for this Not-NEET project is eased by advice and output from a local curriculum committee where Fernley, Whitby and Peisley join specialists and other partners in local agencies invited to contribute to the design of teaching and learning programmes: including but not confined to Datblygiadau Egni Gwledig, representatives from Betsi Cadwaladr University Health Board working with education representatives from Undeb Cenedlaethol Athrawon Cymru (UCAC), NASUWT Cymru, NEU Cymru, ASCL Cymru, Gwynedd Council, GwE, Coleg Menai and Bangor University, and other educational institutions.

14–16 Qualification offer in Wales

This allied Not-NEET project could connect young people with innovative or vocational qualifications to deliver skill-oriented engineering courses and practical training, at each level of the QCF such as those offered by City and Guilds, or the vocational GCSE pathway in engineering. These could then lead to recognised trade certification and/ or apprenticeships work experiences and academic qualifications such as electrical engineering and environmental sciences. This project supports the four purposes of the *Curriculum for Wales* but also links to the Welsh Baccalaureate Skills certificate in the areas of the individual project, the enterprise and employability challenge, the global citizenship challenge and the community challenge.

Potential business partners in associated industries

- Uchelgais Gogledd Cymru (Regional Skills Partnership);
- ADRA (local housing association) on retro-fitting social housing with renewable-heating and energy efficiency;
- Renew Wales's coordinators and mentors;
- Citizen's Advice Bureau, given that it has employed energy experts;
- Datblygiadau Egni Gwledig (DEG) as local energy and engagement experts;
- Travis Perkins;
- Grŵp Llandrillo Menai (partners with ADRA and five community enterprises on the Community Renewal Fund-funded project Sero Net Gwynedd Net Zero. There is a centre of excellence in development in Penygroes that will provide training opportunities aligned to the net zero policies of both Westminster and Cardiff governments.

Facilitation Fund

Like the other Not-NEET projects, this one would benefit from a Facilitation Fund to be managed by the Trem y Mynydd Cooperative with a board to be comprised of local residents and frontline workers and governed in line with cooperative models.[1] This means:

- a start-up grant for a feasibility study £2,000 on renewable energy on Trem y Mynydd;
- a study of research reports on local community energy projects £1,000;

- a pilot study £5,000 to set up curriculum committee and produce sample teaching materials;
- an evaluation £3,000 with advice on scale-up into four areas that participated in the 2018 *Children First* needs assessment;
- a full-scale 'Powering the estate' project subject to a feasibility study report.

Allied businesses and industries

- recycling and new technologies;
- eco-services suppliers;
- trade qualifications (as above) aligned with installers and the qualifications required to install this tech (inc. retrofitting);
- support services to help people learn the new skills and behaviours required to use the new technologies efficiently;
- electrical cable and component supply and manufacture.

Note

1   The Facilitation Fund was so named by one of the residents, Owen MacLean (see chapter 7) and the co-operative was suggested by Pete Whitby, another resident contributing a local solution (see chapter 5), while community development worker Gwen Thirsk provided advice on the legalities: see *www.cwmpas.coop* (see chapter 6).

Appendix 5: the Not-NEET project tied to chapter 6

Starting out for the future: 0–2 years on-site crèche

Preamble

Just before Covid-19 and lockdown, fifteen mothers of pre-school-age children on the Trem y Mynydd estate banded together to initiate a partnership and approached a Flying Start nurse, a community development officer and a Communities4Work worker for support. These three recruited an academic partner to bring ideas on enhancing the 0-2 educational experience through play. They developed a proposal to co-design, co-produce and obtain qualifications to lead a community crèche as a social enterprise. Their bid to Wales's Foundational Economy Challenge Fund was submitted but not funded, yet their circumstances remain much the same although exacerbated by Covid-19 and now the cost-of-living crisis. They are mostly in insecure, low-paid and zero hours' work, and they already provide chaotic informal childcare for each other, as well as rely on friends/family to help them escape a spiral of intergenerational poverty marked by unemployment.

Locally devised solution

This local solution to the problem of accessible and suitable childcare addresses an unmet need given that the closest provision is more than two miles away in one of the city's privatised childcare settings, which is neither affordable nor easily accessible for those families that can ill-afford the time and bus fare to take their babies and toddlers twice daily there and back. By establishing an on-site crèche run by qualified parents with others in training, these mothers' vision is to build capacity in their own community to provide childcare marked by local knowledge of babies' and toddlers' needs and family circumstances. Simultaneously these mothers want childcare available 24/7 to fit with flexible working hours, particularly patterns of shift work, which means that they want to remove barriers to accessing employment, education and training, and family services. This also means that this more accessible and suitable childcare will enable resident families to get work, education and training with skills and recognition.

Precedents

There is no provision for a dedicated crèche for 0–2-year-olds run by
Gwynedd Council or by the market, though on this housing estate
there is council-run children's support-services; Flying Start-funded
childcare for 2–3 years; the Childcare Offer for Wales reiterated
by Gwynedd Council for 3–4 year olds; and Gwynedd Council
LEA-funded childcare for 4–5 years. The need is for resources to
develop this on-site crèche as an asset with social value. The mothers
want childcare and a family-friendly centre, allowing an access-point
for family services and for community-driven solutions to family
problems to emerge. They want to facilitate early intervention where
needs are high and build a seamless approach to multi-service access
for whole family needs.

Links to *Curriculum for Wales*

This Not-NEET project facilitates teaching and learning about
childcare and early childhood where children are respected,
their talents nurtured and their abilities to thrive as UNICEF
recommends in cross-curriculum projects on safe and inspiring
places to learn with potential for expansion locally, regionally and
nationally. There are several statements of 'What matters' to guide
curriculum design that are directly relevant here: see *https://gov.wales/
sites/default/files/publications/2021-11/curriculum-for-wales-statement
s-of-what-matters-code.pdf*. This project also supports the four purposes
of the curriculum, specifically helping young people become:
ambitious, capable learners who are ready to learn throughout their
lives; enterprising, creative contributors, ready to play a full part in
life and work.

Logistics

The burden of work on school Heads and teaching staff for this
Not-NEET project is eased by advice and output from a local curriculum
committee where Thirsk and Mead Sylvester join a delegation of parents,
specialists and other partners in local agencies invited to contribute
to the design of teaching and learning programmes: including
but not confined to early education practitioners, representatives

from Betsi Cadwaladr University Health Board working with education representatives from Undeb Cenedlaethol Athrawon Cymru (UCAC), NASUWT Cymru, NEU Cymru, ASCL Cymru, Gwynedd Council, GwE, Coleg Menai and Bangor University, and other educational institutions.

14–16 qualifications on offer in Wales

This Not-NEET project also draws on further collaboration to highlight vocational 14–16 qualification pathways, including child development, childcare and early childhood studies. There are vocational qualifications available as well as a GCSE pathway in health and social care. There are opportunities for work experience and there are also links to the Welsh Baccalaureate Skills certificate in the areas of the individual project, the enterprise and employability challenge, and the community challenge.

Potential partners

- Uchelgais Gogledd Cymru (Regional Skills Partnership);
- Gwynedd Council youth services;
- Early Years Wales;
- Mudiad Meithrin;
- Department of Work and Pensions;
- Ysgol Trem y Mynydd;
- Betsi Cadwaladr University Health Board Children's Services;
- Bangor University;
- Coleg Menai.

Facilitation Fund

Like the other Not-NEET projects, this one would benefit from a Facilitation Fund to be managed by the Trem y Mynydd Cooperative with a board to be comprised of local residents and frontline workers and governed in line with cooperative models.[1] This means:

- a start-up grant for a feasibility study £2,000 on architecture and business;
- a pilot study £5,000 to set up curriculum committee and produce sample teaching materials;

- an evaluation £3,000 with advice on expansion into four areas that participated in the 2018 *Children First* needs assessment;
- an additional £2,000 to facilitate an application for funding the crèche as a capital asset to be made to the Big Lottery's Rural Fund, Gwynedd Council and/or Bangor's regeneration programme;
- a full-scale 'Starting out for the future' project subject to a feasibility study report and funding applications.

Allied businesses and industries

- a crèche for 0–2-year-olds run by Gwynedd Council;
- council-run children's support-services;
- Flying Start-funded childcare for 2–3 years;
- the Childcare Offer for Wales reiterated by Gwynedd Council for 3–4 year olds;
- Gwynedd Council LEA-funded childcare for 4–5 years.

NB. This requires the renewal of Gwynedd youth services and there is pressure on the timeline because parents want to see their babies and toddlers in the crèche to get the care and experiential learning before they lose these very early years' opportunities and move on.

Note

1   The Facilitation Fund was so named by one of the residents, Owen MacLean (see chapter 7) and the co-operative was suggested by Pete Whitby, another resident contributing a local solution (see chapter 5), while community development worker Gwen Thirsk provided advice on the legalities: see *www.cwmpas.coop* (see chapter 6).

Appendix 6: the Not-NEET project tied to chapter 7

Acting on the future: student expression in the Performing Arts

Preamble

Most children and young people on this housing estate enjoy a good experience of schooling and education that is reflected in their attendance, participation and learning outcomes. Yet there is a cohort of children and teenagers who do not fare well within the traditional structures of primary and secondary schools. They have a record of non-participation and non-attendance having struggled with regulation, relationships with teachers, authority and the relevance of education. This contributes to their alienation and disengagement, which has consequences. However, to counter experiences of miseducation, they do respond to more appealing approaches to teaching and learning in programmes outside the education system.

Locally devised solution

The local solution already in operation is after-school performing arts programmes run by resident artists who design popular learning experiences for the children, teenagers and young adults well known to them. A deep understanding of the challenges that arise from living in poverty underpins their development of term-time sequential sessions to address unmet needs, including language and literacy. They blend the theory and practice of music, poetry, lyricism, oral traditions, life stories and physical activities that enable young people to be fully engaged in performances. These resident artists also encourage school attendance and post-school pathways through their allied Not-NEET project.

Precedents

One resident artist runs hip hop (rap) music workshops, a music hub with photography and filming, an adult music lab, an annual place-based Youth Music Festival, and he contributes to other community-based events on-site and elsewhere. The worth of these programmes is reflected in their popularity with local residents, especially children and young teenagers, who show good participation and regular attendance. As well there is demand from local schools to run one-off extra-curricular sessions. Funding for these time-limited programmes has come from various sources including Community Music Wales, Welsh Government, Gwynedd Council, Mynydd Ni, Invest Local, National Lottery, etc.

Links to *Curriculum for Wales*

This Not-NEET project facilitates teaching and learning about creative expression and creative skills, all leading to performances that combine music, dance, drama, with scriptwriting, film and video production in cross-curriculum school-community music projects with potential for expansion locally, regionally and nationally. By performing, acting and finding their voice, students actively engage in learning, notably about themselves, their local community and place in the wider world. There are several statements of 'What matters' to guide curriculum design that are directly relevant here: see *https://gov.wales/sites/default/files/publications/2021-11/curriculu m-for-wales-statements-of-what-matters-code.pdf*. This project also supports the four purposes of the curriculum, specifically helping young people become: enterprising, creative contributors who are ready to play a full part in life and work; healthy, confident individuals who are ready to lead fulfilling lives as valued members of society.

Logistics

The burden of work on school Heads and teaching staff for this Not-NEET project is eased by advice and output from a local curriculum committee where Maclean and Daws join specialists and other partners in community music invited to contribute to the design of teaching and learning programmes: including but not confined to creative artists, representatives from Betsi Cadwaladr University Health Board working with education representatives from Undeb Cenedlaethol Athrawon Cymru (UCAC), NASUWT Cymru, NEU Cymru, ASCL Cymru, Gwynedd Council, GwE, Coleg Menai and Bangor University, and other educational institutions.

14–16 Qualification offer in Wales

The allied Not-NEET project also draws on these collaborations to facilitate innovative vocational qualifications to provide knowledge and skill sets in regards opportunities to learn about performing arts including music, dance and drama, stagecraft and associated skills, as well as media and social studies, including vlogging, graphic design, entrepreneurship and marketing. While this focus orients students to the performing arts and entertainment industries, their involvement in after-school performances also alerts them to career paths in youth work, which connects with Towler et al.'s (2021) 'Introduction to the First Report of the Interim Youth Board for Wales', *Time to Deliver for Young People in Wales*. There are also links to the Welsh Baccalaureate Skills certificate in the areas of the individual project.

Potential partners

- Uchelgais Gogledd Cymru (Regional Skills Partnership);
- the Interim Youth Board for Wales;
- Pontio and Bangor University;
- Bangor Arts Initiative;
- Wales Arts Council;
- Participatory Arts in Wales;
- Art Works Cymru;
- Community Music Wales.

Facilitation Fund

Like the other Not-NEET projects, this one would benefit from a Facilitation Fund to be managed by the Trem y Mynydd Cooperative with a board to be comprised of local residents and frontline workers and governed in line with cooperative models.[1] This means:

- a start-up grant for a feasibility study £2,000 to build up school-community music;
- a pilot study £5,000 to set up curriculum committee and produce sample teaching materials;
- an evaluation £3,000 with advice on expansion into four areas that participated in the 2018 *Children First* needs assessment;

- an additional interim £10,000 to enable purchase of capital expenditure on equipment;
- a full-scale project 'Acting on the future' subject to a feasibility study report.

Allied businesses and industries

- soliciting the youth voice;
- meeting youth needs;
- reinvigorating the youth work sector;
- advocating for the recommendations in Towler et al.'s (2021) 'First Report of the Interim Youth Board for Wales', *Time to Deliver for Young People in Wales*;
- Pontio/Theatr Clwyd;
- BBC Cymru/S4C.

Note

1   The Facilitation Fund was so named by one of the residents, Owen MacLean (see chapter 7) and the co-operative was suggested by Pete Whitby, another resident contributing a local solution (see chapter 5), while community development worker Gwen Thirsk provided advice on the legalities: see *www.cwmpas.coop* (see chapter 6).

Appendix 7: the Not-NEET project tied to chapter 8

Rooting for the future: Wild Elements outdoor learning

Preamble

There has been a general decline in children and young people accessing outdoor spaces, learning about their environment and taking action to conserve it. This is particularly true after the Covid-19 pandemic where although outdoor spaces were seen as lower risk transmission environments, many children and young people became screen-bound with online schooling and resources and parental concern over letting them out to socialise and play. The physical and mental health benefits of being outside and connecting with nature are well documented, and outdoor learning projects build social capital at the same time as engendering a concern and care for the natural environment.

Locally devised solution

The local solution builds on the work of Wild Elements at Ysgol Trem y Mynydd and on the estate. The programme is to provide STEM learning sessions using outdoor learning within school to support the curriculum. In parallel, an outdoor learning programme operating as an after-school club can engage children and young people in environmental conservation activities, learning about sustainable living at the same time as building social capital. This is structured using the John Muir Award (JMA) scheme, an existing and well-resourced free award scheme that recognises outdoor learning and a commitment to conservation-focused projects. Whilst both can be facilitated by Wild Elements staff, there are opportunities to train young facilitators who can mentor and work with younger groups.

Precedents

There are many examples of schools engaging in the JMA and conservation activities and some JMA clubs/groups that meet outside school as alternatives or to further develop this work and engage with a wider age range (there is no age limit on the JMA). These are predominantly in the north-east of Wales or the north-west of England, currently.

Links to *Curriculum for Wales*

This Not-NEET project facilitates teaching and learning in outdoor learning sessions but also supporting their delivery and mentoring others. It aligns with several areas within the *Curriculum for Wales*: science and technology, health and well-being and humanities, and contributes to the development of social capital, which is less easily quantified. There are several statements of 'What matters' to guide curriculum design that are directly relevant here: see *https:// gov.wales/sites/default/files/publications/2021-11/curriculum-for-wale s-statements-of-what-matters-code.pdf*. This project also supports the four purposes of the curriculum, specifically helping young people become: ambitious, capable learners who are ready to learn throughout their lives, and there is potential for expansion locally, regionally and nationally.

Logistics

The burden of work on school Heads and teaching staff for this Not-NEET project is eased by advice and output from a local curriculum committee where French and Howard join specialists including outdoor learning teachers, youth workers and those involved in conservation work, who are invited to contribute to the design of teaching and learning programmes: including but not confined to Wild Elements and representatives from Betsi Cadwaladr University Health Board working with education representatives from Undeb Cenedlaethol Athrawon Cymru (UCAC), NASUWT Cymru, NEU Cymru, ASCL Cymru, Gwynedd Council, GwE, Coleg Menai and Bangor University, and other educational institutions.

14–16 qualifications on offer in Wales

This Not-NEET project also draws on further collaboration to highlight an innovative and vocational 14–16 qualification pathway, most relevant here, the Agored Cymru 'Learning in the outdoors' suite of qualifications, some of which are already offered by one of the local secondary schools. It has potential to build onto work in environmental studies and ecology, either through higher level vocational qualifications or university undergraduate work.

There is also the potential to move into teaching following this pathway in science, the humanities or outdoor education; healthy, confident individuals who are ready to lead fulfilling lives as valued members of society. There are also links to the Welsh Baccalaureate Skills certificate in the areas of the individual project, the enterprise and employability challenge, the global citizenship challenge and the community challenge.

Potential partners

- Uchelgais Gogledd Cymru (Regional Skills Partnership);
- John Muir Trust;
- North Wales outdoor learning service;
- Institute for Outdoor Learning;
- Wild Elements;
- outdoor education advisers' panel;
- Natural Resources Wales;
- Coleg Menai outdoor courses;
- Agored Cymru.

Facilitation Fund

Like the other Not-NEET projects, this one would benefit from a Facilitation Fund to be managed by the Trem y Mynydd Cooperative with a board to be comprised of local residents and frontline workers and governed in line with cooperative models.[1] This means:

- pay for a member of WE staff to run a pilot club for 10 weeks, 2 hrs per week, 2 staff per session – £800;
- pay for a member of WE staff to run the STEM sessions, 30 weeks, 4 hrs per week, 2 staff per session – £4,800;
- initial resources (tools/materials/PPE) and administration (registration, safeguarding training, etc.) – covered in WE fee above;
- registration for JMA and the award itself are free.

Allied businesses and industries

- horticulture;
- agriculture;

- DIY suppliers;
- market gardens;
- wildlife trusts/conservation organisations;
- forestry;
- land/game management;
- national park conservation work;

Note

1   The Facilitation Fund was so named by one of the residents, Owen MacLean (see chapter 7) and the co-operative was suggested by Pete Whitby, another resident contributing a local solution (see chapter 5), while community development worker Gwen Thirsk provided advice on the legalities: see *www.cwmpas.coop* (see chapter 6).

Appendix 8: the Not-NEET project tied to chapter 12

Rigging the future: Welsh slate boats and World Heritage

Preamble

From the early days of settlement on this housing estate prior to the Second World War, the families of the men working in Penrhyn Port, on the slate trains and Penrhyn's quarries were well accustomed to poverty as a result of class-based inequalities. This history of disadvantage continues into the present, with their descendants living in a school-community on the edge: they continue to battle the fallout from de-industrialisation, unemployment, exploitation of the working poor, universal credit, benefit cuts, and more recently the cost-of-living crisis. There is promise of economic growth and social regeneration given that the slate landscape of northwest Wales has been designated a UNESCO World Heritage site, but the future is in abeyance.

See *https://www.seren.bangor.ac.uk/news-politics/business/2020/12/16/ a-history-of-the-slate-trail/*.

Locally devised solution

In order for our school-community to accrue some benefits sitting in a corridor area associated with the World Heritage site, our local solution was to lobby Gwynedd Council, specifically the team responsible for the heritage designation and its partners including the National Slate Museum. We came with a proposal to build a replica slate boat (see figure 10) and maritime museum with an education centre and public sculptures. This provides multiple opportunities for both business, education, employment and training via our allied Not-NEET project that draws on archival histories, local and family histories, language, culture and heritage conservation, including maritime heritage conservation considering that in 1897, Lord Penrhyn bought a fleet from the Anglesey Shipping Company that included the *Mary B. Mitchell*, his favoured vessel, built in 1892.

Precedents

There are numerous precedents of shipbuilding for tourism; for example, the Jeannie Johnston famine ship on the Liffey in Dublin, opposite the EPIC Emigration Centre and near the Famine public sculptures. Likewise, Gwynedd Council's tourism plan, in line with UNESCO World Heritage and Sustainable Tourism principles, built on its initial Llechi project developed through Gwynedd Council, the Heritage Lottery Fund, Snowdonia National Park and Arloesi Gwynedd Wledig. This project targeted regeneration through heritage and culture activities such as young slate ambassadors, school art projects and wall murals. Local communities were then asked about their regeneration priorities to plug into Gwynedd Council's area regeneration plans. The National Museum of Wales also identified the Slate Museum as a funding priority, and did some consultation on support for local communities, education and skills for the future.

See *https://www.northwaleschronicle.co.uk/news/19520465.councils-big-plans-slate-landscape-becomes-world-heritage-site/.*

Links to *Curriculum for Wales*

This Not-NEET project facilitates teaching and learning about local and family histories including their place in the Welsh slate industry, maritime heritage conservation, including tall ship culture, slate boats' career narratives and marine art (see Brain Cleare's watercolour of the *Mary B. Mitchell*) in cross-curriculum projects with potential for expansion locally, regionally and nationally. There are several statements of 'What matters' to guide curriculum design that are directly relevant here (see *https://gov.wales/sites/default/files/publications/2021-11/curriculum-for-wales-statements-of-what-matters-code.pdf*. This project also supports the four purposes of the curriculum, specifically helping young people become: enterprising, creative contributors who are ready to play a full part in life and work; healthy, confident individuals who are ready to lead fulfilling lives as valued members of society.

Logistics

The burden of work on school Heads and teaching staff for this Not-NEET project is eased by advice and output from a local curriculum committee where Beckett and French join specialists including archivists, museum curators, economic and maritime historians, all invited to contribute to the design of teaching and learning programmes: including but not confined to representatives from Llechi Cymru – Wales Slate, Betsi Cadwaladr University Health Board working with education representatives from Undeb Cenedlaethol Athrawon Cymru (UCAC), NASUWT Cymru, NEU Cymru, ASCL Cymru, Gwynedd Council, GwE, Coleg Menai and Bangor University, and other educational institutions.

14–16 Qualification offer in Wales

The allied Not-NEET project also draws on these collaborations to facilitate innovative vocational qualifications to provide knowledge and skill sets in regards opportunities to learn about tourism, marine heritage conservation, shipbuilding, seamanship, sailing, essential navigation, cargo operations, sea transport, wreck salvage and restoration. This includes the history of the Anglesey Shipping Company and Paul Rogers's shipbuilding industry in Carrickfergus, which built the *Mary B. Mitchell* though wrecked and lost in the Solway Firth in 1944. There are also links to the Welsh Baccalaureate Skills certificate in the areas of the enterprise and employability challenge, the global citizenship challenge and the community challenge.

Potential partners

- Amgueddfa Llechi Cymru (National Slate Museum);
- Penrhyn Castle (National Trust);
- Comisiwn Brenhinol Henbion Cymru (Royal Commission on the Ancient and Historical Monuments of Wales);
- Uchelgais Gogledd Cymru (Regional Skills Partnership);
- Gwynedd Council cabinet member for Economy and Community;
- National Museum Wales's director of research and collections;
- Port Penrhyn Harbour Office.

Facilitation Fund

Like the other Not-NEET projects, this one would benefit from a Facilitation Fund to be managed by the Trem y Mynydd Cooperative with a board to be comprised of local residents and frontline workers and governed in line with cooperative models.[1] This means:

- a start-up grant for a feasibility study £2,000 on a full-scale project;
- an additional £3,000 to visit Carrickfergus and source timber slate boat designs;
- a pilot study £5,000 to set up curriculum committee and produce sample teaching materials;
- an evaluation £3,000 with advice on expansion into four areas that participated in the 2018 *Children First* needs assessment – for costs of the Bangor PLUS project as a whole, see appendix 8;
- a full-scale 'Rigging the future' project subject to a feasibility study report.

Allied businesses and industries

- chandlery/retail;
- marine preservation and archaeology;
- sailing – race coaching;
- sailing – professional crew;
- boat building – Dickies;
- marine architecture/marine engineering;
- Bo's'n training/boat maintenance and repair;
- sail-making;
- youth work through sail training.

Note

1   The Facilitation Fund was so named by one of the residents, Owen MacLean (see chapter 7) and the co-operative was suggested by Pete Whitby, another resident contributing a local solution (see chapter 5), while community development worker Gwen Thirsk provided advice on the legalities: see *www.cwmpas.coop* (see chapter 6).

BIBLIOGRAPHY

Adamson, D. (2016). 'Class, Politics and Poverty in Devolved Wales', in D. Mannay (ed.), *Our Changing Land. Revisiting Gender, Class and Identity in Contemporary Wales.* Cardiff: University of Wales Press.

Alcock, Pete (2012). *The Big Society: a new policy environment for the third sector?* Working Paper. University of Birmingham. See *http:// epapers.bham.ac.uk/1781/* (accessed 17 April 2023).

Alston, P. (2019). 'A/HRC/41/39/Add.1: Visit to the United Kingdom of Great Britain and Northern Ireland – Report of the Special Rapporteur on Extreme Poverty and Human Rights *United Nations*'. Available at: *https://www.ohchr.org/en/documents/country-reports/ahrc4139add1-visit-united-kingdom-great-britain-and-northern-ireland* (accessed 17 April 2023).

Apple, M. (2009). Foreword in Gewirtz et al. (eds). *Changing teacher professionalism. International trends, challenges and ways forward.* Oxford and New York: Routledge.

Australian Council for Health, Physical Education and Recreation (2022). Available at: *www.achper.org.au.*

Australian Government (2020). Mparntwe Declaration. Canberra. Available at: *https://www.dese.gov.au/alice-springs-mparntwe-education-declaration* (accessed 27 April 2023).

Australian Health Promoting Schools Network (2022). *National Principles for Health Education.* Adelaide: Australian Council for Health, Physical Education and Recreation (ACHPER). Available at: *https://shop.achper.org.au/advocacy/australian-health-promoting-schools-2/national-principles-of-health-education* (accessed 27 April 2023).

Ball, S. (2015). 'What is policy? 21 years later: reflections on the possibilities of policy research'. *Discourse: Studies in the Cultural Politics of Education*, 36/3, 306–13.

Banks, S. et al. (2019). *Co-producing research. A community development approach*. University of Bristol: Policy Press.

Beames, S. and M. Atencio (2008). 'Building social capital through outdoor education'. *Journal of adventure education and outdoor learning*, 8/2, 99–112

Beckett, L. (2016). *Teachers and academic partners in urban schools: Threats to professional practice*. London: Routledge.

Bernstein, B. (2000). *Pedagogy, Symbolic Control and Identity: Theory, research, critique*. Oxford: Rowman and Littlefield.

Calder, G., J. Gass and K. Merrill-Glover (2012). *Changing Directions of the British Welfare State*. Cardiff: University of Wales Press.

Child Poverty Action Group (2017). *Poverty: The Facts*. London: Child Poverty Action Group.

Christie, B., P. Higgins and P. McLaughlin (2015). '"Did you enjoy your holiday?" Can residential outdoor learning benefit mainstream schooling?'. *Journal of adventure education and outdoor learning*, 14/1, 1–23.

Cochran-Smith, M. et al. (eds) (2018). *Reclaiming accountability in teacher education*. New York: Teachers College Press.

Cynulliad Cenedlaethol Cymru (2001). *The Learning Country: A Paving Document*. Available at: *https://dera.ioe.ac.uk/5147/1/learning_country_ paving_document.pdf* (accessed 26 April 2023).

Davidson, J. (2020). *#futuregen. Lessons from a small country*. London: Chelsea Green Publishing.

Donaldson, G. (2015). *Successful Futures*. Cardiff: Welsh Government.

Dorling, D. (2014). *Inequality and the 1%*. London: Verso Books.

Dorling, D. (2018). *Peak Inequality. Britain's Ticking Time Bomb*. Bristol: Policy Press.

Durose, C. et al. (2012). *Towards Co-production in Research with Communities*. Connected Communities, Arts and Humanities Research Council.

Ersoy, A. (ed.) (2017). *The impact of co-production: From community engagement to social justice*. Bristol: Policy Press.

Evans, G. (2021). 'Back to the future? Reflections on three phases of education policy reform in Wales and their implications for teachers'. *J Educ Change*, 23, 371–96: https://doi.org/10.1007/s10833-021-09422-6.

Farver, S. D. (2014). 'Review of *Living on the Edge: Rethinking Poverty, Class and Schooling* by Smyth, John & Wrigley, Terry'. *Education Review*, 16.

The Foundational Economy Collective (2018). *Foundational Economy*. Manchester: University of Manchester Press.

French, G. et al. (2021). *The Impact of the COVID 19 Pandemic in Wales on the Health and Wellbeing of Learners and Practitioners and the Implications for Initial Teacher Education*. Available at: *https://hwb. gov.wales/professional-development/the-national-strategy-for-educational-research-and-enquiry-nsere/research-studies-on-the-impact-of-the-covid-19-pandemic-on-the-welsh-education-system/research-study-6/* (accessed 27 April 2023).

French, G. et al. (2022). 'The current state of outdoor learning in Wales'. Commissioned research awaiting publication via Hwb.

Furlong, J. (2015). *Teaching tomorrow's teachers*. Cardiff: Welsh Government.

Future Generations Commissioner for Wales (2020). *Future Generations Report*. Available at: *https://www.futuregenerations.wales/wp-content/uploads/2020/07/At-A-Glance-FG-Report.pdf* (accessed 21 April 2023).

Gannon, S., R. Hattam and W. Sawyer (2018). *Resisting Educational Inequality. Reframing Policy and Practice in Schools Serving Vulnerable Communities*. Oxford and New York: Routledge.

González, N., L. C. Moll and C. Amanti (2005). *Funds of Knowledge*. NJ: Lawrence Erlbaum Associates.

Gorard, S., N. Siddiqui and B. H. See (2019). 'The Difficulties of Judging What Difference the Pupil Premium Has Made to School Intakes and Outcomes in England'. *Research Papers in Education*:

*https://www.tandfonline.com/doi/full/10.1080/02671522.2019.167775
9* (accessed 27 April 2023).

Gorard, S., B. H. See and N. Siddiqui (2020). 'What is the evidence on the best way to get evidence into use in education?'. *Review of Education*, 8/2, 570–610: https://doi.org/10.1002/rev3.3200.

Gorard, S., N. Siddiqui and B. H. See (2021). 'Assessing the impact of Pupil Premium funding on primary school segregation and attainment'. *Research Papers in Education*, DOI: 10.1080/02671522.2021.1907775.

Gresham, F. M. and S. N. Elliott (1990). *Social Skills Rating System*. American Guidance Service.

Guderjan, M., H. Mackay and G. Stedman (2020). *Contested Britain: Brexit, austerity and agency*. Bristol: Bristol University Press.

Hargreaves, A. et al. (2001). *Learning to change: Teaching beyond subjects and standards*. San Francisco: Jossey-Bass.

Harris, A. and M. Jones (2020). *System Recall*. London: Sage.

Harvey, D. (2005). *A Brief History of Neoliberalism*. Oxford: Oxford University Press.

Ife, J. (2009). *Human Rights from Below*. Cambridge: Cambridge University Press.

Institute for Public Policy Research (2020). *Future Welfare State*. Available at: *https://www.ippr.org/future-welfare-state/* (accessed 21 April 2023).

Ivinson, G. et al. (2017). 'Learning the price of poverty across the UK'. *Policy Futures in Education*, 16/2, 130–43.

Jones, C. S. (1903). *What I Saw in Bethesda*. London: Brimley Johnson.

Jones, O. (2011). *CHAVS: The demonization of the working classes*. London: Verso.

Jones, R. M. (1981). *The North Wales Quarrymen 1874–1922*. Cardiff: University of Wales Press.

Keegan, W. (1984). *Mrs Thatcher's Economic Experiment*. London: Allen Lane.

Lambie-Mumford, H. (2017). *Hungry Britain. The Rise of Food Charity*. Bristol: Policy Press.

Lindsay, J. (1974). *A History of the North Wales Slate Industry*. Newton Abbot: David and Charles.

Lindsay, J. (1987). *The Great Strike. A history of the Penrhyn Quarry dispute of 1900–1903*. Newton Abbot: David and Charles.

Lingard, B., Hayes, D., Mills, M., and Christie, P. (2003) *Leading Learning. Making hope practical in schools*. Maidenhead and Philidephia: Open University Press.

Lingard, B. (2009) *Testing Times: The need for new intelligent accountabilities for schooling*. QTU Professional magazine, November: *https://www.academia.edu/27162545/Testing_times_The_need_for_new_intelligent_accountabilities_for_schooling*.

Lingard, B. (2013). 'Reshaping the message system of schooling in the UK: a critical reflection', in Wyse et al. (eds), *Creating the Curriculum*. London: Routledge.

Lupton, R. (2003). *Poverty Street. The dynamics of neighbourhood decline and renewal*. Bristol: Policy Press.

Lupton, R. et al. (2016). *Social Policy in a Cold Climate. Policies and their consequences since the crisis*. Bristol: Policy Press.

Lupton, R. and Hayes, D. (2021). *Great Mistakes in Education Policy*. Bristol: Policy Press.

McFarlane, F. (2021). *Report on the 5th Annual Child and Family Poverty Surveys*. Available at: *https://www.childreninwales.org.uk/application/files/5816/3663/4886/Child_Poverty_Survey_Report_2021_English_v7.pdf* (accessed 17 April 2023).

McGregor, G. et al. (2017). *Reimagining schooling for education: Socially just alternatives*. London: Palgrave Macmillan.

Main, K. and S. Whatman (2016). 'Building social and emotional efficacy to (re)engage young adolescents: capitalising on the "window of opportunity"'. *International Journal of Inclusive Education*, 20/10, 1054–69: doi:10.1080/13603116.2016.1145265.

Mannion, G., L. Mattu and M. Wilson (2015). *Teaching, learning, and play in the outdoors: a survey of school and pre-school provision in Scotland*. Scottish Natural Heritage Commissioned Report no. 779.

Mills, D. and M. Morton (2013). *Ethnography in Education*. London: Sage.

Mills, M. et al. (2009). 'Productive pedagogies: A redefined methodology for analysing quality teacher practice'. *The Australian Educational Researcher*, 36/3, 67–87.

Moll, L. C. (2019). 'Elaborating Funds of Knowledge: Community-Oriented Practices in International Contexts'. *Literacy Research: Theory, Method, and Practice*, August: https://doi.org/10.1177/2381336919870805.

Mygind, E. (2007). 'A comparison between children's physical activity levels at school and learning in an outdoor environment'. *Journal of adventure education and outdoor learning*, 7/2, 161–76.

Mygind, E. (2009). 'A comparison of children's statements about social relations and teaching in the classroom and in the outdoor environment'. *Journal of adventure education and outdoor learning*, 9/2, 151–69.

Nuttall, A. and L. Beckett (2020). 'Teachers' professional knowledge work on poverty and disadvantage', in L. Beckett (ed.), *Research-informed teacher learning. Critical perspectives on theory, research and practice*. Oxford and New York: Routledge.

OECD (2014). *Improving schools in Wales: An OECD perspective*. OECD.

Owen, K. L., R. C. Watkins and J. C. Hughes (2022). 'From evidence-informed to evidence-based: An evidence building framework for education'. *Review of Education*, 10, e3342: https://doi.org/10.1002/rev3.3342.

Ozga, J. and B. Lingard (eds) (2007). *Globalisation, education policy and politics*. Oxford and New York: Routledge.

Piketty, T. (2014). *Interview: Dynamics of Inequality*. Available at: *https://newleftreview.org/issues/ii85/articles/thomas-piketty-dynamics-of-inequality* (accessed 13 April 2023).

Price Davies, B. (1937). 'Practical Aspects of Housing Design'. Paper no. 14 submitted for open competition to the Public Works, Roads and Transport Congress, 17 November, Islington, London. Caernarfon: Gwynedd Archives.

Priestley, M. (2015). 'Teacher agency: What is it and does it matter?'. *British Educational Research Association (BERA)*. Available at: *https://www.bera.ac.uk/blog/teacher-agency-what-is-it-and-why-does-it-matter* (accessed 27 April 2023).

Putnam, R. (2000). *Bowling alone: The collapse and revival of American community*. New York: Simon and Schuster Ltd.

Queensland Government (2022). 'Every child succeeding: State School Strategy, 2022–2026'. Available at: *https://education.qld.gov.au/curriculums/Documents/state-schools-strategy.pdf*.

Reay, D. (2017). *Miseducation. Inequality, education and the working classes*. Bristol: Policy Press.

Redmond, G. (2022). '"I just go to school with no food" – why Australia must tackle child poverty to improve educational outcomes'. *The Conversation AU*, 10 March 2022. Available at: *https://theconversation.com/i-just-go-to-school-with-no-food-why-australia-must-tackle-child-poverty-to-improve-educational-outcomes-178426* (accessed 27 April 2023).

Rizvi, F. and B. Lingard (2010). *Globalizing Education Policy*. Oxford and New York: Routledge.

Sahlberg, P. (2011). 'The fourth way of Finland'. *Journal of Educational Change*, 12, 173–85.

Sandford, R. A., K. M. Armour and P. C. Warmington (2006). 'Re-engaging disaffected youth through physical activity programmes'. *British Educational Research Journal*, 32/2, 251–71.

Saunders, L. (2007). *Educational Research & Policy-Making*. Oxford: Routledge.

Scanlon, L. (2015). *My School: Listening to parents, teachers and students from a disadvantaged educational setting*. Oxford and New York: Routledge.

Sellars, S. and B. Lingard (2013). 'The OECD and the expansion of PISA: new global modes of governance in education'. *British Educational Research Journal*, 40/6, 917–36.

Smyth, B. and T. Wrigley (2013). *Living on the edge*. New York: Peter Lang.

Smyth, J. (2012). 'The socially just school and critical pedagogies in communities put at a disadvantage'. *Critical Studies in Education*, 53/1, 9–18.

Spratt, V. (2023). *Tenants: The People on the Frontline of Britain's Housing Emergency*. London: Profile Books.

Stoddart, F. (2004). 'Developing social capital through outdoor education in Cumbria: A case study'. Paper presented at the Outdoor Education International Research Conference, La Trobe University Bendigo.

Thompson, I. and G. Ivinson (2020). *Poverty in Education across the UK. A Comparative Analysis of Policy and Place*. Bristol: Policy Press.

Thomson, P., B. Lingard and T. Wrigley (2012). 'Ideas for changing educational systems, educational policy and schools'. *Critical Studies in Education*, 53/1, 1–7, DOI: 10.1080/17508487.2011.636451.

Townsend, P. (1970). *The Concept of Poverty*. Portsmouth, NH: Heinemann Educational Books.

Townsend, P. (1996). *A Poor Future*. London: Lemos & Crane.

Tyler, E. T. et al. (2019). 'The Collaborative Institute for Education Research, Evidence and Impact: A Case Study in developing regional research capacity in Wales'. *Wales Journal of Education*, 21/1, 89–108.

Watkins R. C. et al. (2018). 'Research Note: The Collaborative Institute for Education Research, Evidence and Impact (CIEREI)'. *Wales Journal of Education*, 20/1: https://doi.org/10.16922/wje.20.1.8.

Welsh Government (2012). *Improving Schools.* Cardiff: Welsh Government.

Welsh Government (2014). *Qualified for Life.* Cardiff: Welsh Government.

Welsh Government (2015). *Pupil Deprivation Grant: Essential guidance.* Cardiff: Welsh Government.

Welsh Government (2016). *National School Categorisation System: Guidance document for schools, local authorities and regional consortia.* Cardiff: Welsh Government.

Welsh Government (2017a). *Education in Wales: Our National Mission; Action plan 2017–2021.* Cardiff: Welsh Government.

Welsh Government (2017b). *Evaluation of the Pupil Deprivation Grant.* Cardiff: Welsh Government.

Welsh Government (2017c). 'Prosperity for all'. Available at: *https://gov.wales/docs/strategies/170919-prosperity-for-all-en.pdf* (accessed 4 September 2022).

Welsh Government (2019). 'Child Poverty Progress Report'. Available at: *https://www.gov.wales/sites/default/files/publications/2020-01/child-poverty-strategy-2019-progress-report.pdf* (accessed 21 April 2023).

Welsh Government (2021). *The Co-operation Agreement.* Available at: *https://www.gov.wales/sites/default/files/publications/2021-11/cooperation-agreement-2021.pdf* (accessed 21 April 2023).

Whatman, S. (2008). *Wis Wei Youpla Health? Health Education in the Torres Strait.* Germany: VDM Publishers.

Whatman, S. and P. Singh (2015). 'Constructing health and physical education curriculum for Indigenous girls in a remote Australian community'. *Physical Education and Sport Pedagogy,* 20/2, 215–30.

Whatman, S. L. and K. Main (2018). 'Re-engaging "youth at risk" of disengaging from schooling through rugby league club partnership: unpacking the pedagogic practices of the Titans Learning Centre'. *Sport, Education and Society,* 23/4, 339–53.

Whatman, S., R. Thompson and K. Main (2019). 'The Recontextualisation of Youth Well-being in Australian Schools'. *Health Education*, 119/5–6, 321–40.

Whatman, S. et al. (2021). 'Multi-cities Ethnographies Project: school-community relations and pedagogic rights of students'. *BERA Conference 2021*. Virtual: British Educational Research Association. Available at: *https://www.bera.ac.uk/conference/bera-conference-2021* (accessed 27 April 2023).

Whitty, G. et al. (2016). *Research & Policy in Education*. London: UCL IOE Press.

Williams, A. and N. Wainwright (2015). 'A new pedagogical model for adventure in the curriculum: part one – advocating for the model'. *Physical education and sport pedagogy*, 21/5, 481–500.

Williams, A. and N. Wainwright (2019). 'Re-thinking adventurous activities in physical education: models-based approaches'. *Journal of adventure education and outdoor learning*, 20/20, 217–29.

Williams, B. and D. Macdonald (2015). 'Explaining outsourcing in Health and Physical Education'. *Sport Education and Society*, 20/1, 57–72.

Williams, R. (2003). *Who Speaks for Wales? Nation, Culture, Identity*. Cardiff: University of Wales Press.

World Bank (2022). *Understanding Poverty*. Available at: *https://www. worldbank.org/en/understanding-poverty* (accessed 27 April 2023).

World Health Organisation (WHO) (n.d.). *Health Promoting Schools*. Available at: *https://www.who.int/health-topics/health-promoting-schools#tab=tab_1* (accessed 27 April 2023).

Zipin, L., S. Sellar and R. Hattam (2012). 'Countering and exceeding "capital": a "funds of knowledge" approach to re-imagining community'. *Discourse: Studies in the Cultural Politics of Education*, 33/2, 179–92, DOI: 10.1080/01596306.2012.666074.

INDEX